Acknowledgments

Health Care Marketing: Tools and Techniques represents a milestone in that it is my first book published by Jones and Bartlett. This particular work grew out of a previously published work, entitled *Marketing Tools for Healthcare Executives*, a book that was published by Oxford Crest, a publishing house that I founded in 2002. As *Health Care Marketing: Tools and Techniques* and Jones and Bartlett bring the Oxford Crest era to a close, I must thank several people who helped me make Oxford Crest a success.

Vickie M. Cook, a partner at BKD in Oxford, Mississippi, deserves special thanks for her early recognition of Oxford Crest's value. She and her colleagues have provided much-needed operational assistance to Oxford Crest over the years. The Fortenberry family also played a significant role in the establishment and success of Oxford Crest. My mother, Mary Margaret, deserves special thanks, as she assisted me greatly with a number of operational matters pertaining to the publishing house. My sister, Lisa; my brother, Parrish; and my father, the late John Lamar, Sr.; also deserve recognition.

With the new era beginning at Jones and Bartlett, thanks is extended to several people who have been instrumental in making this new relationship a reality and success. Robert Murray, Vice President of Business Development, must receive special thanks as he placed the initial telephone call to me to discuss business opportunities that ultimately led to my publishing relationship with Jones and Bartlett. I would also like to thank my publisher, Michael Brown, for his ongoing assistance and support. Appreciation is also extended to Katey Birtcher, Catie Heverling, Sophie Fleck, Tracey Chapman, Jeanne Hansen, and Jana Hayward for their guidance throughout the preparation, assembly, and promotion of this text.

Additionally, several of my academic mentors deserve special recognition as they provided me with the foundation, tools, and guidance needed to become a successful academician and author. Drs. Anne Permaloff and Carl Grafton, Emeriti Professors of Political Science and Public Administration at Auburn University at Montgomery, have been supportive of me throughout my career, dating back to my days as a PhD student at Auburn University. Both have greatly influenced me and have been especially supportive of my scholarly writing efforts. Dr. Peter J. McGoldrick, Tesco Professor of Retailing at the University of Manchester's Manchester Business School, also must be recognized as he has had the single greatest influence on me as a marketing academician and author. From his helpful comments and suggestions regarding my books to his role as supervisor of my second PhD, earned from the University of Manchester, to our ongoing academic research endeavors, Professor McGoldrick deserves special thanks.

I also must draw attention to two administrators at Louisiana State University in Shreveport who have been of special assistance to me. Dr. Vincent J. Marsala, Chancellor, and Dr. Patricia F. Doerr, Dean of Graduate Studies, must be recognized for their enduring support. Through their efforts, I was afforded with a productive and enjoyable work environment which permitted me to author this text. Drs. Marsala and Doerr have been among the strongest of advocates for me, my scholarly research, and associated publications.

Finally, a member of the extended family of Louisiana State University in Shreveport, James K. Elrod, deserves to be recognized. Mr. Elrod, President and Chief Executive Officer of Willis-Knighton Health System, has worked extensively with me over the years, providing important feedback regarding my scholarly writing endeavors, offering me interesting and enlightening research opportunities, and serving as an advocate for me both on campus at LSUS and in the healthcare community of Shreveport, Louisiana. I am very proud to be the holder of the James K. Elrod Professorship in Health Administration.

I am deeply appreciative of the guidance and support offered by the individuals noted above. They each have played a unique and beneficial role in helping me author *Health Care Marketing: Tools and Techniques*.

Health Care Marketing: Tools and Techniques
Third Edition

**John L. Fortenberry, Jr., MBA, PhD
(Public Administration and Public Policy),
PhD (Business Administration)**
Health Administration Department Chair
MHA Program Director
James K. Elrod Professor of Health Administration
and Professor of Marketing
College of Business
Louisiana State University in Shreveport
Shreveport, Louisiana

JONES AND BARTLETT PUBLISHERS
Sudbury, Massachusetts
BOSTON   TORONTO   LONDON   SINGAPORE

World Headquarters

Jones and Bartlett Publishers
40 Tall Pine Drive
Sudbury, MA 01776
978-443-5000
info@jbpub.com
www.jbpub.com

Jones and Bartlett Publishers
Canada
6339 Ormindale Way
Mississauga, Ontario L5V 1J2
Canada

Jones and Bartlett Publishers
International
Barb House, Barb Mews
London W6 7PA
United Kingdom

Jones and Bartlett's books and products are available through most bookstores and online booksellers. To contact Jones and Bartlett Publishers directly, call 800-832-0034, fax 978-443-8000, or visit our website www.jbpub.com.

Substantial discounts on bulk quantities of Jones and Bartlett's publications are available to corporations, professional associations, and other qualified organizations. For details and specific discount information, contact the special sales department at Jones and Bartlett via the above contact information or send an email to specialsales@jbpub.com.

This publication is designed to provide accurate and authoritative information in regard to the Subject Matter covered. It is sold with the understanding that the publisher is not engaged in rendering legal, accounting, or other professional service. If legal advice or other expert assistance is required, the service of a competent professional person should be sought.

Production Credits
Publisher: Michael Brown
Production Director: Amy Rose
Production Editor: Tracey Chapman
Associate Editor: Katey Birtcher
Editorial Assistant: Catie Heverling
Marketing Manager: Sophie Fleck
Manufacturing and Inventory Control Supervisor: Amy Bacus
Composition: Publishers' Design and Production Services, Inc.
Cover Design: Brian Moore
Cover Image: © Handy Widiyanto/ShutterStock, Inc.
Printing and Binding: Malloy, Inc.
Cover Printing: Malloy, Inc.

ISBN: 978-1-4496-2221-3

Library of Congress Cataloging-in-Publication Data
Fortenberry, John L.
    Health care marketing : tools and techniques / John L. Fortenberry, Jr. —3rd ed.
        p. ; cm.
    Rev. ed. of.: Marketing tools for healthcare executives / John L. Fortenberry, Jr., 2nd ed., c2005
    Includes bibliographical references and index.
    ISBN-13: 978-0-7637-6327-5 (casebound)
    ISBN-10: 0-7637-6327-6 (casebound)
    1. Medical care—Marketing. 2. Health services administration. I. Fortenberry, John L. Marketing tools for healthcare executives. II. Title.
    [DNLM: 1. Marketing of Health Services—methods. W 74.1 F737h 2009]
    RA410.56.F675 2009
    362.1068'8—dc22
                                                                          2008028575

6048

Printed in the United States of America
16 15   10 9 8 7 6 5 4

In Memory of my Grandmother
Dr. Margaret James Mosal
1911–1987

About the Author

John L. Fortenberry, Jr. serves as Health Administration Department Chair, MHA Program Director, James K. Elrod Professor of Health Administration, and Professor of Marketing in the College of Business at Louisiana State University in Shreveport where he teaches a variety of courses in both health administration and marketing. He received a BBA in Marketing from the University of Mississippi; an MBA from Mississippi College; a PhD in Public Administration and Public Policy, with concentrations in Health Administration, Human Resource Management, and Organization Theory, from Auburn University; and a PhD in Business Administration, with a major in Marketing, from the University of Manchester in the United Kingdom.

Dr. Fortenberry's academic research interests are centered on marketing, notably including the components of advertising, consumer behavior, and strategy. His specific sector interests include health, retail, and transportation industries. *Health Care Marketing: Tools and Techniques* represents his fourth book and his first published by Jones and Bartlett.

Contents

Preface

Healthcare entities compete in what might be considered the most competitive of industries in an environment of immense complexity. On an ongoing basis, hospitals, medical clinics, pharmaceutical manufacturers, and other healthcare establishments vie against one another in their respective markets for the opportunity to serve customers. Each of these healthcare organizations ultimately is in search of growth and prosperity, and the best managed of these entities will indeed realize this goal.

Marketing is possibly the most critical management responsibility associated with the pursuit and realization of growth and prosperity. Marketing can broadly be defined as *a management process that involves the assessment of customer wants and needs, and the performance of all activities associated with the development, pricing, provision, and promotion of product solutions that satisfy those wants and needs.*

Although most often associated with advertising and sales, marketing is much more encompassing, as its definition implies. Aside from promotions activities, marketing includes such critical functions as environmental scanning, wants and needs assessment, new product development, target marketing, product pricing, product distribution, and market research.

For anyone engaged in the healthcare industry, the importance of understanding marketing cannot be understated. As the healthcare industry is characterized by intense and ever increasing rivalry, marketing becomes all the more essential as a mechanism for achieving success. To assist healthcare administrators, clinicians, students, and other interested parties in gaining an understanding of this important discipline, I authored *Health Care Marketing: Tools and Techniques.*

Written from the perspective of the healthcare marketing professional, *Health Care Marketing: Tools and Techniques* presents a series of 39 essential marketing tools and demonstrates their application in the healthcare environment. The tools presented in this work cover a fairly broad spectrum of marketing, including product development and portfolio analysis, branding and identity management, target marketing, consumer behavior and product promotions, environmental analysis and competitive assessment, marketing management, and marketing strategy and planning. The specific tools selected from these broad categories range from time-tested marketing classics to new models that will undoubtedly become classics in time.

Each chapter of this work focuses on a specific marketing tool and, if desired, can be read as a stand-alone document—a convenience that greatly increases the utility of *Health Care Marketing: Tools and Techniques*. For those who are new to marketing, a brief introduction to the discipline is offered in the appendix of this book. A glossary of marketing terminology is also included at the conclusion of this work.

It is my hope that you will find the tools and techniques presented in this book useful in your study of healthcare marketing.

John L. Fortenberry, Jr.

New to This Edition

Health Care Marketing: Tools and Techniques includes significant upgrades that distinguish it from its predecessor, *Marketing Tools for Healthcare Executives*. The chapter count has increased by one from 38 to 39, adding George Day's R-W-W Screen to the book's collection of marketing tools. Readers familiar with *Marketing Tools for Healthcare Executives* will appreciate this new tool as it perfectly complements existing instruments.

Additionally, the beginnings and endings of chapters in this updated work are much improved, with learning objectives situated initially within each chapter, providing a useful outline of chapter content, and exercises situated at chapter conclusions. Importantly, exercises for each chapter include a theoretical inquiry, challenging readers to provide comprehensive overviews of profiled tools and share associated insights, and a practical one, calling on readers to engage in field assessments within their respective local markets, demonstrating their ability to make practical sense of given instruments.

For instructors, the upgrades continue. For the first time, a comprehensive set of instructor resources is available through Jones and Bartlett to those who adopt this text for use in the classroom. Such resources include PowerPoint slides, a test bank, and teaching insights for each chapter. These resources will greatly assist instructors who use *Health Care Marketing: Tools and Techniques* in their efforts to educate and enlighten their students.

PART ONE

Product Development & Portfolio Analysis Tools

CHAPTER 1

The Product Life Cycle

LEARNING OBJECTIVES

After examining this chapter, readers will have the ability to:

- Recognize that all healthcare products possess limited life spans, necessitating appropriate product succession planning efforts.
- Appreciate the value of the Product Life Cycle as a tool for product succession planning and related product management activities, including portfolio planning, strategy formulation, and forecasting.
- Identify the four stages of the Product Life Cycle and understand methods for strategically and tactically managing products during each of these stages.
- Utilize the Product Life Cycle in the healthcare industry to effect enhanced marketing outcomes.

INTRODUCTION

As with all living things, products have finite life spans. This is particularly evident in the healthcare industry where continuous innovation and change have become commonplace. Regardless of the particular healthcare component examined—medical technologies, pharmaceutical products, surgical techniques and procedures, durable medical equipment manufacturing, service delivery systems, and so on—innovation is pervasive. Rapid innovation, while beneficial to society, drives existing products into obsolescence very quickly, creating obvious challenges—logistical, financial, and otherwise—for marketers who are dually charged with managing current product offerings while actively seeking to develop new products that will succeed those entering decline.

Not only do products possess limited life spans, but like their living counterparts, their life spans consist of a number of developmental stages, with each of these stages presenting its own unique array of opportunities and constraints. Products must be managed differently during the different stages of their life cycles, making it imperative for marketing managers to understand these stages and the appropriate strategies to be employed—a task facilitated by a model known as the Product Life Cycle.

Illustrated in Figure 1-1, the Product Life Cycle consists of a vertical axis representing sales, a horizontal axis representing time, a curve illustrating sales growth in relation to time, and four stages of development: introduction, growth, maturity, and decline. These stages of development are defined as follows.

STAGE 1: INTRODUCTION

The introduction stage of the Product Life Cycle involves the initial presentation of a product in the market. During this stage, sales growth slowly begins to increase as the public begins to gain awareness of newly introduced product offerings through promotional efforts. Competitors are few or nonexistent at this point. Here, marketers are primarily concerned with developing innovative promotional strategies that will increase *product* awareness in the market.

STAGE 2: GROWTH

The growth stage of the Product Life Cycle is characterized by rapidly escalating sales, courtesy of increased product awareness. This rapid sales growth generates large amounts of cash, but it also attracts competitors to the market. This necessitates that organizations reinvest the resulting cash windfalls back into these products to fend off new entrants. During this stage, marketers shift their attention from building *product* awareness to building *brand* awareness.

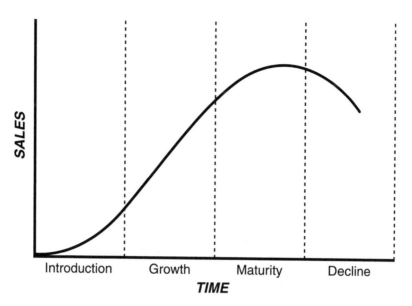

FIGURE 1-1 The Product Life Cycle

STAGE 3: MATURITY

During the maturity stage of the Product Life Cycle, sales growth levels off in what has now become an established market. Plateauing sales growth causes weaker competitors to exit the market, leaving their stronger counterparts who intensely compete for market dominance. At this point, products are the most lucrative for their organizations. Because mature offerings are established in the market, it is not necessary to reinvest the entirety of cash that these products generate. Here, marketers seek to increase market share by further differentiating their products from competitive offerings.

STAGE 4: DECLINE

During the decline stage of the Product Life Cycle, sales growth rapidly decreases, as well as the number of competitors in the marketplace. Falling consumer demand leads marketers to either eliminate these products or seek to extend the life spans of declining offerings through the discovery of new product uses or through product repositioning.

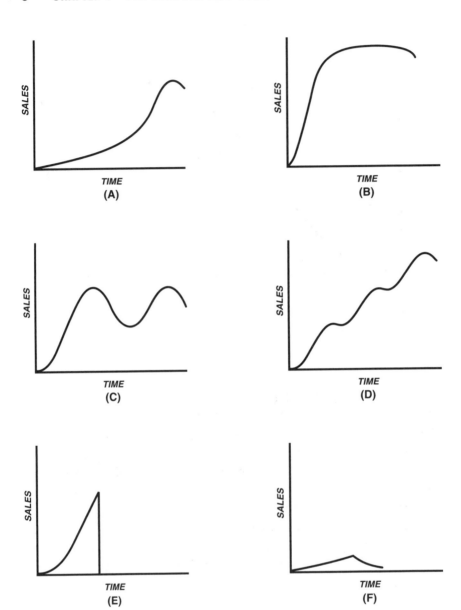

FIGURE 1-2 Product Life Cycle Variants

PRODUCT LIFE CYCLE VARIANTS

Although typically illustrated as an S-shaped curve, the appearance of the Product Life Cycle varies based on the marketplace experiences of product offerings. Figure 1-2 illustrates six curves that could potentially develop.

Figure 1-2A illustrates the life cycle of a product that witnessed a very lengthy ascent to maturity, possibly because the public was not ready or willing to quickly accept the new offering or perhaps because the entity had difficulties informing the public of the new product's existence. Newly established medical clinics, pharmacies, dental offices, etc. seeking to enter established markets with established providers would likely face this type of life cycle scenario as they strive to develop a customer base.

Figure 1-2B depicts the life cycle of a product that gained immediate acceptance followed by a period of enduring maturity. Such a curve would possibly develop upon the discovery of a medical breakthrough that was immediately welcomed by customers, such as the discovery of a therapeutic intervention for a previously untreatable illness.

Figure 1-2C depicts the life cycle of a product that entered maturity, declined, reentered maturity, and reentered decline. This cyclical pattern would be representative of, for example, a medical therapy that experienced provider and patient interest and disinterest over time.

Figure 1-2D illustrates the life cycle of a product that reentered the growth stage multiple times after reaching maturity. Such a curve would be representative of, for example, a pharmaceutical product that was found to be useful for purposes beyond its original scope, resulting in extended growth beyond its initial maturity stage.

Figure 1-2E illustrates the life cycle of a product that experienced a period of rapid growth followed by an immediate decline. This type of curve would be representative of, for example, a pharmaceutical product that was suddenly pulled from the market due to newly discovered health concerns. This curve would also be illustrative of a home health agency that was forced to close because of reduced reimbursement rates.

Figure 1-2F illustrates the life cycle of a product that failed after its introduction into the market. This unfortunate life cycle could possibly represent any of the multiple new product offerings that are introduced into the market but fail to achieve commercial success.

These examples illustrate only a few of the many Product Life Cycle variants that could possibly develop. Obviously, there are no guarantees that products will move through any or all of the stages of development. Given the unpredictable nature of product and market dynamics, it stands to reason that Product Life Cycles cannot be predetermined.

OPERATIONAL MATTERS

Given that all products have limited lives, marketers must actively assemble and manage product portfolios that are formulated to achieve long-term growth and prosperity. The Product Life Cycle assists marketers in this endeavor, serving as a useful portfolio planning tool.

Ideally, firms will have products at all stages of the Product Life Cycle. Established offerings provide excess amounts of cash that can be used to develop and grow new products that will ensure the future viability of organizations. By assembling balanced product portfolios, marketers position their organizations for consistent, enduring growth.

In addition to its strength as a portfolio planning tool, the Product Life Cycle also serves as a guide for designing marketing strategies. Because different developmental stages require different marketing actions, the Product Life Cycle provides marketers with a decision-making tool for formulating marketing strategy.

The Product Life Cycle can also be used, as Theodore Levitt suggested in his classic article entitled "Exploit the Product Life Cycle," as a forecasting tool where marketers attempt to predict the Product Life Cycles of new and anticipated product offerings. Even though Product Life Cycles cannot be predetermined, marketing strategy can be improved by formulating potential life cycle scenarios.

SUMMARY

The Product Life Cycle provides marketers with an effective tool for portfolio planning, strategy formulation, and forecasting. It serves as a reminder of the limited life spans possessed by products and hence the necessity for product succession planning—an essential marketing task in the innovation-rich healthcare marketplace. The insights offered by the Product Life Cycle can greatly improve the marketing performance of organizations.

EXERCISES

1. Define and comprehensively discuss the Product Life Cycle and its four associated stages, providing an illustration of this important marketing tool. Ensure that appropriate attention is directed toward the Product Life Cycle's use in portfolio planning, strategy formulation, and forecasting. Share your thoughts regarding the tool's implications and uses in the healthcare industry.

2. Contact a local healthcare entity (e.g., hospital, retail pharmacy, medical clinic) and arrange an informational interview with a marketing executive. Present the Product Life Cycle and request insights regarding the appearance of the particular curves for several of the entity's product offerings. Does the given marketing department actively use the Product Life Cycle as a tool for portfolio planning, strategy formulation, and forecasting? What other tools does the marketing executive employ for such endeavors? Report your findings in detail.

REFERENCE

Levitt, Theodore. 1965. Exploit the product life cycle. *Harvard Business Review* (November–December): 81–94.

2

Booz, Allen & Hamilton's New Product Process

LEARNING OBJECTIVES

After examining this chapter, readers will have the ability to:

- Recognize the importance of healthcare entities engaging in new product development as a means of ensuring enduring growth and prosperity.
- Understand unique barriers to new product development that complicate associated initiatives in the healthcare industry.
- Appreciate the value provided by Booz, Allen & Hamilton's New Product Process, guiding new product development activities from strategy development and idea generation through to commercialization.

INTRODUCTION

Given that all products possess limited life spans, a fact that is especially evident in the innovation-rich healthcare marketplace, organizations must continually seek to develop new product offerings that will ensure long-term growth and prosperity. These new products, of course, do not automatically appear in the healthcare marketplace. Instead, new products result from labor intensive and expensive efforts that eventually lead to market entry.

Market entry for new offerings is further complicated by the immense rules and regulations governing many healthcare goods and services. Pharmaceutical products and medical devices, for example, must successfully pass through the rigorous processes of the US Food and Drug Administration. Hospitals and nursing homes must, in many states, acquire certificates of need that authorize, among other things, the establishment of patient beds. Even if market entry is attained, there are no guarantees of commercial success, as indicated by the high incidence of new product failure.

In addition to the effort, expense, and bureaucracy associated with new product development, healthcare entities face yet another concern. Every time new products are presented in the market, organizations place their reputations in jeopardy. New products that are poorly developed can be quite damaging to existing offerings, presenting yet another potential disaster and an incentive for institutions to work diligently to ensure new product success.

MINIMIZING RISK

Although risk is inherent in new product development, it can be lessened by adopting a systematic framework for managing new product activities. One such framework for managing new product activities is offered by the management consulting firm of Booz, Allen & Hamilton. Illustrated in Figure 2-1, Booz, Allen & Hamilton's New Product Process divides new product development into seven sequential stages: new product strategy development, idea generation, screening and evaluation, business analysis, development, testing, and commercialization. These stages are explained as follows.

STAGE 1: NEW PRODUCT STRATEGY DEVELOPMENT

Booz, Allen & Hamilton's New Product Process begins with the development of new product strategies. Here, marketers lay the foundation for the new product process by reviewing corporate objectives and identifying roles that new products might play in satisfying those objectives. This information clarifies the strategic business requirements for new products and

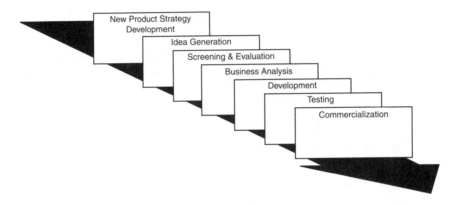

From *New Products Management for the 1980s* by Booz, Allen & Hamilton. Copyright ©
1982 by Booz, Allen & Hamilton. Reprinted by permission of Booz, Allen & Hamilton.

FIGURE 2-1 Booz, Allen & Hamilton's New Product Process

provides a point of reference for subsequent new product development
stages.

STAGE 2: IDEA GENERATION

During the idea generation stage, entities search for product ideas that are
compatible with the goals and objectives determined in the preceding stage.
The idea generation stage usually begins by conducting a self-assessment
to determine the product categories that are of primary interest to given
entities. When areas of interest have been determined, organizations scan
the environment in search of growth opportunities that can be exploited.
Ideas should actively be solicited from any potential idea source, including
employees, customers, and vendors. The ultimate purpose of the idea generation stage is to produce a wealth of ideas. Here, every idea should be
welcomed and initially considered on a "can do" basis.

STAGE 3: SCREENING & EVALUATION

The screening and evaluation stage involves the analysis of all of the ideas
gathered during the idea generation stage to determine which discoveries
should be further investigated. Here, each idea should be envisioned as a
product in the market where it can be evaluated on its potential contribution to given entities. Through screening and evaluation, organizations

seek to narrow down the number of ideas generated during the preceding stage by focusing only on those that offer the greatest potential.

During this stage, new product ideas decrease; however, the expenses associated with new product development increase—a trend that continues through the remaining stages of the new product process, as indicated in Figures 2-2 and 2-3, respectively. Organizations can only afford to

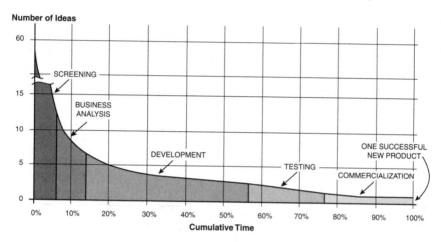

From *Management of New Products* by Booz, Allen & Hamilton. Copyright © 1968 by Booz, Allen & Hamilton. Reprinted by permission of Booz, Allen & Hamilton.

FIGURE 2-2 Mortality of New Product Ideas

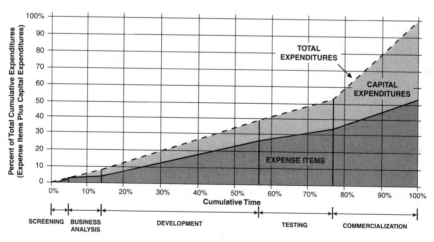

From *Management of New Products* by Booz, Allen & Hamilton. Copyright © 1968 by Booz, Allen & Hamilton. Reprinted by permission of Booz, Allen & Hamilton.

FIGURE 2-3 Cumulative New Product Expenditures

develop those ideas that possess the greatest potential for success in the market. The most promising ideas move to the business analysis stage, and all others are eliminated.

STAGE 4: BUSINESS ANALYSIS

During the business analysis stage, the most promising product ideas are subjected to intense scrutiny to determine their potential for translation into commercially successful offerings. Here, hypothetical business plans are formulated for these offerings, which identify product attributes, barriers to entry, current and potential competitors, target markets, market growth information, financial projections, promotional methods, and so on in an effort to formulate preliminary business recommendations. Successful product ideas graduate to the development stage.

STAGE 5: DEVELOPMENT

During the development stage, product ideas that have successfully met the scrutiny forwarded during prior stages are translated into actual product offerings. For goods, development involves the actual physical assembly of the offerings. For services, development involves the assembly of all components required for the services to be offered, such as office space, equipment, operating permits, and personnel. During this stage, product offerings may go through many alterations—a usual occurrence when on-paper ideas are translated into real-world offerings. Alterations continue through the remaining stages of the new product process as goods and services are readied for the market.

STAGE 6: TESTING

Testing seeks to validate earlier business projections associated with new offerings through commercial experimentation. Here, new products are readied for commercialization by conducting trials to determine marketplace suitability, with the nature of the testing being dependent on the characteristics of the particular products under development and the markets sought.

Because of their tangibility, goods are particularly well suited for laboratory testing, as well as test marketing—a practice where marketers directly or indirectly seek consumer feedback regarding their new products. Durable medical equipment manufacturers, for example, subject their products to intensive laboratory testing to ensure that their offerings meet designated quality standards. These firms might also test market their products by providing individuals with wheelchairs, hospital beds, and other items in exchange for their comments regarding the utility and comfort of the particular product offerings. Of course, one of the most notable examples of new product testing in health care involves the highly regulated and expensive clinical trial process that pharmaceutical firms undergo in pursuit of FDA approval for their new offerings. These firms are also actively engaged in test marketing. They might, for example, test market a newly developed pain reliever in several major cities to assess consumer demand, making adjustments as needed prior to the product's national introduction.

Like their tangible counterparts, services can also be tested and test marketed, albeit in a different manner. Certainly, prior to its grand opening, a medical clinic would undergo an intensive battery of tests to ensure that equipment is working properly, that necessary supplies are available, that employees understand their duties and responsibilities, etc. The medical clinic might even decide to test market its services by assembling a group of consumers to receive service offerings and provide feedback. The clinic might, for example, offer free physical examinations to individuals in exchange for their comments and opinions regarding the clinic's accessibility, decor, practitioner skill and concern, customer service, and so on.

The feedback generated through testing provides marketers with yet another opportunity to ready their products for entry into the marketplace. After any necessary alterations have been made, products are ready for commercialization.

STAGE 7: COMMERCIALIZATION

Commercialization involves the full-scale market introduction of newly developed products. As new products enter the market, ongoing customer feedback should actively be sought to ensure that products meet and, ideally, exceed customer expectations. Any new product "bugs" that are identified should quickly be remedied. Aside from ensuring a trouble-free marketplace introduction, marketers must carefully monitor competitor reactions to their new product offerings, taking steps when necessary to counteract competitive responses.

RISK & FAILURE

Risk is an inherent part of new product development where new product failures routinely outnumber successes. These failures are caused by a variety of factors, as illustrated in Table 2-1. New product difficulties are prevalent

Table 2-1 Causes of New Product Failure

1. Market/marketing failure
   Small size of the potential market
   No clear product differentiation
   Poor positioning
   Misunderstanding of customer needs
   Lack of channel support
   Competitive response
2. Financial failure
   Low return on investment
3. Timing failure
   Late in the market
   Too early—market not yet developed
4. Technical failure
   Product did not work
   Bad design
5. Organizational failure
   Poor fit with the organizational culture
   Lack of organizational support
6. Environmental failure
   Government regulations
   Macroeconomic factors

From "Managing New Product Development for Strategic Competitive Advantage" by Dipak Jain in *Kellogg on Marketing*, edited by Dawn Iacobucci. Copyright © 2001 by John Wiley & Sons, Inc. Reprinted with permission of John Wiley & Sons, Inc.

across all industries but are further amplified in the intensely regulated healthcare marketplace where oversight bodies demand that innovators ensure the efficacy of their healthcare goods and services and, oftentimes, demonstrate that a community need exists for given healthcare offerings. These healthcare industry-specific aspects greatly increase the costs of new product development and hence the associated risks.

Despite these risks, healthcare entities must engage in the new product process if they wish to endure and prosper. Only through the adoption of a systematic framework for managing new product activities can marketers minimize associated risks and increase their chances of developing new goods and services that achieve commercial success.

SUMMARY

Booz, Allen & Hamilton's New Product Process serves as a useful guide for new product development. Its seven sequential stages—new product strategy development, idea generation, screening and evaluation, business analysis, development, testing, and commercialization—provide invaluable guidance to healthcare marketers seeking to develop new products in a comprehensive and orderly fashion.

EXERCISES

1. Provide a detailed account profiling Booz, Allen & Hamilton's New Product Process, identifying and explaining each of its seven steps, accompanied by an appropriate illustration. Discuss the rigors of new product development as they impact general industry and offer insights regarding how and why these burdens are magnified in the healthcare industry. Share your thoughts on the degree to which modern healthcare organizations follow a systematic new product development process, such as that offered by Booz, Allen & Hamilton.

2. Contact an area healthcare establishment (e.g., medical center, nursing home, cosmetic surgery clinic) and arrange an informational interview with a member of the executive team to learn about their new product development practices. Specifically request information about the trials and tribulations associated with any recent or historic

product launches. Present Booz, Allen & Hamilton's New Product Process to the executive and ask about the degree to which his or her organization follows such a process. Report your findings in detail.

REFERENCES

Booz, Allen & Hamilton. 1968. *Management of new products.* New York: Booz, Allen & Hamilton.

———. 1982. *New products management for the 1980s.* New York: Booz, Allen & Hamilton.

Jain, Dipak. 2001. Managing new product development for strategic competitive advantage. In *Kellogg on marketing*, ed. Dawn Iacobucci. New York: Wiley.

CHAPTER **3**

George Day's
R-W-W Screen

LEARNING OBJECTIVES

After examining this chapter, readers will have the ability to:

- Understand that new product development in the healthcare industry involves the assumption of risk but offers the potential for reward.
- Realize that the increasingly competitive nature of the healthcare marketplace mandates that healthcare entities engage in new product development to increase the likelihood of survival, growth, and prosperity.
- Recognize that, as new product development represents a mandatory pursuit, reduction of risk becomes the prevailing consideration.
- Appreciate George Day's R-W-W Screen as a tool for reducing the risk associated with new product development, increasing the likelihood of successful new product endeavors.

INTRODUCTION

New product development in the healthcare industry is a process teeming with risk but also reward. The risk is associated with the huge investments of time and money required to launch new offerings. Difficulties are magnified in the healthcare industry because such offerings are heavily scrutinized by myriad regulatory bodies, adding an intensive layer of bureaucracy

19

to the process. Of course, when new products are fielded, institutions place their reputations on the line, representing yet another risk.

The risk associated with new product development certainly represents a deterrent to engagement in this process, but only through the development and launch of new and improved offerings can institutions position themselves for enduring marketplace success, yielding associated rewards. Given this, new product development should be viewed as a mandatory pursuit. Reduction of risk becomes the prevailing consideration.

While there are no guarantees that new products will be successful in the healthcare marketplace, there are techniques that can be employed to reduce associated risk and increase the likelihood of success. One such technique, offered by George Day, is known as the R-W-W Screen. Presented in Figure 3-1, Day's R-W-W Screen essentially consists of three primary questions, each containing an array of more specific questions, which are to be addressed in any new product venture. The R-W-W descriptor is derived from the first letter of key words in the set of primary questions: (1) Is it Real? (2) Can we Win? and (3) Is it Worth doing? These three questions and associated inquiries are explained as follows.

IS IT REAL?

The "Is it real?" inquiry pertains to market and product viability, calling on evaluators to answer two second-level questions ("Is the market real?" and "Is the product real?") and a series of related inquiries flowing from each.

As for the market, evaluators must assess whether it is of adequate size and whether targeted customers want or need the offering and have the means and desire to purchase the product. For example, highly specialized medical services offered in rural communities might indeed fill a marketplace want or need, and patients may very well have the means and desire to effect purchase, but the population may simply be too small to support such services. Of course, there are circumstances where populations in such rural locales might be capable of supporting these services. Only through prudent market research can such determinations be made.

As for the product, assessments must determine if the given offering is well conceptualized, can actually be produced, and is capable of satisfying customers. A hospital venturing into, say, cardiac medicine clearly is faced with myriad decisions associated with offering services in that particular

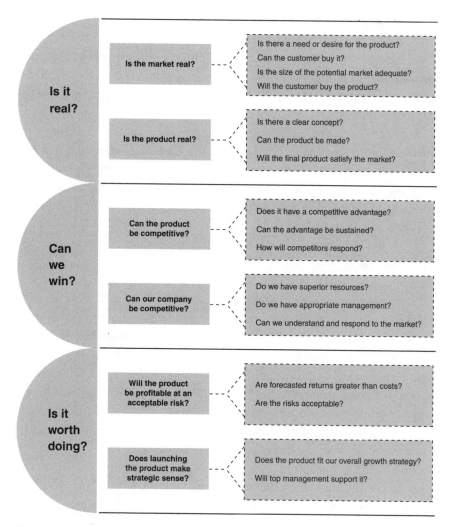

FIGURE 3-1 George Day's R-W-W Screen

area of medicine. Highly trained personnel must be acquired, along with specialized medical equipment, and, in some jurisdictions, the support of regulatory bodies must be obtained. Even if the provision of cardiac services is feasible, one still must investigate whether the offering will be capable of meeting and ideally exceeding customer wants and needs.

CAN WE WIN?

The "Can we win?" inquiry pertains to product and company competitiveness, calling on evaluators to answer two second-tier questions ("Can the product be competitive?" and "Can our company be competitive?") and associated inquiries.

As for product competitiveness, assessments must ascertain whether new offerings have a sustainable competitive advantage over other offerings and what, if any, response will be forwarded by competitors with the launch of the potential new offering. A healthcare product without a competitive advantage will struggle for market share, and even if the offering has an initial edge, if it is not sustainable, any gains generated will be lost to more savvy rivals. Therefore, it is imperative that healthcare products incorporate a sustainable competitive advantage that will distinguish them from current and potential offerings. Of course, regardless of advantage, competitive responses to new offerings must be envisioned, with the operative task being the incorporation of appropriate defenses into new products.

As for company competitiveness, evaluators must investigate the availability of resources and presence of qualified managers. Behind every healthcare product stands the organization that produces and provides the offering. A poorly resourced healthcare entity is sure to encounter difficulties even if its new product development efforts yield a successful launch. With such a launch, one would expect obvious market demand to attract competitors. If those competitors possess superior resources, opportunities abound for them to capture market share. Of course, management officials must be astute observers of the marketplace, being ready, willing, and able to act on any potential opportunity while avoiding or eliminating threats.

IS IT WORTH DOING?

The "Is it worth doing?" inquiry pertains to risk/return and strategic appropriateness, calling on evaluators to answer two second-tier questions ("Will the product be profitable at an acceptable risk?" and "Does launching the product make strategic sense?") and a series of related inquiries flowing from each.

As for risk/return, evaluators must determine if returns will be greater than costs and whether risks are acceptable. Quite obviously, if a healthcare offering is not anticipated to generate adequate financial returns, it would not make business sense to proceed with development of the product. However, there are situations in the healthcare industry where entities are compelled to offer services that are not profitable but are necessary to fulfill their given missions. In such cases, financial considerations would only be part of the formula for determining given return on investment, further demonstrating that healthcare marketers intensively must understand their products and associated roles within and outside of their particular organizations. Of course, risk is ever present in new product development, but such risk must not exceed a tolerable level.

As for strategic appropriateness, assessments must determine if products are suited for the overall growth strategy of given healthcare organizations and whether top management will offer support. New healthcare offerings must be viewed in the context of the existing offerings held by given entities and must make sense as new additions within associated product portfolios. They, too, must be championed by top-level healthcare executives because new product pursuits require ongoing attention and resources that can only be provided by executive ranks.

OPERATIONAL MATTERS

Implementation of Day's R-W-W Screen simply involves asking each of the questions indicated in Figure 3-1 and answering the inquiries intelligently and honestly. Clearly, the instance of any definite "no" answer for questions in the first and second columns of the diagram is grounds for immediate termination of the idea, and the instance of a definite "no" answer in third column inquiries strongly signals that development should not be pursued.

Because the information needed to address the inquiries identified in Day's R-W-W Screen is intensive, and the impact of new products affects multiple units within healthcare organizations, it is advised that interdisciplinary teams be created to assess each inquiry. Such teams must endeavor to avoid viewing the instrument as an obstacle to overcome, something that can occur when team members are especially passionate about new product ideas and look for ways to circumvent barriers that suggest idea termination. It is absolutely imperative that inquiries identified in Day's R-W-W Screen be addressed in a completely objective fashion.

It is important to realize that Day's R-W-W Screen should be used on multiple occasions throughout the stages of product development. This repeated use is essential because initial conceptions of products often change as they work their way through the various developmental processes, sometimes emerging as manifestations far removed from initial designs. Deployment of Day's R-W-W Screen across the multiple stages of product development ensures that new product efforts remain worthwhile pursuits.

SUMMARY

George Day's R-W-W Screen provides much needed guidance to healthcare marketers in their endeavors to determine the viability of new product ideas. Importantly, this tool can be utilized to minimize the risk associated with new product development, increasing the likelihood that new goods and services will launch productively and achieve sustained success in the healthcare marketplace.

EXERCISES

1. Provide a detailed account profiling George Day's R-W-W Screen, identifying and explaining its components, purposes, methods of implementation, and practical applications, accompanied by an appropriate illustration. Preface your discussion by offering an overview of the risk and return associated with new product development in the healthcare industry. Share your thoughts regarding the tool's implications and uses in the healthcare marketplace.
2. Conduct a review of trade journals, Web sites, and other sources in an effort to identify articles that describe various healthcare product failures. From these accounts, identify and describe the mistakes that were made which led to failure. Could the use of George Day's R-W-W Screen have prevented these mistakes/failures? If so, how?

REFERENCE

Day, George S. 2007. Is it real? Can we win? Is it worth doing? Managing risk and reward in an innovation portfolio. *Harvard Business Review* (December): 110–120.

Theodore Levitt's Total Product Concept

LEARNING OBJECTIVES

After examining this chapter, readers will have the ability to:

- Recognize that healthcare products consist of multiple levels of attributes, ideally assembled in such a manner to attract and retain the patronage of target audiences.
- Understand that, given ever-increasing customer expectations, product attributes must continually be enhanced and improved to meet and exceed the wants and needs of target audiences.
- Realize the value of Theodore Levitt's Total Product Concept as an aid in developing these multiple levels of attributes to increase the likelihood that associated healthcare offerings continually will meet and exceed customer wants and needs.

INTRODUCTION

Products are much more than one-dimensional items. Instead, they represent complex bundles of attributes that are purchased and consumed by customers to satisfy wants and needs. The success of goods and services in the marketplace is largely based on the skillful assembly of associated product attributes in a manner that will attract and retain customers. Therefore, marketers must possess a thorough understanding of the multidimensional nature of products.

The Total Product Concept, which was formulated by Theodore Levitt, illustrates the multidimensional nature of products and provides guidance to marketers seeking to develop goods and services that meet and exceed the expectations of customers. Presented in Figure 4-1, Levitt's Total Product Concept depicts four product levels—generic, expected, augmented, and potential—which are illustrated by four concentric circles.

As products move from inner levels to outer levels, they become increasingly complex and offer marketers enhanced opportunities to differentiate goods and services from competitive offerings. The four product levels are defined as follows.

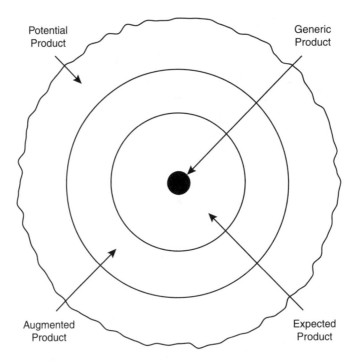

FIGURE 4-1 Levitt's Total Product Concept

THE GENERIC PRODUCT

The generic product, which could also be referred to as the core product, is an offering in its most basic and rudimentary form. At this level, competitive products are virtually indistinguishable from one another as they represent only core offerings and nothing more. Customers expect more than base offerings.

THE EXPECTED PRODUCT

The expected product consists of the generic product along with features that allow it to be distinguished from competitive offerings. Expected products add branding, product features, product quality, packaging, and like elements to generic products to create offerings that can easily be recognized by customers. At this level, goods and services meet the minimum expectations of customers. In essence, these offerings represent what customers *expect* to receive.

THE AUGMENTED PRODUCT

The augmented product consists of the expected product plus additional features that extend beyond the expectations of customers. Product augmentations vary based on the nature of given offerings, but typical examples include personalized service, warranties and guarantees, extended service plans, and financial assistance. Augmentations allow marketers to further differentiate their products from competitive offerings. The differentiation offered by specific augmentations may decline over time as consumers become accustomed to the enhancements and come to expect these additions, necessitating that marketers discover new ways to augment their products.

THE POTENTIAL PRODUCT

The potential product represents all things that can potentially be incorporated into offerings to attract and retain customers. Whereas augmented products represent everything that is *currently* being done to attract and retain customers, potential products represent everything that *might* be done. As current augmentations become expected by customers, marketers must formulate future methods to augment, and thus differentiate, their products. The potential product level identifies these future augmentations.

OPERATIONAL MATTERS

To assess products using Levitt's Total Product Concept, marketers simply (1) identify the product to be evaluated, (2) construct the Total Product Concept diagram, as illustrated in Figure 4-1, (3) identify and/or formulate the generic, expected, augmented, and potential components for the product under evaluation, and (4) place the identified components on the diagram accordingly. The resulting Total Product Concept diagram is then analyzed to gain product insights.

Figure 4-2 identifies an example of Levitt's Total Product Concept applied to a hospital's labor and delivery unit. The core offering provided by the unit is its ability to deliver babies. This generic offering is transformed into an expected product through a variety of additions; for example, labor and delivery classes, private patient rooms, skilled healthcare providers, and superior technology. The labor and delivery unit hopes to further differentiate itself from its competitors through a series of augmentations; namely, newborn gift packs, labor/delivery/recovery (LDR) rooms, infant care classes, and related enhancements. Future differentiation could occur through renovations, upgraded technology, personal care assistants, and so on.

Figure 4-3 identifies an example of Levitt's Total Product Concept applied to an assisted living center. The center's generic product consists of the shelter and assistance that it offers to occupants. This base offering is transformed into the expected product through various features; namely, private occupant rooms, round-the-clock security, daily meals, weekly laundry service, and related amenities. Augmentations include weekly excursions to area attractions, access to transportation, private dining facilities, and so on. Future differentiation opportunities exist through overnight accommodations for guests, enhanced room amenities, personal care assistants assigned to each occupant, and related product upgrades.

Clearly, Levitt's Total Product Concept reminds marketers that products represent complex bundles of attributes that must skillfully be assembled to satisfy customers. It also serves as an excellent product planning

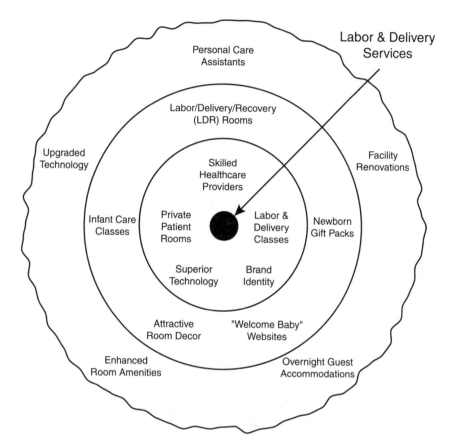

Constructed using design methodologies in Levitt, Theodore. "Marketing Success through Differentiation—of Anything." *Harvard Business Review* (January-February) 1980: 83–91.

FIGURE 4-2 A Labor & Delivery Unit's Total Product Concept

and analysis tool for the level-by-level dissection of current, and even proposed, products. Through this dissection, marketers can identify and, if necessary, enhance those attributes that differentiate products from competitive offerings. They also can formulate strategies for the future differentiation of goods and services. These points of differentiation are especially useful in the development of effective promotional campaigns.

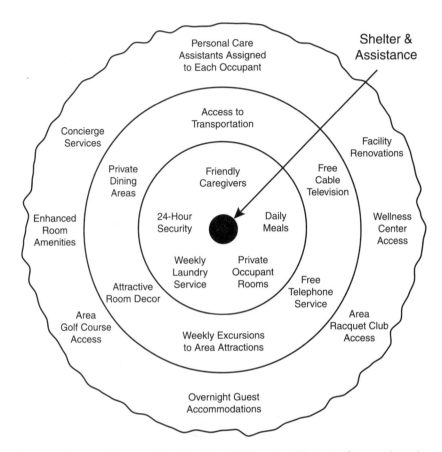

Constructed using design methodologies in Levitt, Theodore. "Marketing Success through Differentiation—of Anything." *Harvard Business Review* (January-February) 1980: 83–91.

FIGURE 4-3 An Assisted Living Center's Total Product Concept

SUMMARY

Levitt's Total Product Concept clearly illustrates the multidimensional nature of products. By understanding the product levels identified in the Total Product Concept, marketers are better prepared to assemble the multiple attributes of goods and services in a manner that will attract and retain customers.

EXERCISES

1. Provide a comprehensive overview of Theodore Levitt's Total Product Concept, explaining its purpose, components, uses, and benefits, accompanied by an associated illustration. Be sure to indicate how the model focuses not only on current product manifestations but also on future perspectives of product offerings. Share your views regarding how this instrument can be used to effect better product management outcomes in the healthcare industry.

2. Place yourself in the position of a healthcare entrepreneur seeking to investigate opportunities for a new product offering of your choice in your local market. Using Theodore Levitt's Total Product Concept, develop an associated diagram for the given offering, identifying attributes pertaining to each level indicated in the model. Provide a narrative to accompany this diagram, discussing your thought processes for assembling the product in the manner illustrated.

REFERENCES

Levitt, Theodore. 1980. Marketing success through differentiation—of anything. *Harvard Business Review* (January-February): 83–91.

———. 1986. *The marketing imagination*. Exp. ed. New York: The Free Press.

5

The Boston Consulting Group's Growth/ Share Matrix

LEARNING OBJECTIVES

After examining this chapter, readers will have the ability to:

- Understand the importance of assembling balanced product portfolios as a means of ensuring extended success in the healthcare marketplace.
- Realize the value of The Boston Consulting Group's Growth/ Share Matrix as a device for assessing the product portfolios of healthcare entities.
- Effect prudent product management decisions on the basis of the growth and market share characteristics of given healthcare goods and services, as determined by the positioning of such offerings in The Boston Consulting Group's Growth/ Share Matrix.

INTRODUCTION

Successful healthcare entities must strive to assemble balanced product portfolios that will ensure long-term growth and prosperity. Because all products have defined life spans, it is necessary to plan for the future by developing new products that will eventually succeed mature offerings.

Successful, established products generate large amounts of cash, while new, developing products rarely generate any revenue. It is with the excess cash generated by established offerings that new products emerge and gain market share in their high-growth environments.

The successful assembly of a balanced product portfolio requires that marketers maintain a keen awareness of the characteristics of the products they are responsible for managing. This awareness is attained, in part, by conducting a portfolio analysis. Through such an analysis, marketers comprehensively review their product offerings in an effort to identify strengths and weaknesses, making alterations and enhancements as necessary.

To analyze product portfolios, marketers often rely on The Boston Consulting Group's Growth/Share Matrix. Illustrated in Figure 5-1, the Growth/Share Matrix evaluates products based on market growth and market share characteristics.

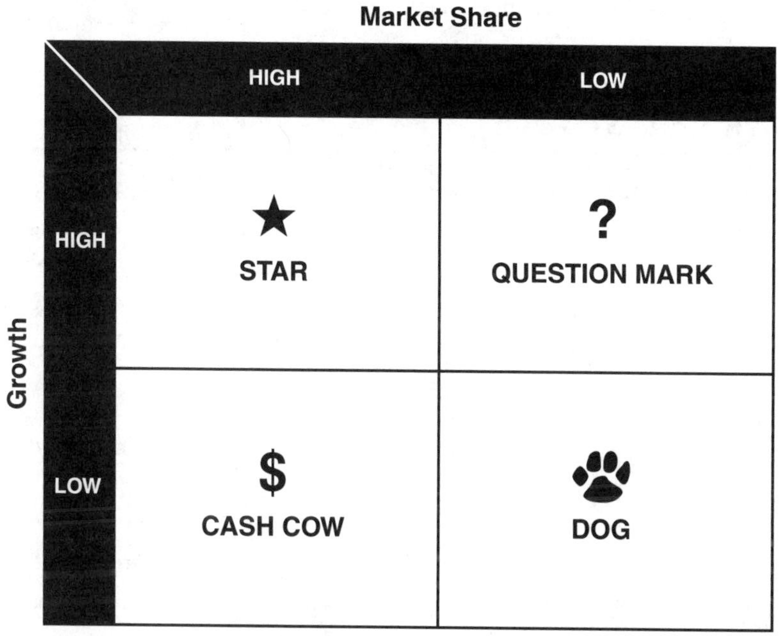

Market Share

	HIGH	LOW
HIGH	★ STAR	? QUESTION MARK
LOW	$ CASH COW	🐾 DOG

Growth

Taken from "The Product Portfolio" (1970) by Bruce D. Henderson in *The Boston Consulting Group on Strategy*, edited by Carl W. Stern and Michael S. Deimler. Copyright © 2006 by The Boston Consulting Group, Inc. Reprinted with permission of The Boston Consulting Group, Inc.

FIGURE 5-1 The Boston Consulting Group's Growth/Share Matrix

Market growth is a measure of a market's momentum or lack thereof, while market share is a measure of an entity's portion of the total sales generated by a given product in a given market. The Growth/Share Matrix consists of a vertical axis representing market growth (high and low), a horizontal axis representing market share (high and low), and four cells identified as cash cows, stars, question marks, and dogs. These four cells are explained as follows.

CASH COWS (LOW GROWTH, HIGH MARKET SHARE)

A cash cow is a product that possesses a strong market position in a low growth market. Cash cows generate large amounts of cash, typically in excess of that required to maintain market share. Hence, cash cows are very profitable. The sizeable revenues that they generate can be used to develop other goods and services in associated portfolios.

STARS (HIGH GROWTH, HIGH MARKET SHARE)

A star is a product that possesses a significant share of a rapidly growing market. Although stars generate large amounts of cash, the cash must be reinvested to maintain market share in their high growth environments. If stars maintain their market positions, they will eventually become cash cows when market growth levels off along with the associated reinvestment requirements.

QUESTION MARKS (HIGH GROWTH, LOW MARKET SHARE)

A question mark is a product that has a weak market position in an environment of rapid growth. Although the market is quite attractive, the market share possessed by these product offerings is not. If question marks maintain their market positions, they will eventually become dogs. However, if market share can be increased, question marks can become stars and eventually cash cows. Increasing market share, however, requires significant investment, which must come from other sources, most notably cash cows, because question marks cannot independently generate the necessary cash.

DOGS (LOW GROWTH, LOW MARKET SHARE)

A dog is a product that possesses a weak market position in an environment of little growth. Dogs are generally cash drains on entities, and even when they do show an accounting profit, the profit must be reinvested to maintain market share. Unless compensating factors exist, dogs should ideally be divested, freeing resources to be directed toward more profitable pursuits.

MARKET DYNAMICS

Because market growth eventually slows down, all products will eventually become either cash cows or dogs. This fact necessitates that marketers diligently pursue market leadership positions for all of their products during periods of growth. Leadership positions will pay dividends when growth slows and reinvestment requirements become minimal.

OPERATIONAL MATTERS

To assess products using The Boston Consulting Group's Growth/Share Matrix, marketers simply (1) identify the offerings they wish to evaluate, (2) construct the Growth/Share Matrix, as illustrated in Figure 5-1, (3) gather product-related growth/share data, and (4) plot each product on the Growth/Share Matrix using circles, with larger circles representing products with larger shares of the market.

This visual representation is then analyzed to determine the strengths and weaknesses associated with given product portfolios. If additional detail is desired, marketers can forecast the market positions of products at some point in the future and plot these predictions on the Growth/Share Matrix using contrasting circles.

Figure 5-2 identifies a Growth/Share Matrix (current and forecasted) that was developed for a rural medical center. The eight white circles identify the medical center's eight product offerings designated by departmental unit. These units include the medical center's nursing home, surgery

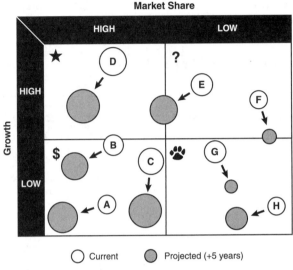

Constructed using design methodologies in Henderson, Bruce D. "The Product Portfolio" (1970). In *The Boston Consulting Group on Strategy: Classic Concepts and New Perspectives*, 2nd ed., edited by Carl W. Stern and Michael S. Deimler. New York: Wiley, 2006.

FIGURE 5-2 A Rural Medical Center's Growth/Share Matrix

department, emergency department, occupational health clinic, assisted living center, home health agency, primary care clinic, and wellness center. The eight shaded circles represent the market share estimates for these products in 5 years. A review of this diagram indicates that the medical center currently has three cash cows, one star, two question marks, and two dogs.

Overall, the current and forecasted portfolios of this facility appear to be very strong. The medical center is fortunate to have three cash cows generating revenues that can be used to fund other product offerings. With continued investment, its star can be converted into a cash cow as its market matures. The question marks must carefully be evaluated to determine each unit's potential contribution. If the 5-year forecast is accurate, it appears that the assisted living center represents a worthwhile investment because it is anticipated to become a star. However, the home health agency is expected to lose market share and drift into the dog quadrant.

The home health agency, along with the two dogs (i.e., the primary care clinic and wellness center), should be divested unless compensating factors exist.

Figure 5-3 identifies a Growth/Share Matrix (current and forecasted) that was developed for a home health agency with operations in five different geographic locations: Washington County, Adams County, Jefferson County, Madison County, and Lincoln County. Currently, the agency possesses one cash cow, one star, no question marks, and three dogs. Washington and Adams markets are clearly beneficial and are expected to remain so in the future. The Jefferson, Madison, and Lincoln markets, however, represent portfolio liabilities. Obviously, the home health agency would do well to exit these markets and concentrate exclusively on the prosperous Washington and Adams markets, unless compensating factors exist, of course.

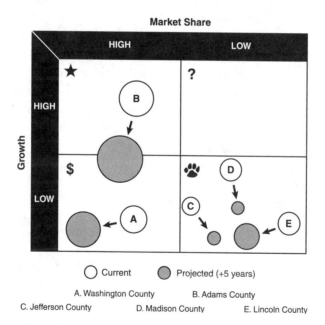

Constructed using design methodologies in Henderson, Bruce D. "The Product Portfolio" (1970). In *The Boston Consulting Group on Strategy: Classic Concepts and New Perspectives*, 2nd ed., edited by Carl W. Stern and Michael S. Deimler. New York: Wiley, 2006.

FIGURE 5-3 A Home Health Agency's Growth/Share Matrix

SUMMARY

The Boston Consulting Group's Growth/Share Matrix provides marketers with a simple, yet highly effective, portfolio analysis tool. Notably, the matrix assists marketers in their endeavors to assemble balanced product portfolios. Given the importance of assembling such portfolios, progressive marketers will find The Boston Consulting Group's Growth/Share Matrix to be an invaluable resource that greatly improves marketing efforts.

EXERCISES

1. Define and comprehensively discuss The Boston Consulting Group's Growth/Share Matrix, providing insights regarding its uses, features, methods of interpretation, and value, accompanied by an appropriate illustration. Be sure to include in your discussion an overview of the instrument's importance as a strategic marketing device in the healthcare industry.
2. Contact a retail pharmacy in your local market and request permission to walk through the aisles noting various product categories. Next, arrange a meeting with the store manager, explain The Boston Consulting Group's Growth/Share Matrix, ask for insights as to how each of the noted categories would be presented in the matrix, and prepare an associated illustration. Lastly, prepare a narrative discussing your experiences.

REFERENCES

Henderson, Bruce D. 1998. The product portfolio (1970). In *Perspectives on strategy from The Boston Consulting Group*, ed. Carl W. Stern and George Stalk Jr. New York: Wiley.

———. 2006. The product portfolio (1970). In *The Boston Consulting Group on strategy: Classic concepts and new perspectives*, 2nd ed., ed. Carl W. Stern and Michael S. Deimler. New York: Wiley.

CHAPTER 6

General Electric's Strategic Business-Planning Grid

LEARNING OBJECTIVES

After examining this chapter, readers will have the ability to:

- Recognize the necessity for portfolio planning endeavors in the healthcare industry to ensure productive marketing operations.
- Understand General Electric's Strategic Business-Planning Grid and its role in assessing the product portfolios of healthcare entities.
- Formulate effective product management strategies and tactics based on the market attractiveness and business strength characteristics of given healthcare offerings and their resulting locations in General Electric's Strategic Business-Planning Grid.

INTRODUCTION

Portfolio analysis, a rigorous endeavor entailing the comprehensive review of the goods and services offered by given entities, is an essential marketing management activity. The reason for this is obvious: Marketers must thoroughly understand their products if they are to successfully manage them.

The particular portfolio analysis tool used by marketers is dependent on the specific issues at hand and the level of analytical detail desired. Some portfolio analysis tools are very basic, while others are more sophisticated. One of the more elaborate portfolio analysis tools is known as the Strategic Business-Planning Grid, an evaluative device introduced by General Electric.

Illustrated in Figure 6-1, General Electric's Strategic Business-Planning Grid evaluates products based on industry attractiveness—here termed *market* attractiveness, which is more appropriate for the healthcare industry—and business strength. Market attractiveness is a measure of a particular market's desirable attributes. Business strength is a measure of organization/product prowess, or lack thereof, in a particular market.

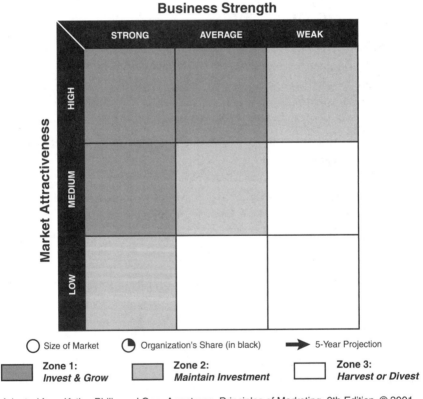

Adapted from Kotler, Philip and Gary Armstrong, Principles of Marketing, 9th Edition, © 2001, Pg. 55. Reprinted by permission of Pearson Education, Inc., Upper Saddle River, NJ.

FIGURE 6-1 General Electric's Strategic Business-Planning Grid

General Electric's Strategic Business-Planning Grid consists of a vertical axis representing market attractiveness (high, medium, and low), a horizontal axis representing business strength (strong, average, and weak), and nine cells divided into three zones (1, 2, and 3) differentiated by color. Zone 1 encompasses the three cells located in the upper left corner of the grid. Products falling within these cells represent offerings that should receive further investment for growth. Zone 2 includes the three cells running diagonally from the upper right to lower left corners of the grid. For products falling within these cells, investment should be maintained. Zone 3 encompasses the three cells located in the lower right corner of the grid. Products falling within these cells represent drains on portfolios and should be harvested or divested, unless compensating factors exist.

The strength of General Electric's Strategic Business-Planning Grid rests with the fact that its axes are designed to incorporate multiple factors associated with attractiveness and strength. This multifactor feature allows marketers to develop axes that incorporate variables that are deemed most relevant to their particular operations. The result is a customized evaluative tool.

Variables that are commonly used to compose the attractiveness axis include market size, market growth, profitability, and number of competitors. Variables that are commonly used to compose the strength axis include technological innovation, institutional capabilities, personnel, and distribution channels. The particular variables selected to compose each axis are completely up to the evaluating marketers. The only requirement is that the selected variables appropriately relate to market attractiveness and business strength.

OPERATIONAL MATTERS

To assess products using General Electric's Strategic Business-Planning Grid, marketers (1) identify the product offerings they wish to evaluate, (2) construct the Strategic Business-Planning Grid, as illustrated in Figure 6-1, (3) determine the variables that will compose the attractiveness and strength axes, weighting variables as deemed appropriate if increased detail is desired, (4) gather relevant product and market data, and (5) plot each product on the diagram using circles (which indicate market size, with larger circles indicating larger markets) and slices within each circle (which indicate the market share of given offerings).

This visual representation is then analyzed to determine the strengths and weaknesses associated with given product portfolios. If additional detail is desired, marketers can use arrows to indicate anticipated attractiveness-strength characteristics at some point in the future.

Figure 6-2 identifies a Strategic Business-Planning Grid (with forecast arrows) that was developed for a pharmaceutical retailer. Here, the retailer evaluated its seven retail pharmacies—Georgetown, Colony, Northtown, Meadowbrook, Riverview, Midtown, and Oakdale—based on market attractiveness (defined by market size and market growth) and business strength (defined by store location and product line).

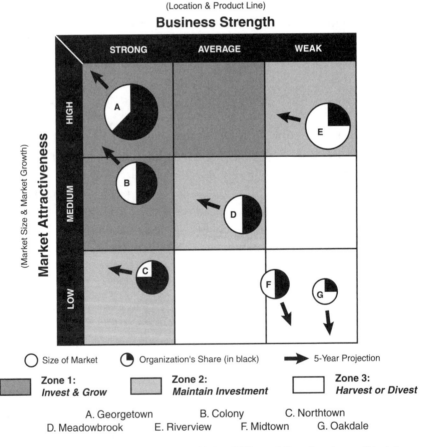

Constructed using design methodologies in Kotler, Philip, and Gary Armstrong. *Principles of Marketing.* 9th ed. Upper Saddle River, NJ: Prentice Hall, 2001.

FIGURE 6-2 A Pharmaceutical Retailer's GE Grid

A review of the grid indicates that the retailer currently has two Zone 1 offerings (i.e., Georgetown and Colony), three Zone 2 offerings (i.e., Northtown, Meadowbrook, and Riverview), and two Zone 3 offerings (i.e., Midtown and Oakdale). Of the establishments identified in Zone 1, Georgetown is most favorably situated, with Colony closely following. Given the combination of market attractiveness and business strength characteristics, the retailer would be wise to further invest in these locations in an effort to build these positions, especially given the positive 5-year forecast, as indicated by the diagram's arrows.

Northtown, Meadowbrook, and Riverview are situated in Zone 2. These establishments deliver neither superior nor inferior performance; however, the 5-year forecast indicates positive attractiveness-strength characteristics. Given their placement in Zone 2, coupled with the positive forecast, the retailer would be wise to maintain its level of investment in these locations.

Midtown and Oakdale are situated in Zone 3. These offerings possess inferior attractiveness-strength characteristics that are not expected to improve in the future. Unless compensating factors exist, these locations should be eliminated from the retailer's portfolio.

SUMMARY

General Electric's Strategic Business-Planning Grid provides marketers with a useful evaluative tool that can shed significant light on the product portfolios of healthcare entities. With its ability to incorporate multiple variables into its attractiveness and strength axes, the grid offers marketers a truly flexible device that can be customized to address almost any situation. Progressive marketers will undoubtedly find General Electric's Strategic Business-Planning Grid to be very useful in their endeavors to successfully manage product portfolios.

EXERCISES

1. Define and comprehensively discuss General Electric's Strategic Business-Planning Grid, its three associated zones, and methodology associated with placing products in the diagram. A diagram of the grid should be included to add value to your narrative. Be sure to include in your discussion details pertaining to how the particular

axes are formulated and the advantages associated with such. Share your thoughts regarding the tool's implications and uses in the healthcare industry.

2. Compare and contrast General Electric's Strategic Business-Planning Grid with The Boston Consulting Group's Growth/Share Matrix. Discuss the strengths and weaknesses of these two instruments. Share your thoughts on the particular tool you believe to be most appropriate for use in the healthcare industry, providing justifications for your designated position.

REFERENCE

Kotler, Philip, and Gary Armstrong. 2001. *Principles of marketing.* 9th ed. Upper Saddle River, NJ: Prentice Hall.

CHAPTER 7

Igor Ansoff's Product-Market Expansion Grid

LEARNING OBJECTIVES

After examining this chapter, readers will have the ability to:

- Recognize the importance of continually pursuing opportunities for growth in the healthcare marketplace.
- Understand that, as a result of intense competition, complacency, even for healthcare entities occupying market leadership positions, will eventually lead to market share erosion and ultimately failure.
- Identify expansion opportunities available to healthcare institutions through the use of Igor Ansoff's Product-Market Expansion Grid.
- Understand methods for gaining enhanced insights into growth prospects through the use of Igor Ansoff's Expansion Cube.

INTRODUCTION

The healthcare environment is characterized by innovation, intense competition, and uncertainty. Given this turbulent environment, healthcare marketers must strive to proactively monitor their surroundings to, among other things, detect growth opportunities that can be exploited. No longer can healthcare marketers be satisfied with maintaining the status quo.

Instead, marketers must vigorously pursue and capitalize on growth opportunities to increase the likelihood of institutional survival, growth, and prosperity. To capitalize on growth opportunities, marketers must carefully formulate appropriate expansion strategies—a process that is greatly facilitated by Igor Ansoff's Product-Market Expansion Grid.

Also known as Ansoff's Matrix, the Product-Market Expansion Grid was developed to shed light on the growth options available to organizations. Illustrated in Figure 7-1, the Product-Market Expansion Grid consists of a vertical axis representing markets (current and new), a horizontal axis representing products (current and new), and four cells that identify the four basic growth alternatives: market penetration, market development, product development, and diversification. These four growth strategies are defined as follows.

Products / Markets	Current	New
Current	*Market Penetration*	*Product Development*
New	*Market Development*	*Diversification*

Adapted from *Corporate Strategy: An Analytic Approach to Business Policy for Growth and Expansion* by H. Igor Ansoff. Copyright © 1965 by McGraw-Hill, Inc. Published by McGraw-Hill. Reprinted by permission of the estate of H. Igor Ansoff.

FIGURE 7-1 Ansoff's Product-Market Expansion Grid

MARKET PENETRATION (CURRENT PRODUCTS, CURRENT MARKETS)

Market penetration is a growth strategy that seeks to increase the use of current product offerings by current customers. Here, marketing managers seek growth by identifying ways to increase consumption of the goods and services that are currently offered in existing markets. Marketing techniques used to achieve deeper market penetration include increased advertising, identification of new uses for products, price reductions, use of incentives, and so on. These techniques, when aimed at current markets, can stimulate consumption, resulting in increased growth.

MARKET DEVELOPMENT (CURRENT PRODUCTS, NEW MARKETS)

Market development is a growth strategy that involves the introduction of current products into new markets. This is achieved by identifying new target audiences and directing current offerings accordingly. Current products may, for example, be placed in different geographic markets or directed toward new demographic segments to stimulate demand and increase growth. These new markets offer new opportunities to increase the consumption of current product offerings.

PRODUCT DEVELOPMENT (NEW PRODUCTS, CURRENT MARKETS)

Product development is a growth strategy that involves the introduction of new products into current markets. These products might be completely different offerings or they might be modified versions of existing products. With this strategy, marketers focus their efforts on developing new goods and services that will be attractive to current customers.

DIVERSIFICATION (NEW PRODUCTS, NEW MARKETS)

Diversification is a growth strategy that involves the introduction of new products into new markets. By focusing on new products and new markets, this strategy calls for organizations to enter completely unfamiliar territory.

Given that both aspects of this pursuit—product and market—are new to entities, diversification is the riskiest of the four growth strategies.

OPERATIONAL MATTERS

To formulate growth strategies using Ansoff's Product-Market Expansion Grid, marketers (1) construct the Product-Market Expansion Grid, as illustrated in Figure 7-1, (2) formulate growth options for each of the four growth strategies, and (3) place these growth options in their respective cells on the Grid. The resulting Product-Market Expansion Grid provides a simple, yet highly useful, depiction of available expansion opportunities.

Figure 7-2 identifies a Product-Market Expansion Grid that was developed for an assisted living center. Here, marketers could potentially achieve deeper market penetration by increasing consumer awareness through expansion of the facility's current advertising campaign. This more prominent

Products / Markets	Current	New
Current	*Market Penetration* — Expansion of the current advertising campaign	*Product Development* — Construction of an on-site senior wellness center
New	*Market Development* — Construction of a new facility in a neighboring community	*Diversification* — Acquisition of a nursing home

Adapted from *Corporate Strategy: An Analytic Approach to Business Policy for Growth and Expansion* by H. Igor Ansoff. Copyright © 1965 by McGraw-Hill, Inc. Published by McGraw-Hill. Reprinted by permission of the estate of H. Igor Ansoff.

FIGURE 7-2 An Assisted Living Center's Expansion Grid

campaign could direct more interest and attention toward the facility and potentially increase the center's occupancy rate. Growth could also be achieved by developing a new geographic market through the construction of a new assisted living center in a neighboring community. Another growth option involves the construction of an on-site senior wellness center to serve the current market. This new amenity could give the facility a competitive advantage over other area assisted living centers, improving occupant retention and encouraging potential occupants to select it for their assisted living needs. Finally, the assisted living center could seek growth through diversification by purchasing and operating a nursing home.

Figure 7-3 presents a Product-Market Expansion Grid that was developed for a medical clinic. The medical clinic could potentially achieve deeper market penetration by organizing several on-site health fairs that would encourage current and potential customers to visit the facility. These events could build awareness in the market and ultimately increase

Products / Markets	Current	New
Current	**Market Penetration** On-site health fairs to stimulate interest and attention	**Product Development** Introduction of an evening and weekend clinic
New	**Market Development** Direction of promotional efforts toward minority and senior citizen groups	**Diversification** Acquisition of a renal dialysis center

Adapted from *Corporate Strategy: An Analytic Approach to Business Policy for Growth and Expansion* by H. Igor Ansoff. Copyright © 1965 by McGraw-Hill, Inc. Published by McGraw-Hill. Reprinted by permission of the estate of H. Igor Ansoff.

FIGURE 7-3 A Medical Clinic's Expansion Grid

patient encounters. Growth could also be achieved by targeting new demographic segments and encouraging their members to visit the clinic. The medical clinic might, for example, develop advertising campaigns that focus on minority and senior health issues to attract members of these groups to the establishment. To improve its position in the current market, the medical clinic could introduce an evening and weekend clinic to serve clients who find it difficult to schedule appointments during normal business hours. Lastly, the medical clinic could seek expansion through diversification by purchasing and operating a renal dialysis center.

It should be noted that although each strategy in the Product-Market Expansion Grid represents a distinct path toward growth, most organizations pursue multiple growth strategies simultaneously. Importantly, the Product-Market Expansion Grid does not communicate which strategy or strategies organizations should pursue. Instead, it focuses attention on the growth opportunities that are available to entities.

AN UPDATED VERSION

It should be mentioned that Igor Ansoff developed an updated version of his Product-Market Expansion Grid, which might be termed Ansoff's Expansion Cube. Illustrated in Figure 7-4, Ansoff's Expansion Cube incorporates three dimensions: market need, product technologies, and market geography. These three dimensions create a cube that illustrates a variety of growth options, ranging from addressing current needs and current markets with current technologies (Section A) to addressing new needs and new markets with new technologies (Section B). Quite obviously, Ansoff's Expansion Cube offers enhanced insights into growth opportunities, making it highly useful for marketers seeking additional detail.

SUMMARY

The long-term viability of hospitals, clinics, home health agencies, and other healthcare entities largely depends on the successful identification and exploitation of growth opportunities. Igor Ansoff's Product-Market Expansion Grid provides marketers with a very powerful and effective tool for recognizing and evaluating these opportunities. This tool greatly assists marketers in the development of appropriate expansion strategies.

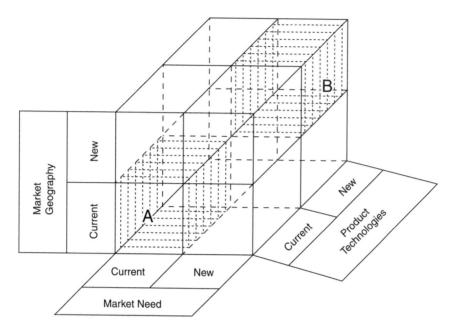

From *The New Corporate Strategy*, Rev. ed. by H. Igor Ansoff. Copyright © 1988 by H. Igor Ansoff. Published by John Wiley & Sons, Inc. Reprinted by permission of the estate of H. Igor Ansoff.

FIGURE 7-4 Ansoff's Expansion Cube

EXERCISES

1. Compare and contrast Igor Ansoff's Product-Market Expansion Grid with his Expansion Cube, identifying the components of each, supported by illustrations. Which model possesses the most utility for use in the healthcare industry? Why do you view this to be the case?

2. Select a local healthcare establishment and gain insights into its current array of product offerings. Based on your knowledge of the market and the local healthcare establishment, formulate one growth option for each of the four growth strategies identified in Igor Ansoff's Product-Market Expansion Grid. Identify the particular option you believe to be most viable. Be sure to provide justifications for your selection.

REFERENCES

Ansoff, H. Igor. 1965. *Corporate strategy: An analytic approach to business policy for growth and expansion.* New York: McGraw-Hill.
————. 1988. *The new corporate strategy.* Rev. ed. New York: Wiley.

PART TWO

Branding & Identity Management Tools

CHAPTER 8

Schmitt & Simonson's Drivers of Identity Management

LEARNING OBJECTIVES

After examining this chapter, readers will have the ability to:

- Understand the critical pursuit of identity management and its role in helping healthcare entities build strong, recognizable brands.
- Realize the importance of establishing brands and other elements of identity as a means of differentiating given products from competitive offerings in the marketplace.
- Appreciate the value and guidance offered by Schmitt and Simonson's Drivers of Identity Management as a tool for informing healthcare marketers of the circumstances that necessitate addressing elements of identity within their given institutions.

INTRODUCTION

Healthcare marketers must continually be concerned with how their organizations and related product offerings are perceived by target audiences. Customer perceptions are, at least in part, influenced by the efforts of marketers to create desirable identities for given product offerings.

Identity is achieved through branding activities, with such activities generating logos, product names, slogans, jingles, product packaging, building signage, and related identity vehicles for the purpose of conveying desired images to target audiences. Branding activities assist customers in identifying goods and services in the marketplace, importantly helping them to distinguish such products from competitive offerings. Attending to these activities is often termed *identity management*—one of the most important responsibilities of healthcare marketers.

Given the importance of identity management activities, it is helpful for healthcare marketers to possess an understanding of the primary forces that drive such efforts. To assist marketers in achieving this understanding, Bernd Schmitt and Alex Simonson identified nine drivers of identity management, which are illustrated in Figure 8-1. These nine drivers—change in corporate structure, low loyalty or losing share, outdated image, incon-

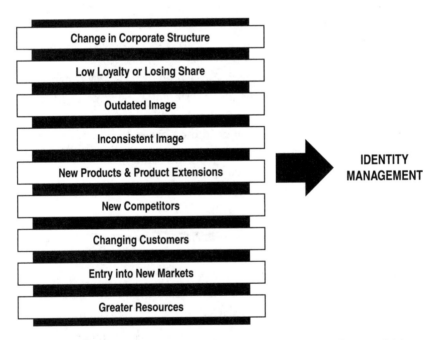

FIGURE 8-1 Schmitt & Simonson's Drivers of Identity Management

sistent image, new products and product extensions, new competitors, changing customers, entry into new markets, and greater resources—are defined as follows.

CHANGE IN CORPORATE STRUCTURE

Alterations in the corporate structures of establishments are quite common across all industries, including the healthcare industry. Mergers and acquisitions, for example, occur for any number of reasons, but both are prefaced by beliefs that combined, rather than singular, efforts will yield enhanced benefits for the organizations under examination.

Any time two or more healthcare organizations combine to form a single establishment, identity management issues must be addressed. Possibly the most pressing identity management issue associated with mergers and acquisitions is the determination of an appropriate name for the newly combined entity. Should the two healthcare organizations be allowed to carry their existing, separate identities (e.g., Ridgewood Medical Center *and* Valley Medical Center)? Should the two establishments agree to accept one name over the other (e.g., Ridgewood Medical Center)? Should the entities select some sort of a hybrid name (e.g., Ridgewood Valley Medical Center)?

These questions may or may not be easy to answer depending on the particular circumstances associated with given transactions. Factors to consider include the strength, or lack thereof, of given brand names, the real or anticipated preferences of target markets, and so on—issues that must thoroughly be investigated prior to making such determinations.

As with mergers and acquisitions, spin-offs elicit an equally intensive need for identity management activities. Clearly, changes in the corporate structures of healthcare entities serve as drivers of identity management.

LOW LOYALTY OR LOSING SHARE

Customer loyalty is an essential ingredient for marketing success. Loyalty not only delivers the benefits associated with customer retention but also results in such customers echoing their support to members of their social circles through the very powerful communications medium of word-of-mouth publicity. Customer loyalty bolsters market share, increasing the likelihood of growth and prosperity.

Naturally, low customer loyalty and market share attrition are causes of concern for any healthcare marketer, and such occurrences may, at least in part, be the result of identity problems. Valuable identities are the result of brand characteristics that are attractive to target audiences and strategically well managed. Healthcare establishments must ensure that they possess such identities.

OUTDATED IMAGE

Brand imagery, with the passage of time, is subject to stagnation in the eyes of customers. Healthcare entities, in the interest of being current, often select progressive logos and related visual references. This modern symbolism is quite appropriate in such a technology-oriented industry and is highly relevant upon initiation. Unfortunately, however, these designs can rapidly become outdated, requiring periodic alterations to remain current. Even more traditional imagery, which typically possesses a longer life span, is not immune to stagnation, necessitating updates over time. Simply stated, diminished imagery equates with diminished identity and thus serves as a driver of identity management.

INCONSISTENT IMAGE

Consistency in the imagery associated with identity is a must. Ideally, logos, building signage, promotional materials, and so on should be coordinated to achieve a consistent, orderly appearance. Unfortunately, such consistency is not always the case.

Inconsistent imagery is confusing to customers, resulting in difficulties in identifying given establishments and their product offerings. It also typically conveys the impression of disorder—a disastrous image for any organization, but especially for healthcare establishments, which are entrusted with the personal health of individuals.

NEW PRODUCTS & PRODUCT EXTENSIONS

When new products and product extensions are introduced into the marketplace, identity creation decisions are required. Such decisions range from being very simple to being very complex, depending on the nature of the new offering and its placement within a given product portfolio.

A pharmaceutical manufacturer, for example, would face a simple identity creation decision with the introduction of an extra-strength version of an existing pain reliever. Such identity creation simplicity, however, would not be possible in a situation involving an entirely different pharmaceutical product resulting from a recent discovery. Likewise, a medical center would not encounter a very rigorous identity creation decision if it decided to simply enhance its existing array of maternity services. If, instead, the medical center decided to enter a completely different arena, say, occupational health services, the identity creation decision would be much more difficult.

Regardless of the level of difficulty involved in creating effective identities, new products and product extensions clearly hasten the identity management process.

NEW COMPETITORS

Identity management is one of many activities that healthcare marketers must engage in when new competitors enter the market. Among other things, new competitors bring their new identities into the marketplace, and these identities might impact consumer perceptions of existing ones in the given environment. Such competitive entry minimally calls for healthcare marketers to review their existing identity management efforts and may call for the alteration and enhancement of given identities. Ultimately, healthcare marketers would like for their identities, rather than those of their competitors, to be viewed most favorably by consumers, making the introduction of new competitors into the marketplace a driver of identity management.

CHANGING CUSTOMERS

Customers, their wants and needs, their tastes and preferences, their perceptions, and their environments are constantly changing. In an effort to stay relevant in the minds of customers, the identities of establishments and their product offerings must change in tandem with changing customers.

On an ongoing basis, healthcare marketers must study their desired customer populations and objectively analyze their identity management efforts, seeking to view such efforts from the perspective of target audiences. By doing this, healthcare marketers stay abreast of changing customer characteristics, allowing them to alter identities accordingly to meet the current expectations of target markets.

ENTRY INTO NEW MARKETS

Whenever healthcare entities enter new markets, identity management efforts must carefully be evaluated. Here, healthcare marketers must determine whether to use existing identities, related identities, or entirely new identities in these new markets. Because different markets quite frequently possess different characteristics, existing identity schemes may not be transferable to new settings. This necessitates that healthcare marketers carefully investigate identity management issues associated with newly targeted markets and design their identities accordingly.

GREATER RESOURCES

Burgeoning resources afford healthcare marketers with more identity options (e.g., more appealing facility signage, more elaborate product packaging, enhanced marketing communications initiatives) which are worthy of exploration in attempts to build customer perceptions regarding given product offerings. Whenever an infusion of resources occurs (e.g., more prosperous economic periods), healthcare marketers must comprehensively review their identity management efforts to determine the most productive methods for utilizing these funds to effect the greatest identity gains in the marketplace.

SUMMARY

Because marketing success requires effective identity management efforts, healthcare marketers must ensure that they are aware of the circumstances and events that drive such endeavors. The typology offered by Schmitt and Simonson effectively portrays the forces that drive identity management, reminding healthcare marketers of their important responsibilities.

EXERCISES

1. Provide a detailed overview of Schmitt and Simonson's Drivers of Identity Management, noting facets regarding its purpose, use, and value in healthcare organizations. Share your thoughts and ideas regarding the degree to which modern healthcare organizations actively engage in routine endeavors to ensure appropriate identities.

2. Select a healthcare organization in your local market and study its logo and other elements of brand identity. Using guidance provided by Schmitt and Simonson's Drivers of Identity Management regarding *inconsistent image*, prepare a report detailing the degree to which you believe the chosen facility's logo and associated branding elements convey an image of consistency and order. If you believe that changes are necessary, what do you recommend? If you believe that changes are not necessary, why do you consider this to be the case?

REFERENCE

Schmitt, Bernd, and Alex Simonson. 1997. *Marketing aesthetics: The strategic management of brands, identity, and image*. New York: The Free Press.

Calder & Reagan's Brand Design Model

LEARNING OBJECTIVES

After examining this chapter, readers will have the ability to:

- Recognize the value of assigning appropriate brand identities to represent healthcare goods, services, and institutions.
- Understand the functions of brands and the value that brands offer both buyers and sellers.
- Understand that for brands to attract the patronage of target audiences, they must convey customer-focused meaning.
- Realize that the process of brand development must be conducted in a systematic, orderly fashion to ensure successful brand identities.
- Recognize the value of Calder and Reagan's Brand Design Model as a device for systematically guiding healthcare marketers through the process of formulating brands.

INTRODUCTION

Brands are names, logos, slogans, and other references that identify goods and services, thus allowing customers to distinguish products from competitive offerings. In essence, brands give products *identity*, a component that is absolutely essential for the purpose of product differentiation.

Brands can be used to identify individual products, product lines, or entire organizations, and they benefit both producers and consumers, as presented in Figure 9-1. These benefits illustrate the critical importance of brands, making the successful establishment of brand identity one of the most essential tasks of marketing management.

Despite the importance of branding, the process of brand development is often conducted in an unsystematic, haphazard fashion, typically as a derivative of either marketing plans or advertising. In an effort to bring order to this process and improve branding results, Bobby Calder and Steven Reagan developed the Brand Design Model.

Illustrated in Figure 9-2, the Brand Design Model consists of an inner circle representing the meaningful relevant value of a product and an outer circle representing verbal and visual brand expressions. The Brand Design Model challenges marketers to first identify product-related meaning (i.e., meaningful relevant value) and then formulate methods to convey this meaning to customers through an arrangement of verbal and visual

FIGURE 9-1 Functions of a Brand

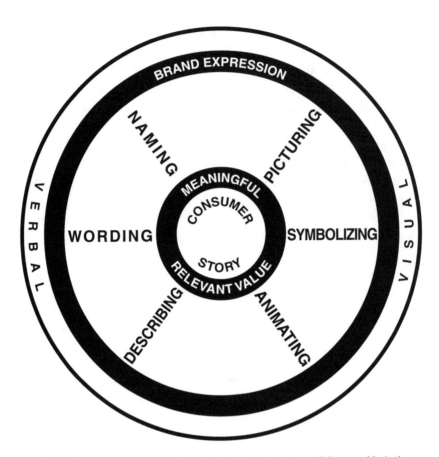

From "Brand Design" by Bobby J. Calder and Steven J. Reagan in *Kellogg on Marketing*, edited by Dawn Iacobucci. Copyright © 2001 by John Wiley & Sons, Inc. Reprinted with permission of John Wiley & Sons, Inc.

FIGURE 9-2 Calder & Reagan's Brand Design Model

elements (i.e., brand expressions). Meaningful relevant value and brand expressions of the Brand Design Model are explained as follows.

MEANINGFUL RELEVANT VALUE

Through branding, marketers seek to make products more meaningful to customers, and one of the best methods for accomplishing this entails viewing products from the perspective of target markets. To view products through the eyes of customers, marketers must ask themselves how their products positively impact the lives of customers. When viewing products in this manner, marketers focus their attention on the prime motivator of consumer purchase activity—the ability of products to satisfy wants and needs. These inquiries ultimately yield consumer stories that are meaningful to target markets. When consumer stories have been formulated, marketers then focus on conveyance of these stories to target markets through the formulation of brand expressions.

BRAND EXPRESSIONS

Brands can be expressed using verbal and visual elements. Verbal brand expressions include naming (i.e., the assignment of names to products), wording (i.e., the development of specialized vocabularies to describe product attributes—catch phrases, slogans, etc.), and describing (i.e., the scripting of phrases and sentences that elaborate upon the attributes of products—product uses, safety information, durability information, customer testimonials, etc.).

Visual brand expressions include picturing (i.e., the presentation of products using still photography and other static, illustrative methods), symbolizing (i.e., the development and use of logos and other abstract, symbolic methods to identify products), and animating (i.e., the use of "moving" pictures, including video photography and computer animation, to present products).

In formulating brand expressions, the ultimate goal is to develop verbal and visual components that will accurately convey the meaning of products—the consumer stories revealed through meaningful relevant value inquiries—to target markets.

OPERATIONAL MATTERS

To develop brands using Calder and Reagan's Brand Design Model, marketers simply (1) identify the product to be branded, (2) construct the Brand Design diagram, as illustrated in Figure 9-2, (3) identify and/or formulate a product-related story that is of interest to target markets along with verbal and visual brand expressions that will convey this story to customers, and (4) place these elements on the Brand Design diagram accordingly. The resulting diagram yields a customer-focused brand identity for the given product offering.

Figure 9-3 illustrates a Brand Design Model that was developed for a newly established ambulance company. Here, the company has identified a relevant story of consumer interest—quick access to emergency transportation—and has designed its verbal and visual expressions around this story. Quite clearly, each verbal and visual element directly relates to all-inclusive, expeditious access to quality emergency transportation. Courtesy of the Brand Design Model, the company has successfully formulated a customer-focused brand identity that will allow it to effectively market ambulance transportation to its target audience. Coordinated promotional efforts can now be initiated.

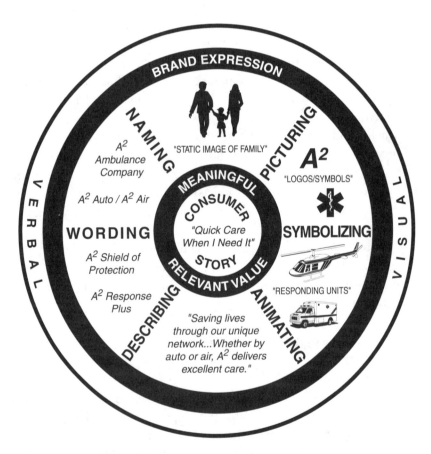

FIGURE 9-3 An Ambulance Company's Brand Design Model

The ambulance company's completed schematic clearly illustrates the power of the Brand Design Model. In one simple diagram, marketers can view the strategic and tactical brand fundamentals associated with given product offerings. This centralized source of carefully prepared information is particularly useful in achieving consistency of presentation across advertising media. Given the increasing array of available media, along with desires for more precise target marketing, the Brand Design Model offers marketers a method for ensuring integrated marketing communications.

It should be noted that the Brand Design Model is to be formulated in an inclusive fashion where input from all organizational members involved in the development and management of associated products is actively encouraged. The multiple perspectives offered by this extended group of individuals can greatly enhance resulting Brand Designs.

SUMMARY

Brands allow customers to distinguish goods and services from competitive offerings and are, therefore, essential for the purpose of product differentiation. Given the importance of brands, marketers can significantly benefit from the branding process offered by Calder and Reagan's Brand Design Model.

The Brand Design Model systematically guides marketers through the process of formulating brands that convey customer-focused meaning—an absolute requirement for attracting the patronage of target markets. Despite its simplicity, the Brand Design Model significantly enhances branding results. Progressive marketers will undoubtedly find it to be an invaluable resource that greatly improves marketing efforts.

EXERCISES

1. Provide a detailed overview of Calder and Reagan's Brand Design Model, illustrating its use and value as a device for systematically guiding healthcare marketers through the process of formulating brands. Share your perspectives regarding the degree to which healthcare organizations in your local community are communicating consistent messages across their various communications platforms.
2. Place yourself in the role of a healthcare industry entrepreneur who is contemplating the development of a healthcare good, service, or

institution of your choice. Using Calder and Reagan's Brand Design Model, create this particular item's consumer story, assemble verbal and visual brand expressions, and place these elements in an appropriate Brand Design diagram. Provide a brief narrative explaining your thoughts and ideas.

REFERENCES

Berthon, Pierre, James M. Hulbert, and Leyland F. Pitt. 1999. Brand management prognostications. *MIT Sloan Management Review* 40 (2): 53–65.

Calder, Bobby J., and Steven J. Reagan. 2001. Brand design. In *Kellogg on marketing*, ed. Dawn Iacobucci. New York: Wiley.

CHAPTER 10

Martin Lindstrom's 5-D Brand Sensogram

LEARNING OBJECTIVES

After examining this chapter, readers will have the ability to:

- Understand the essential role of brands and their importance in product differentiation in the healthcare marketplace.
- Realize that brands can incorporate facets that extend into five dimensional realms, incorporating sight, sound, taste, touch, and smell.
- Recognize the assistance that Martin Lindstrom's 5-D Brand Sensogram offers healthcare marketers in assessing their efforts to incorporate sight, sound, taste, touch, and smell into their various goods and services.

INTRODUCTION

Successful branding initiatives result in the establishment of appropriate and effective identities and associated representations (e.g., names, logos, slogans, and other identifiers) for healthcare organizations and the products they offer to target audiences. Because brands are used by customers to recognize goods and services and, significantly, distinguish them from competitive offerings, the importance of branding and associated identity management activities cannot be understated.

Brands have traditionally been viewed as verbal and visual manifestations that are designed and developed to represent organizations and their product offerings. While verbal and visual elements are, and will continue to be, core components for the establishment of institutional and product identity, such attributes only tap into the sight (i.e., visual) and sound (i.e., verbal) senses. Remaining senses—taste, touch, and smell—have largely gone unaddressed in branding but represent potential opportunities for healthcare marketers to further distinguish their given offerings.

An understanding of the brand enrichment opportunities afforded by addressing the five senses led Martin Lindstrom to suggest that marketers move beyond the traditional, two-dimensional (2-D) view of branding and, instead, embrace a more comprehensive, five-dimensional (5-D) perspective that incorporates all five senses—sight, sound, taste, touch, and smell—providing marketers with enhanced opportunities to communicate with customers.

To assist marketers in their efforts to design 5-D brands, Lindstrom developed the 5-D Brand Sensogram. As illustrated in Figure 10-1, the Brand

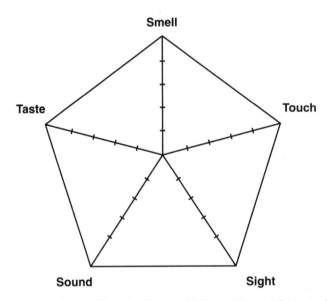

FIGURE 10-1 Lindstrom's 5-D Brand Sensogram

Sensogram is depicted as a pentagon with each point identifying a different sense—sight, sound, taste, touch, and smell. Five-point scales running from the center of the diagram outward to associated points indicate the strength of given senses pertaining to the brand under examination, with greater distance from the center indicating greater strength. Prefaced by descriptions of the five senses of sight, sound, taste, touch, and smell, Lindstrom's 5-D Brand Sensogram is explained as follows.

SIGHT

Sight-related brand manifestations include logos, slogans, illustrations, and photographs, along with the marketing communications devices that incorporate these items, including business cards, facility signage, product packaging, and visual advertisements. Beyond items that are traditionally associated with marketing communications, however, numerous other sight-related branding opportunities are available to healthcare entities. Such possibilities include institutional cleanliness; well-groomed, appropriately attired employees; and well-appointed waiting, examination, and patient rooms. These sight-related elements of branding, if designed effectively, clearly have the potential to positively impact customers and their perceptions of healthcare institutions.

SOUND

Sound-related brand manifestations include jingles, musical scores, and customer testimonials, along with the marketing communications tools that incorporate these items, including music-on-hold programming, corporate sound systems, and audio advertisements. Sound offers healthcare entities many creative branding opportunities. Original promotional tunes, for example, can play when corporate computers boot up or they can be converted into ringtones for employee-issued cellular telephones, bolstering the brand identity of given healthcare establishments.

TASTE

Taste represents a departure from the traditional sight and sound mindset of branding, but opportunities, under the right circumstances, clearly exist for taste to bolster brands. Pharmaceutical firms, for example, are highly concerned with taste for the various medicines that they produce because pleasant flavors are welcomed by individuals of all ages. Hospitals are often said to serve food that is not particularly desirable, affording these entities with opportunities to bolster consumer perceptions by ensuring that dietary departments endeavor to prepare excellent meals for patients and hospital guests. While achieving taste-related brand characteristics is not possible in all circumstances, healthcare marketers are encouraged to take advantage of such opportunities when they present themselves.

TOUCH

As with taste, touch represents a nontraditional characteristic of branding with much potential to bolster identity in given situations. Durable medical equipment manufacturers, for example, are presented with many opportunities to incorporate touch-related elements into their products. Quality wares, such as hospital beds and wheelchairs, are often said to feel very secure and offer significant support—all touch-related items. Pharmaceutical manufacturers, too, can incorporate touch by, say, distributing their medicines in distinctive bottles that are safe but also easy to open. Likewise, hospitals can incorporate quality fabrics and linens that are pleasing to the touch for their patient populations. Each of these facets illustrates the use of touch as an opportunity to bolster the brand identity efforts of healthcare organizations.

SMELL

The nontraditional brand manifestation of smell affords healthcare entities with a wealth of opportunities to bolster brand identity efforts. Pharmaceutical manufacturers, for example, are very interested in developing desirable scents for medicinal creams, gels, and related products. Hospitals, medical centers, and nursing homes are highly concerned with maintaining good air quality—a smell-related element—to, in part, establish perceptions of safe and clean clinical environments. These establishments are equally concerned with ensuring that linens possess fresh scents that further bolster cleanliness initiatives. Smell clearly influences customer perceptions of healthcare entities and their product offerings, making smell an important element in the establishment of brand identity.

THE 5-D BRAND SENSOGRAM

Lindstrom's 5-D Brand Sensogram allows healthcare marketers to measure their efforts at establishing 5-D brands. To do this, marketers simply (1) identify the product offering to be evaluated, (2) construct the Brand Sensogram, as illustrated in Figure 10-1, (3) rank the offering's brand characteristics related to each of the five senses, plotting discoveries on the diagram accordingly, and (4) connect the plotted points. This visual representation is then analyzed to determine the given brand's sensory awareness properties, allowing marketers the opportunity to bolster their identity management efforts.

Enhanced insights can be afforded by noting the specific brand characteristics which prompted the rankings in completed Brand Sensograms. Additional detail can be gained by plotting competitive brands over completed Brand Sensograms to comparatively assess branding initiatives.

As Figures 10-2 and 10-3 illustrate, completion of this simple, yet highly effective, diagram yields considerable insights into efforts to establish

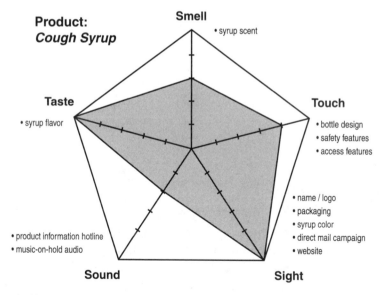

FIGURE 10-2 A Pharmaceutical Firm's 5-D Brand Sensogram

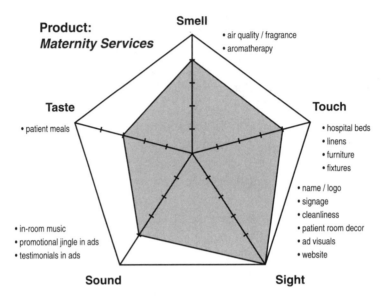

FIGURE 10-3 A Medical Center's 5-D Brand Sensogram

multidimensional brands and hence serves as an essential brand management tool.

SUMMARY

Lindstrom's 5-D Brand Sensogram draws significant attention to the multidimensional nature of brands, affording healthcare marketers with a convenient tool for assessing their efforts to incorporate sight, sound, taste, touch, and smell into their goods and services. By addressing each of the senses within Lindstrom's 5-D Brand Sensogram, healthcare marketers can deliver enriched product offerings that are attractive to target audiences on many levels.

EXERCISES

1. Define and comprehensively discuss Martin Lindstrom's 5-D Brand Sensogram, providing insights into the five dimensional realms of sight, sound, taste, touch, and smell. Share your thoughts regarding the tool's implications and uses in the healthcare industry. Provide your perspectives regarding the degree to which you believe brand managers in modern healthcare institutions address each of the five dimensions.

2. Select a local healthcare facility and arrange to visit the institution. On your tour of the facility, look for identity elements that relate to the five senses of sight, sound, taste, touch, and smell. With this information, prepare a 5-D Brand Sensogram for the establishment. Are branding opportunities available? If so, how might you address these opportunities in a manner to maximize facility identity?

REFERENCE

Lindstrom, Martin. 2005. *Brand sense: Build powerful brands through touch, taste, smell, sight, and sound.* New York: The Free Press.

CHAPTER 11

Lederer & Hill's Brand Portfolio Molecule

LEARNING OBJECTIVES

After examining this chapter, readers will have the ability to:

- Understand that brands exist not in isolation but in a larger environment that includes other brands.
- Realize that brands impact one another; sometimes positively, sometimes neutrally, and sometimes negatively.
- Appreciate the value of Lederer and Hill's Brand Portfolio Molecule as a tool for understanding brand relationships.

INTRODUCTION

Brands are names, logos, slogans, and other identifiers that are developed and assigned to products to help customers distinguish goods and services from competitive offerings. By successfully branding products, marketers greatly increase the likelihood that customers will recognize their goods and services—an essential prerequisite for purchase activity.

Given the obvious importance of branding, healthcare marketers must diligently work to ensure that they thoroughly understand the brands they are responsible for managing. The better marketers understand brands, the better prepared they will be to appropriately manage these offerings.

One of the most effective tools for understanding brands is known as the Brand Portfolio Molecule which, as illustrated in Figure 11-1, presents brand portfolios in the form of atoms. Developed by Chris Lederer and

Sam Hill, the Brand Portfolio Molecule multidimensionally illustrates the relationships that exist among brands within given product portfolios. The Brand Portfolio Molecule also identifies, in the same multidimensional fashion, associated external brands that impact these portfolios.

COMPONENTS OF THE BRAND PORTFOLIO MOLECULE

A Brand Portfolio Molecule consists of a large central atom (i.e., the lead brand), which represents the most influential brand within a given portfolio; midsized atoms (i.e., strategic brands), which heavily influence customer purchases; and small atoms (i.e., support brands), which mildly influence customer purchases.

The color of atoms in the Brand Portfolio Molecule indicates the influence that particular brands have within given portfolios. A light color indicates a positive influence, a medium color indicates a neutral influence, and a dark color indicates a negative influence.

Nodes are atoms (i.e., brands) that have relationships with other atoms (i.e., brands), with direct connections indicating direct relationships and indirect connections indicating indirect relationships. The width of the link between nodes indicates the degree of control that one brand commands over the other. Thicker links indicate greater control.

Proximity indicates the positioning characteristics of brands. Brands that are close in proximity are similarly positioned. Brands that are more distant in proximity are more distinctly positioned.

OPERATIONAL MATTERS

To assemble a Brand Portfolio Molecule, marketers (1) list all of the brands within a given portfolio, as well as associated external brands, (2) classify each brand as lead, strategic, or support, (3) establish the network of relationships that exist among these brands, and (4) map the Brand Portfolio Molecule either by hand or with the assistance of illustration software. When mapped, marketers use the Brand Portfolio Molecule to assess given brand portfolios.

Figure 11-1 illustrates a Brand Portfolio Molecule that was developed for a medical clinic. From the molecule, it is easily determined that City Clinic

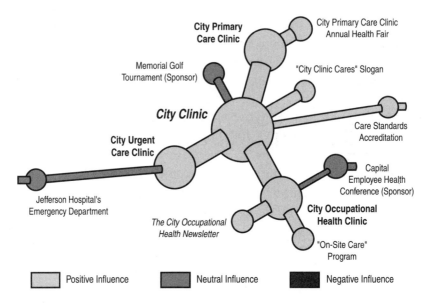

Constructed using design methodologies in Lederer, Chris, and Sam Hill. "See Your Brands through Your Customers' Eyes." *Harvard Business Review* (June) 2001: 125-133.

FIGURE 11-1 A Medical Clinic's Brand Portfolio Molecule

is the lead brand because it is the largest atom in the diagram. City Clinic is positively influenced by its "City Clinic Cares" slogan and its Care Standards accreditation. The entity is neutrally influenced by its sponsorship of the Memorial Golf Tournament. City Clinic serves as the umbrella brand for three distinct units that provide positive influences: City Primary Care Clinic, City Urgent Care Clinic, and City Occupational Health Clinic.

City Primary Care Clinic is positively influenced by its relationship with its parent, City Clinic, as well as the annual health fair that it holds for community citizens. City Urgent Care Clinic is positively influenced by its relationship with City Clinic and neutrally influenced by its relationship with Jefferson Hospital's emergency department. City Occupational Health Clinic is positively influenced by its relationship with City Clinic, its distribution of *The City Occupational Health Newsletter*, and its "On-Site Care" program that is offered to various enterprises. City Occupational Health Clinic is neutrally influenced by its sponsorship of the Capital Employee Health Conference.

The Brand Portfolio Molecule clearly illustrates that City Clinic possesses a strong array of brands, with positive influences dominating its portfolio. The establishment is particularly fortunate not to have any brands that negatively influence the portfolio. With this information, City Clinic can focus its attention on maintaining the numerous positive components of its brand portfolio.

SUMMARY

Lederer and Hill's Brand Portfolio Molecule provides marketers with a valuable tool for understanding the relationships that exist within brand portfolios. By clearly demonstrating internal brand relationships, as well as relationships that exist with associated external brands, the Brand Portfolio Molecule allows marketers to easily identify strong, neutral, and weak points associated with their brands. With its succinct presentation of given brand portfolios and associated relationships, the Brand Portfolio Molecule clearly facilitates brand management activities.

EXERCISES

1. Provide a detailed overview of Lederer and Hill's Brand Portfolio Molecule, identifying and explaining its assembly methods and its features and benefits. Support this overview by drawing an example illustration of the Brand Portfolio Molecule. Share your thoughts regarding the tool's implications and uses in the healthcare industry.
2. Assume that you have been hired as the marketing director for a newly established company known as Century Care Pharmaceuticals, a firm that will soon produce one product, an ibuprofen pain reliever, known as Century Care Relief. After visiting a local retail pharmacy to gain insights into direct and indirect competitors and possible substitutes, assemble a Brand Portfolio Molecule for Century Care Relief. As Century Care's product is in its developmental stages, concentrate only on Century Care Relief's potential relationships with external brands. Provide a brief narrative explaining your illustration.

REFERENCE

Lederer, Chris, and Sam Hill. 2001. See your brands through your customers' eyes. *Harvard Business Review* (June): 125–133.

12

Kevin Lane Keller's Brand Report Card

INTRODUCTION

Branding—the development, assignment, and management of names, logos, slogans, and other identifiers associated with products—is one of the most important activities of marketing management. Through branding, marketers give their products *identity*. This identity allows customers to distinguish goods and services from competitive offerings.

Branding activities do not cease with the introduction of products into the marketplace. Instead, these activities are ongoing. Consumers, their wants and needs, their preferences, their perceptions, and their environments are constantly changing. Brands and the products they represent must keep up with these changes—a task which necessitates that marketing managers devote significant attention to branding throughout the product life cycle.

Given the dynamic nature of the marketplace and its consumers, marketers must periodically assess the brand performance of their given offerings in an effort to ensure that brands are meeting strategic and tactical goals and objectives. To assist marketers in the process of brand evaluation, Kevin Lane Keller developed the Brand Report Card, a useful tool that allows marketers to evaluate their offerings based on 10 characteristics possessed by excellent brands.

Illustrated in Figure 12-1, Keller's Brand Report Card requires that marketers (1) read each of the 10 brand characteristics, (2) rate their brands on a scale of 1 to 10 for each characteristic, with 1 being extremely poor and 10 being extremely good, and (3) create a bar chart that reflects the results of the evaluation. This chart is then analyzed to determine strengths and weaknesses associated with brand management. The 10 characteristics possessed by excellent brands are identified as follows.

CHARACTERISTIC 1

The brand excels at delivering the benefits customers truly desire.

When customers purchase products, they are buying collections of tangible and intangible attributes that satisfy wants and needs. In arranging these tangible and intangible characteristics, marketers must strive to ensure that their products incorporate the attributes that customers indeed are seeking. This, of course, first requires the identification of customer-desired features.

Identification of customer-desired attributes can be accomplished through a variety of methods. One such method is known as environmental scanning, an externally focused activity where marketers seek to assess the environment in an effort to identify marketplace trends. Externally focused activities are ideally supplemented by internally focused activities. One such internally focused activity is the customer satisfaction survey, which requests feedback from customers regarding their experiences, perceptions, and opinions concerning the ability of entities to appropriately address wants and needs.

Rating Your Brand

Instructions: Rate your brand on a scale of one to ten (one being extremely poor and ten being extremely good) for each characteristic below. Then create a bar chart that reflects the scores. Use the bar chart to generate discussion among all those individuals who participate in the management of your brands. Looking at the results in that manner should help you identify areas that need improvement, recognize areas in which you excel, and learn more about how your particular brand is configured.

It can also be helpful to create a report card and chart for competitors' brands simply by rating those brands based on your own perceptions, both as a competitor and as a consumer. As an outsider, you may know more about how their brands are received in the marketplace than they do.

Keep that in mind as you evaluate your own brand. Try to look at it through the eyes of consumers rather than through your own knowledge of budgets, teams, and time spent on various initiatives.

 The brand excels at delivering the benefits customers truly desire.

Have you attempted to uncover unmet consumer wants and needs? By what methods? Do you focus relentlessly on maximizing your customers' product experiences? Do you have a system in place for getting comments from customers to the people who can effect change?

 The brand stays relevant.

Have you invested in product improvements that provide better value for your customers? Are you in touch with your customers' tastes? With the current market conditions? With new trends as they apply to your offering? Are your marketing decisions based on your knowledge of the above?

 The pricing strategy is based on customers' perceptions of value.

Have you optimized price, cost, and quality to meet or exceed customers' expectations? Do you have a system in place to monitor customers' perceptions of your brand's value? Have you estimated how much value your customers believe the brand adds to your product?

 The brand is properly positioned.

Have you established necessary and competitive points of parity with competitors? Have you established desirable and deliverable points of difference?

 The brand is consistent.

Are you sure that your marketing programs are not sending conflicting messages and that they haven't done so over time? Conversely, are you adjusting your programs to keep current?

FIGURE 12-1- A Keller's Brand Report Card

The brand portfolio and hierarchy make sense.

Can the corporate brand create a seamless umbrella for all brands in the portfolio? Do the brands in that portfolio hold individual niches? How extensively do the brands overlap? In what areas? Conversely, do the brands maximize market coverage? Do you have a brand hierarchy that is well thought out and well understood?

 The brand makes use of and coordinates a full repertoire of marketing activities to build equity.

Have you chosen or designed your brand name, logo, symbol, slogan, packaging, signage, and so forth to maximize brand awareness? Have you implemented integrated marketing activities that target customers? Are you aware of all the marketing activities that involve your brand? Are the people managing each activity aware of one another? Have you capitalized on the unique capabilities of each communication option while ensuring that the meaning of the brand is consistently represented?

 The brand's managers understand what the brand means to customers.

Do you know what customers like and don't like about a brand? Are you aware of all the core associations people make with your brand, whether intentionally created by your organization or not? Have you created detailed, research-driven portraits of your target customers? Have you outlined customer-driven boundaries for brand extensions and guidelines for marketing programs?

 The brand is given proper support and that support is sustained over the long run.

Are the successes or failures of marketing programs fully understood before they are changed? Is the brand given sufficient R&D support? Have you avoided the temptation to cut back marketing support for the brand in reaction to a downturn in the market or a slump in sales?

 The organization monitors sources of brand equity.

Have you created a brand charter that defines the meaning and equity of the brand and how it should be treated? Do you conduct periodic brand audits to assess the health of your brand and to set strategic direction? Do you conduct routine tracking studies to evaluate current market performance? Do you regularly distribute brand equity reports that summarize all relevant research and information to assist marketers in making decisions? Have you assigned explicit responsibility for monitoring and preserving brand equity?

FIGURE 12-1- B Keller's Brand Report Card—continued

The activity of discovering customer-desired benefits is highly complex in any environment but even more so in the intensely competitive, complex, and innovative healthcare industry. Such complex environments pose even greater challenges for marketers as they seek to assess customer wants and needs.

Identification of customer wants and needs is, however, only part of the equation. The other part, of course, involves the development and delivery of innovative product solutions that satisfy the identified wants and needs.

CHARACTERISTIC 2

The brand stays relevant.

Brands must stay relevant in the eyes of customers. This relevance is maintained not only by incorporating the latest new features and benefits into given healthcare offerings but also by taking steps to ensure that the imagery associated with brands accurately reflects modern society.

Brands are image laden. They convey feelings and emotions—aspects of human life that change over time. Given this, marketers must ensure that they devote significant attention to both the tangible and intangible aspects of branded products in an effort to keep their brands relevant in the eyes of customers.

CHARACTERISTIC 3

The pricing strategy is based on customers' perceptions of value.

Pricing in the healthcare marketplace is highly complex, largely due to the fact that third-party payers—health insurance companies; managed care firms; and government health insurance programs, such as Medicare and Medicaid—backed by their associated bureaucracies, often cover the costs of medical care on behalf of the clients they serve. Regardless of who ultimately pays for healthcare offerings, marketers must ensure that product pricing equates with the value delivered by the particular goods and services. In essence, a balance must be struck between the price of healthcare offerings and associated product features and benefits. The more balanced the relationship, the more likely marketers can meet the value expectations of customers and associated third-party payer entities.

CHARACTERISTIC 4

The brand is properly positioned.

As identity vehicles, brands are essential to the practice of product positioning, where marketers seek to influence customer perceptions of their offerings by determining an appropriate and effective image for products to convey to target audiences. In positioning products, marketers must determine, for example, whether they have established appropriate *points of parity* (i.e., areas where products meet the strengths of competitive offerings) and *points of difference* (i.e., areas where products outperform competitive offerings).

A medical clinic that successfully incorporates these points essentially communicates to customers that it offers all of the benefits provided by competing clinics plus value-added features (e.g., friendlier service, more convenient hours of operation) that distinguish it from rivals.

Products that are poorly positioned are destined to fail because they do not elicit desired perceptions in the minds of customers. Given this, marketers must place significant attention on this important marketing aspect.

CHARACTERISTIC 5

The brand is consistent.

One of the most important aspects of branding involves consistency in the presentation of brands in the marketplace. Given the ever-increasing array of advertising media that marketers have at their disposal, achieving consistency in presentation has become a most challenging task.

If a hospital simultaneously portrays itself as "the leader in the altruistic delivery of patient care" in its radio and television campaigns; "the leader in the technological delivery of patient care" in its print and outdoor media campaigns; and "the leader in the economical delivery of patient care" in its Internet campaign, customers will undoubtedly be confused by the conflicting messages that are being sent.

For given promotional campaigns over given periods of time, it is essential for marketers to deliver the same consistent message to customers across all advertising media, thus alleviating the confusion associated with multiple conflicting messages.

CHARACTERISTIC 6

The brand portfolio and hierarchy make sense.

The number of brands held by organizations varies considerably depending on the characteristics of associated entities. Medical clinics, home health agencies, and similar healthcare organizations that offer a limited array of products will likely need only one brand to represent both the given entity and its product offerings. Comprehensive medical centers, medical device firms, pharmaceutical manufacturers, and other large entities, however, will need to develop multiple brands that accurately represent their many product offerings.

When multiple brands exist, it is very important for marketers to ensure that their *brand portfolios* (i.e., the overall collection of brands held by an organization) and *brand hierarchies* (i.e., the method of organizing brands within a brand portfolio) are appropriate. Importantly, marketers must ensure that they do not place too many products under one brand name. They also must ensure that they avoid overlapping two brands within the same portfolio.

All brands impact the value of associated brand portfolios. The better organized the brands, the more likely the arrangement will make sense to marketers and their target audiences. Appropriately arranged hierarchies, in essence, facilitate brand performance.

CHARACTERISTIC 7

The brand makes use of and coordinates a full repertoire of marketing activities to build equity.

Every marketing effort represents an opportunity to increase brand awareness, thus increasing *brand equity*—the value of a brand. Marketers must be certain to make use of such opportunities by ensuring that brand names, logos, symbols, etc. are prominently featured in advertisements and other promotional campaigns in an effort to facilitate brand awareness. Brands serve as identity vehicles for goods and services. Failure to appropriately incorporate them into associated marketing campaigns is most wasteful.

CHARACTERISTIC 8

The brand's managers understand what the brand means to customers.

Brands have meaning. Some aspects of brands may be viewed positively by customers, while other aspects may be viewed negatively. By understanding exactly what brands mean to customers, marketers are better prepared to make decisions involving product offerings. Failure to view brands through the eyes of customers can lead to disaster.

A medical clinic that has achieved a reputation for offering timely service to patients would likely lose a considerable portion of its patient base if it initiated a plan to double the number of patient encounters expected of its existing array of practitioners. Such a move would undoubtedly create extended waiting periods and possibly reduce the quality of patient care, immediately eroding the clinic's now *former* brand asset of timely delivery of care.

Progressive marketers understand what brands mean to customers. With this understanding, they can make appropriate decisions that build brand equity.

CHARACTERISTIC 9

The brand is given proper support and that support is sustained over the long run.

Building and maintaining brand equity requires a significant and sustained investment. All too often, however, healthcare entities withdraw funding after initial marketing success, believing that newly established brands have the power to maintain and possibly grow market share without additional resource expenditures. When this occurs, however, it opens the door for competitors to easily take away any market share victories gained by entities.

Whether the retrenchment of resources is in the form of reduced advertising dollars, reduced research and development investments, or even the declining interest of top executives, brand performance will undoubtedly suffer, dramatically increasing the likelihood of product failure.

As with any administrative operation, removal of attention, support, and other resources from branding initiatives results in brand decline and, ultimately, failure. Quite obviously, marketers must work to ensure that appropriate, sustained resources are devoted to brands.

CHARACTERISTIC 10

The organization monitors sources of brand equity.

Prudent brand management requires the ongoing assessment of brand performance in the marketplace. Ideally, marketers should periodically conduct a *brand equity audit* that includes a *brand inventory* (i.e., an internal compilation identifying all of the brands held by an organization along with detailed information outlining how each brand is to be marketed) and a *brand exploratory* (i.e., an external analysis that seeks to discover what brands mean to customers).

If this information is then placed in a *brand equity charter* (i.e., a formal document that identifies and describes brand management fundamentals associated with given product offerings), marketers are afforded with an invaluable tool that (1) assesses current brand performance and (2) provides guidance for brand management. Without such evaluative instruments, brand equity and its associated sources cannot accurately be assessed.

OPERATIONAL MATTERS

Figure 12-2 illustrates a bar chart that reflects the results of a Brand Report Card that was completed by a medical clinic. This diagram clearly depicts the organization's brand performance, notably indicating strengths in characteristics 1, 2, 5, and 9 and weaknesses in characteristics 3, 6, and 10. With this information, marketers can take steps to build upon strengths and reduce or eliminate weaknesses, thus increasing brand performance. Any adjustments, however, should be made cautiously, making sure not to disrupt current strengths.

If desired, marketers can gain additional insights by completing Brand Report Cards for competing products because this would likely yield useful information regarding rival offerings.

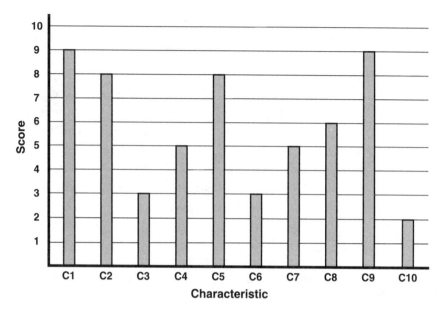

FIGURE 12-2 A Medical Clinic's Brand Report Card Bar Chart

SUMMARY

Through its identification of 10 characteristics possessed by excellent brands, Keller's Brand Report Card provides marketers with a useful tool for assessing brands. This evaluative device greatly simplifies the activity of monitoring brand performance, providing marketers with concise brand assessments that can be used to improve brand management activities, thus increasing brand equity.

EXERCISES

1. Provide a detailed overview of Kevin Lane Keller's Brand Report Card, explaining its importance as an evaluative tool for assessing brand performance in the healthcare industry. Be sure to add into your discussion details regarding the imperative of analyzing brand performance throughout the product life cycle and methods for operationalizing the Brand Report Card accordingly. Based on your

knowledge of your local healthcare marketplace, do you view area healthcare entities to be actively engaged in maintaining their brand identities? Why do you believe this to be the case?

2. Select a local healthcare organization and arrange to meet its marketing director. Present Kevin Lane Keller's Brand Report Card to the director and request that he or she complete the instrument. On completion of the Brand Report Card, interview the marketing director to ascertain the bases for given rankings. Conclude the interview by asking the marketing director about his or her perceptions regarding the value of the Brand Report Card. Prepare a written narrative of your interview experiences and findings.

REFERENCE

Keller, Kevin Lane. 2000. The brand report card. *Harvard Business Review* (January–February): 147–157.

CHAPTER 13

David Taylor's Brand Stretch Spectrum

LEARNING OBJECTIVES

After examining this chapter, readers will have the ability to:

- Understand the importance of evaluating newly developed healthcare products in an effort to determine whether they will carry existing brand names or be assigned new ones.
- Realize the tradeoffs associated with the use of brand extensions in the healthcare marketplace.
- Appreciate the value of David Taylor's Brand Stretch Spectrum as a tool for formulating a variety of brand extension pathways.

INTRODUCTION

On an ongoing basis, healthcare marketers forward intensive efforts to develop the brands they are responsible for managing. Such concentrated attention to brand management responsibilities is to be expected because of the many benefits that successful brands afford to healthcare entities. Most notably, brands establish product identity, allowing customers to easily locate the goods and services of given organizations and differentiate them from competitive offerings. When healthcare marketers develop successful brands, they deliver valuable institutional assets that, if well managed, will yield enduring benefits for their associated healthcare organizations.

Brand management initiatives are called upon for a variety of reasons, one of which is new product development. When new products are developed, healthcare marketers encounter numerous, related branding issues, with one of the most notable being the determination of whether new goods and services will carry existing brand names, termed *brand extensions*, or be assigned entirely new ones.

Whether to field brand extensions or introduce new brands requires careful consideration. Brand extensions carry the benefit of familiarity in that target audiences already possess an awareness of associated brand names. This certainly affords advantages for new offerings in that the burden of building a base identity is significantly reduced and might even be outright eliminated depending on the strength of established brand names.

Despite this powerful benefit, brand extensions are not always desirable. Brand portfolios can occasionally be overextended with too many products carrying given badges, resulting in confusion for both healthcare marketers and their customer populations. New product offerings also might not logically fit under existing brand names, warranting that such offerings carry newly developed identities.

Significantly, brand extensions carry risks associated with the application of successful brand names to new and unproven product offerings. If these new products are not successful, such offerings will likely diminish the overall value of the brand names that they carry, negatively impacting all of the other product offerings in given brand portfolios. Regardless, the extension of established brand names to newly developed product offerings represents a practice worthy of consideration any time new goods and services present themselves.

Interestingly, in the course of managing brands, healthcare marketers may discover logical additions to existing product arrays, resulting in various brand extensions. Hence, brand extensions can spur new product development even in the absence of formal initiatives to do so.

For assistance whenever brand extensions are under consideration, healthcare marketers can turn to the Brand Stretch Spectrum, a tool developed by David Taylor. Illustrated in Figure 13-1, Taylor's Brand Stretch Spectrum identifies three paths for extending, or stretching, existing brands: the core range extension, the direct stretch extension, and the indirect stretch extension. Each of these paths presents opportunities for growth and expansion under the right circumstances, with risk increasing as extensions move further away from core product offerings. These three brand extension pathways, accompanied by examples in Figures 13-2 and 13-3, are explained as follows.

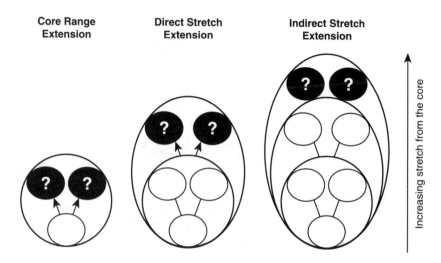

Adapted from *Brand Stretch: Why 1 in 2 Extensions Fail and How to Beat the Odds* by David Taylor. Copyright © 2004 by John Wiley & Sons Limited. Reproduced with permission.

FIGURE 13-1 Taylor's Brand Stretch Spectrum

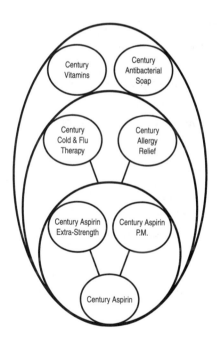

Constructed using design methodologies in Taylor, David. *Brand Stretch: Why 1 in 2 Extensions Fail and How to Beat the Odds*. Chichester, West Sussex, UK: Wiley, 2004.

FIGURE 13-2 A Pharmaceutical Firm's Brand Stretch Spectrum

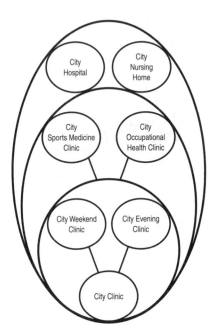

Constructed using design methodologies in Taylor, David. *Brand Stretch: Why 1 in 2 Extensions Fail and How to Beat the Odds.* Chichester, West Sussex, UK: Wiley, 2004.

FIGURE 13-3 A Medical Clinic's Brand Stretch Spectrum

THE CORE RANGE EXTENSION

The core range extension represents the application of a brand name to a new version (i.e., a product form variant) of an existing branded product. Because the brand is applied to a product with common core characteristics, such extensions are quite logical and reasonably safe pursuits.

An extra-strength version of a branded aspirin product offered by a pharmaceutical manufacturer, for example, would represent a core range extension. So, too, would a newly established weekend medical clinic that carried the brand name of an existing weekday clinic. Yet another core range extension would be that of a deluxe wheelchair line offered by a durable medical equipment company that was placed under the same brand name as an existing wheelchair line possessing a standard array of features.

Core range extensions are essentially equivalent product offerings, distinguished only by moderate feature and benefit differences. With such products, brand extensions make perfect sense because the given offerings are so closely related to each other. This affords excellent opportunities for newly developed goods and services to benefit from existing brand awareness in the marketplace.

THE DIRECT STRETCH EXTENSION

The direct stretch extension involves the application of an existing brand name to a broadened array of goods and services that differs from the core offering upon which the extension was based. This extension essentially stretches the brand name to cover items within a particular product class, which extends beyond the specific product form from which the brand name was derived.

A pharmaceutical manufacturer that introduces cold and flu, allergy, and cough remedies under an existing brand associated with its array of aspirin products has effected a direct stretch extension. A medical clinic offering primary care services would, too, effect a direct stretch extension by placing a new specialty care clinic under its existing brand name. Likewise, a durable medical equipment company that introduces a new line of walkers, canes, and crutches under the brand name of its successful array of wheelchairs effects a direct stretch extension.

Although direct stretch extensions differ from the core offerings that provided their associated brand identities, these extensions do fit into like product classes. Regardless, direct stretch extensions carry a greater degree of risk than core range extensions because the associated product offerings are different. This necessitates that healthcare marketers carefully evaluate direct stretch initiatives to ensure that these extensions represent appropriate applications for existing brand names.

THE INDIRECT STRETCH EXTENSION

The indirect stretch extension involves entry into a new product class. The degree of differentiation between the existing product class and the newly pursued one can range from mild to substantial. Because indirect stretch extensions branch out into unrelated product classes, they stretch brand names across a wide array of diverse product offerings, essentially creating umbrella brands.

A pharmaceutical manufacturer exclusively focused on the pain relief product class would effect an indirect stretch extension by introducing a vitamin product under the brand name carried by its pain relief products.

A medical clinic focused on the provision of comprehensive medical services in outpatient settings would effect an indirect stretch extension if the establishment decided to construct and operate a hospital or nursing home. A durable medical equipment company providing a comprehensive array of personal mobility products would effect an indirect stretch extension by introducing a new line of hospital beds under the brand name associated with its array of personal mobility products.

Indirect stretch extensions pierce through the current product classes pursued by healthcare entities, placing them in new product classes containing goods and services that may be closely associated with, or very distant from, the goods and services offered in existing product classes. Clearly, indirect stretch extensions carry the highest level of risk associated with stretching brand names because established identities are being applied to product classes that are new and different. Given this, healthcare marketers must ensure that a goodness of fit exists between new product classes and existing brand identities because weak connections might possibly diminish existing brand equity.

OPERATIONAL MATTERS

Taylor's Brand Stretch Spectrum clearly identifies three potential paths for extending brand names to cover products that are increasingly distant from the core offerings upon which the associated brand names originated. Each of these extensions can be successfully effected under the right circumstances.

As with any new product pursuit, extensions should carefully be evaluated to ensure that markets for given products exist and that the application of existing brand names to new offerings makes sense to both internal and external audiences. If these conditions are met, the brand extension route affords many opportunities for marketing success. If, however, new goods and services appear to possess great potential, but existing brand names do not seem to represent appropriate identities for these new offerings, the establishment of entirely new brand identities would likely yield better marketing results.

Significantly, Taylor's Brand Stretch Spectrum can be used to spark new product ideas. By understanding the various pathways for stretching brands, healthcare marketers can review their existing product arrays and ask themselves how they might go about effecting core range, direct, and indirect stretch extensions. This activity can yield very productive new product insights even if formal systems for new product development do not exist. It is not uncommon for some of the best new product ideas to grow out of existing product offerings and, when this happens, the application of existing brand names to these new goods and services offers excellent opportunities to quickly connect with target audiences.

SUMMARY

David Taylor's Brand Stretch Spectrum provides healthcare marketers with a useful portrayal of potential paths for effecting brand extensions. Aside from its use as a tool for understanding such extensions, Taylor's Brand Stretch Spectrum can be used to foster new product development initiatives by encouraging healthcare marketers to envision how they might potentially extend their product arrays beyond core offerings.

EXERCISES

1. Define and comprehensively discuss David Taylor's Brand Stretch Spectrum, providing insights into its guidance and use as a device for the extension of core brands. Preface your discussion by reflecting on the advantages and disadvantages associated with brand extensions. How would you characterize the prevalence of brand extensions in the healthcare industry? What is the basis of your characterization?

2. Select a healthcare good or service of your choice and assign the product an appropriate brand name. Using David Taylor's Brand Stretch Spectrum, envision potential brand extensions to this hypothetical healthcare offering by formulating core range extensions, direct stretch extensions, and indirect stretch extensions. Provide an illustration of your Brand Stretch Spectrum and offer a narrative explaining your rationale for assembling the brand portfolio as you did.

REFERENCE

Taylor, David. 2004. *Brand stretch: Why 1 in 2 extensions fail and how to beat the odds.* Chichester, West Sussex, UK: Wiley.

PART THREE

Target Marketing Tools

The Market-Product Grid

INTRODUCTION

In an effort to more effectively address the wants and needs of customers, marketers engage in target marketing, a practice that involves three inter-related activities: market segmentation, targeting, and product positioning. Market segmentation is the process of dividing a market into groups (i.e., segments) of individuals who share common characteristics. When the market has been segmented, marketers engage in targeting where they se-lect (i.e., target) attractive segments and focus their efforts on satisfying the wants and needs of these groups. These targeted segments are known as an entity's target market. Product positioning follows targeting and involves the determination of an appropriate and effective image for products to convey to customers.

Target marketing developed out of desires to more appropriately address the various wants and needs of different customer groups. The practice stands in contrast to mass marketing, which involves offering products to the market as a whole without regard for individual tastes and preferences.

Target marketing makes sense. Women of childbearing age, for example, have potential needs for labor and delivery services. Parents have needs, courtesy of their infants and young children, for pediatric medical services. Elderly individuals have needs for home health care, assisted living, and nursing home services.

By focusing on the specific wants and needs of market segments, marketers can deliver goods and services that are specifically tailored for the associated groups. This practice not only improves customer satisfaction but also allows for better use of promotions resources through the selection of communications vehicles that precisely reach desired populations.

A useful tool for target marketing is known as the Market-Product Grid, an instrument that specifically addresses the segmenting and targeting aspects of the practice. Illustrated in Figure 14-1, the Market-Product Grid, as depicted by Roger Kerin, Eric Berkowitz, Steven Hartley, and William Rudelius, consists of a matrix with markets identified on its vertical axis and products identified on its horizontal axis. The actual number of cells in the matrix is, of course, dependent on the number of markets and products identified. As a result, Market-Product Grids range from being quite small for entities with few markets and few products to being very large for entities that offer multiple markets an extensive array of products.

To create a Market-Product Grid, marketers simply (1) construct a matrix of sufficient size, (2) list potential markets on the vertical axis, (3) list product offerings on the horizontal axis, and (4) evaluate each of the resulting market-product combinations, characterizing them as large, medium, small, or nonexistent markets.

The activity of listing the goods and services of entities on the Market-Product Grid is quite simple, but identifying and listing potential markets can be somewhat challenging without some point of reference. This point of reference can often be found by consulting a breakdown of segmentation variables, such as the one listed in Table 14-1.

This table provides examples of specific segments that exist within each of the four major segmentation categories: geographic, demographic, psychographic, and behavioral. It, however, presents only a few of the almost

Products Markets	Product 1	Product 2	Product 3
Market 1	?	?	?
Market 2	?	?	?
Market 3	?	?	?

3 = Large Market, 2 = Medium Market, 1 = Small Market, 0 = No Market

Adapted from *Marketing*, 7th ed. by Roger A. Kerin, Eric N. Berkowitz, Steven W. Hartley, and William Rudelius. Copyright © 2003, 2000, 1997, 1994, 1992, 1989, 1986 by The McGraw-Hill Companies, Inc. Published by McGraw-Hill. Reproduced with permission of The McGraw-Hill Companies.

FIGURE 14-1 The Market-Product Grid

Table 14-1 Major Segmentation Variables

GEOGRAPHIC

World region/country	North America, Western Europe, Middle East, Pacific Rim, China, India, Canada, Mexico
Country region	Pacific, Mountain, West North Central, West South Central, East North Central, East South Central, South Atlantic, Middle Atlantic, New England
City or metro size	Under 5000; 5000–20,000; 20,000–50,000; 50,000–100,000; 100,000–250,000; 250,000–500,000; 500,000–1,000,000; 1,000,000–4,000,000; 4,000,000+
Density	Urban, suburban, rural
Climate	Northern, southern

(continues)

Table 14-1 Major Segmentation Variables—continued

DEMOGRAPHIC

Age	Under 6, 6–11, 12–19, 20–34, 35–49, 50–64, 65+
Gender	Male, female
Family size	1–2, 3–4, 5+
Family life cycle	Young, single; young, married, no children; young, married with children; older, married with children; older, married, no children under 18; older, single; other
Income	Under $10,000; $10,000–$20,000; $20,000–$30,000; $30,000–$50,000; $50,000–$100,000; $100,000+
Occupation	Professional and technical; managers, officials, and proprietors; clerical; sales; craftspeople; supervisors; operatives; farmers; retired; students; homemakers; unemployed
Education	Grade school or less; some high school; high school graduate; some college; college graduate
Religion	Catholic, Protestant, Jewish, Muslim, Hindu, other
Race	Asian, Hispanic, black, white
Generation	Baby boomer, Generation X, Generation Y
Nationality	North American, South American, British, French, German, Italian, Japanese

PSYCHOGRAPHIC

Social class	Lower lowers, upper lowers, working class, middle class, upper middles, lower uppers, upper uppers
Lifestyle	Achievers, strivers, strugglers
Personality	Compulsive, gregarious, authoritarian, ambitious

BEHAVIORAL

Occasions	Regular occasion, special occasion
Benefits	Quality, service, economy, convenience, speed
User status	Nonuser, ex-user, potential user, first-time user, regular user
User rates	Light user, medium user, heavy user
Loyalty status	None, medium, strong, absolute
Readiness stage	Unaware, aware, informed, interested, desirous, intending to buy
Attitude toward product	Enthusiastic, positive, indifferent, negative, hostile

endless market segments that marketers could potentially pursue. Such a table serves as a useful starting point for identifying markets for placement on the Market-Product Grid.

OPERATIONAL MATTERS

Figure 14-2 illustrates a Market-Product Grid that was developed for a home health agency. Here, the agency used the grid to assess the market potential of different areas of Jackson County. The grid indicates that the south and central sections of Jackson County possess large markets, the east section possesses a medium market, and the north and west sections contain small markets. The grid clearly identifies the most prominent markets (i.e., the south and central regions) for home health services within the county—information that can greatly assist the agency in determining which markets it wishes to pursue.

Products / Markets	Home Health Services
North	1
South	3
East	2
West	1
Central	3

(Jackson County)

3 = Large Market, 2 = Medium Market, 1 = Small Market, 0 = No Market

Constructed using design methodologies in Kerin, Roger A., Eric N. Berkowitz, Steven W. Hartley, and William Rudelius. *Marketing.* 7th ed. New York: McGraw-Hill, 2003.

FIGURE 14-2 A Home Health Agency's Market-Product Grid

Figure 14-3 presents a more complex Market-Product Grid that was developed for a sports medicine clinic. Here, the clinic sought to examine Washington County's market potential for various sports medicine procedures by type of sport. The grid notably reveals a prominent market across all sports for foot and ankle procedures, followed closely by knee procedures. It also reveals that, among sports types, the tennis and golf sports populations possess the largest markets for broad sports medicine procedures—details that shed significant light on segment opportunities.

It should be noted that although the largest markets might seem to represent the most productive marketing pursuits, such markets are not always appropriate targets. Organizations must, for example, factor in marketplace competitors, their dominance in certain segments, and their overall numbers. Certain segments, although large, may be saturated with competitors or dominated by market leaders. In such situations, smaller markets with fewer competitors may be more desirable segments to pursue. Aside from competitive elements, healthcare organizations might select smaller markets based on the particular missions they embrace. Entities that cater to under-

Products / Markets		Sports Medicine Procedures					
		Shoulder	Elbow	Hand	Hip	Knee	Foot & Ankle
Washington County	Football Players	1	1	0	1	2	2
	Basketball Players	1	0	0	1	1	2
	Baseball Players	0	1	1	0	1	1
	Soccer Players	0	0	0	0	1	2
	Tennis Players	3	2	1	2	3	3
	Golfers	3	1	2	2	2	2

3 = Large Market, 2 = Medium Market, 1 = Small Market, 0 = No Market

Constructed using design methodologies in Kerin, Roger A., Eric N. Berkowitz, Steven W. Hartley, and William Rudelius. *Marketing.* 7th ed. New York: McGraw-Hill, 2003.

FIGURE 14-3 A Sports Medicine Clinic's Market-Product Grid

served, rural populations represent excellent examples of institutions engaging in this practice.

It should also be noted that Market-Product Grids are only as accurate as the information that is used to complete them. Although they remain useful even with informally collected data, the use of data derived from formal market research can greatly improve their accuracy.

SUMMARY

The Market-Product Grid provides a simple, yet highly useful, method for segmenting and targeting markets. By using this tool, marketers can more precisely identify and target appropriate customer groups. The Market-Product Grid also ensures that marketers consider multiple market opportunities.

EXERCISES

1. Define and comprehensively discuss the Market-Product Grid and its role as an instrument for segmenting markets and targeting appropriate segments. Preface your discussion by sharing insights regarding the value of target marketing in the healthcare industry.
2. Visit the Web site of an area healthcare institution and identify as many of its product offerings as possible. Based on your knowledge of your local region, identify potential markets for these products. With this information, construct a Market-Product Grid for the given healthcare entity, being sure to evaluate the resulting market-product combinations. Then, prepare a narrative describing the most appropriate targets based on your analysis. Are the targets you selected consistent with the perceived selections of the given healthcare entity? Explain your rationale.

REFERENCES

Kerin, Roger A., Eric N. Berkowitz, Steven W. Hartley, and William Rudelius. 2003. *Marketing*. 7th ed. New York: McGraw-Hill.
Kotler, Philip, and Gary Armstrong. 2004. *Principles of marketing*. 10th ed. Upper Saddle River, NJ: Prentice Hall.

15

Kotler & Trias de Bes' Lateral Marketing Strategy

LEARNING OBJECTIVES

After examining this chapter, readers will have the ability to:

- Appreciate the value of target marketing as an important healthcare marketing activity.
- Understand the practice of vertical segmentation, the traditional approach to market segmentation, which involves identifying viable segments by drilling down into markets.
- Understand the practice of lateral segmentation, a nontraditional approach to market segmentation, which encourages marketers to look broadly at markets to identify previously overlooked opportunities.
- Appreciate the value of Kotler and Trias de Bes' Lateral Marketing Strategy as an instrument, when used in tandem with traditional approaches, for realizing the true depth and breadth of marketplace opportunities.

INTRODUCTION

Target marketing—the three interrelated activities of market segmentation, targeting, and product positioning—represents one of the most important marketing practices. This practice essentially tailors products for specific market segments in an effort to encourage exchange. Clearly more productive than mass marketing, which involves marketing goods and services to broad markets without regard for individual tastes and preferences, target marketing places a defined emphasis on serving specific customer populations and represents a very common marketing practice.

Despite the obvious benefits that the practice of target marketing affords to marketers and their customers, there are refinements that can be effected to improve the practice. One area of improvement concerns the first step of target marketing—market segmentation.

Specifically, market segmentation is the process of dividing a market into groups (i.e., segments) of individuals who share common characteristics. Market segmentation is typically effected by drilling down into markets, bypassing layers that are deemed undesirable until desirable layers of associated markets have been identified. Appealing market segments are then targeted. This very common, drill-down orientation of market segmentation can be termed *vertical segmentation.*

Vertical segmentation is clearly a viable method for segmenting markets, but as illustrated in Figure 15-1, the practice of drilling down into markets results in many missed opportunities. Such opportunities, although historically passed up, will become all the more important as the competitive intensity of the marketplace continues to increase and vertically defined segments become increasingly saturated.

To assist marketers in improving their segmentation results by identifying missed opportunities, Philip Kotler and Fernando Trias de Bes formulated Lateral Marketing Strategy, a method for introducing *lateral segmentation* into the array of segmentation tools already possessed by marketers.

Kotler and Trias de Bes developed Lateral Marketing Strategy to encourage marketers to look broadly at their markets in an attempt to identify opportunities to serve customer groups that have previously been overlooked, courtesy of the drill-down orientation of vertical marketing. The technique benefits marketers through the identification of valuable segments to

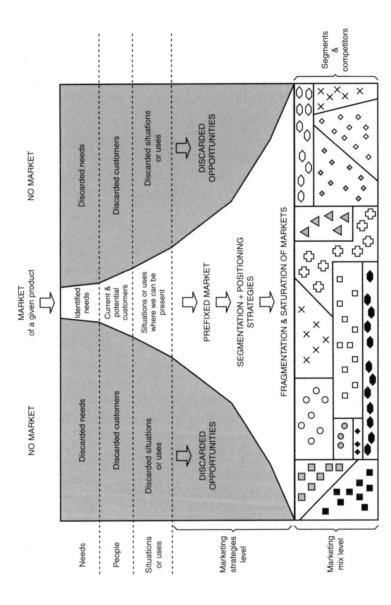

FIGURE 15-1 Vertical Segmentation & Missed Opportunities

From *Lateral Marketing: New Techniques for Finding Breakthrough Ideas* by Philip Kotler and Fernando Trias de Bes. Copyright © 2003 by Philip Kotler and Fernando Trias de Bes. Reprinted with permission of John Wiley & Sons, Inc.

110

pursue. Significantly, it also benefits customers whose wants and needs might otherwise go unnoticed.

THE LATERAL MARKETING STRATEGY APPROACH

Lateral Marketing Strategy essentially requires that healthcare marketers carefully examine their served market segments and the products that are used to address those segments. Specifically, healthcare marketers must endeavor to determine what market segment opportunities, if any, have been overlooked or bypassed over the course of serving current customer populations. Previously forgone segments are then evaluated to determine whether they are worthy of pursuit, with valuable segments becoming potential target markets.

Consider an assisted living facility that has, as part of its product array, constructed a wellness center to serve its elderly population. The wellness center clearly provides benefits for its target market—the elderly residents of the facility—but in drilling down to this target population, what potential opportunities were overlooked? Depending on the capacity of the wellness center, opportunities for it to also serve as a fitness center for members of the community might be possible. The array of wellness center equipment, coupled with the skills of current employees, might also provide opportunities for the establishment of a physical therapy clinic.

Each of these options—true departures from vertical segmentation initiatives—can potentially improve the revenues earned by the assisted living facility, illustrating the benefits offered by Lateral Marketing Strategy. As this example demonstrates, lateral segmentation initiatives require a degree of exploration and creativity on the part of healthcare marketers, but they afford a range of segmentation opportunities that might otherwise be neglected.

Importantly, Kotler and Trias de Bes note that lateral segmentation is not a substitute for vertical segmentation. Instead, it is a complementary technique that increases the potential for the identification of productive market segments. When vertical and lateral segmentation approaches are combined, healthcare marketers significantly increase the range of growth opportunities at their disposal—an important benefit given the ever-increasing competitive intensity of the healthcare marketplace.

SUMMARY

Kotler and Trias de Bes' Lateral Marketing Strategy provides healthcare marketers with an innovative method for broadly viewing segment opportunities in the marketplace. By adding lateral segmentation to their existing array of segmentation tools, healthcare marketers better position themselves and their organizations for enduring marketing success.

EXERCISES

1. Define and discuss the vertical segmentation and lateral segmentation techniques and provide details regarding their respective deployment in the healthcare industry. Do you view Kotler and Trias de Bes' Lateral Marketing Strategy as a technique that will compel healthcare marketing managers to reevaluate their segmentation practices? Explain your rationale.
2. Reflect on the various healthcare organizations in your local community and their respective targets. Can you identify any attractive opportunities that were possibly overlooked? If so, what are they?

REFERENCE

Kotler, Philip, and Fernando Trias de Bes. 2003. *Lateral marketing: New techniques for finding breakthrough ideas.* Hoboken, NJ: Wiley.

CHAPTER 16

Kim & Mauborgne's Blue Ocean Strategy

LEARNING OBJECTIVES

After examining this chapter, readers will have the ability to:

- Understand the increasingly saturated state of the healthcare marketplace, necessitating innovative efforts to locate target markets.
- Realize the value of looking to both established and developing markets for market share growth opportunities.
- Appreciate the value of Kim and Mauborgne's Blue Ocean Strategy as a tool for guiding target marketing innovations.

INTRODUCTION

Healthcare marketers routinely endeavor to segment given markets, target desirable customer populations, and position their products in a manner that will be attractive to designated customer groups. These three interrelated activities—market segmentation, targeting, and product positioning—combine to form the essential and increasingly important practice known as target marketing.

Now more than ever, to be successful at target marketing, healthcare marketers must be open-minded. This open-mindedness is required because the healthcare marketplace is becoming increasingly saturated with competitors, necessitating that healthcare marketers become innovative in their efforts to locate viable target audiences. One approach that can assist

113

healthcare marketers in broadening their perspectives of the marketplace is known as Blue Ocean Strategy, a method for viewing markets that was developed by W. Chan Kim and Renee Mauborgne.

Blue Ocean Strategy encourages marketers to view their markets differently than they have in the past. This new approach stands in contrast to Red Ocean Strategy, the traditional approach to viewing markets, as illustrated in Figure 16-1. Specifically, Blue and Red Ocean Strategies are distinguished from each other by their different philosophies pertaining to five important attributes: market space, competition, demand, the value-cost tradeoff, and differentiation/low cost parameters. These attributes are explained as follows.

MARKET SPACE

Whereas Red Ocean Strategy focuses on competing in ever-saturated markets, Blue Ocean Strategy seeks to identify new markets for given product offerings. Blue Ocean Strategy is so termed as a reference to open, clear blue water in the ocean—a stark contrast to the bloody, red ocean water resulting from attacks of some sort—making it a useful analogy for uncontested market space.

Red Ocean Strategy	Blue Ocean Strategy
Compete in existing market space.	Create uncontested market space.
Beat the competition.	Make the competition irrelevant.
Exploit existing demand.	Create and capture new demand.
Make the value-cost tradeoff.	Break the value-cost tradeoff.
Align the whole system of a firm's activities with its strategic choice of differentiation *or* low cost.	Align the whole system of a firm's activities in pursuit of differentiation *and* low cost.

Reprinted by permission of Harvard Business School Press. From *Blue Ocean Strategy: How to Create Uncontested Market Space and Make the Competition Irrelevant* by W. Chan Kim and Renee Mauborgne. Boston, MA 2005, p. 18. Copyright © 2005 by the Harvard Business School Publishing Corporation; all rights reserved.

FIGURE 16-1 Red Ocean Strategy vs. Blue Ocean Strategy

Smaller markets that have traditionally been overlooked in pursuit of larger ones represent potential blue oceans for healthcare entities. The same would be true of rare, but highly desirable, value-added practices like house calls offered by physicians or home delivery offered by retail pharmacies. As these examples illustrate, the discovery of blue oceans requires imagination, but when identified they afford uncontested market space ready to be acquired by innovative entities.

COMPETITION

Whereas Red Ocean Strategy seeks to battle competition within known markets, Blue Ocean Strategy seeks to pursue uncontested markets, thus avoiding direct competition. Successful market share pursuits into previously untapped markets, however, will likely draw competitors, which may ultimately turn blue oceans into red oceans. Therefore, healthcare marketers must ensure that they maintain the ability to compete in red oceans, regardless of the current fortunes offered by blue oceans.

DEMAND

Whereas Red Ocean Strategy exploits existing demand by engaging in market share battles within known markets, Blue Ocean Strategy involves the pursuit and capture of new demand by opening up new, previously untapped markets. In many established marketplaces, supply exceeds demand, creating the bloodiest of red oceans as competitors struggle for market share in an effort to remain viable. Such pressures do not exist in blue oceans, where potentially substantial, although untapped, demand may, in fact, exist.

THE VALUE-COST TRADEOFF

It has traditionally been accepted that products offering greater value carry higher costs, and vice versa—the domain of Red Ocean Strategy. Blue Ocean Strategy, instead, seeks to break the value-cost tradeoff by increasing value while reducing costs. This practice, termed *value innovation*, is accomplished by embedding enhanced customer-desired features into product offerings, while simultaneously reducing or eliminating elements that are not important to customers. Value innovation essentially provides customers with more for less.

If a retail pharmacy, for example, discovered that its customers favored low cost prescription drugs and quick service over any other shopping concern, the given retailer could concentrate on reducing nonessential elements of the shopping experience. The resulting savings could then be used to offer the lowest priced prescription drugs and bolster expeditious service. Hence, greater value would be afforded to customers at reduced costs.

DIFFERENTIATION/LOW COST PARAMETERS

Closely related to the value-cost tradeoff issue is the differentiation/low cost matter. Whereas Red Ocean Strategy seeks to pursue either differentiation *or* low cost, Blue Ocean Strategy seeks to simultaneously pursue differentiation *and* low cost. A retail pharmacy, for example, seeking to offer the lowest priced prescription pharmaceuticals could provide home delivery for a modest fee, preserving low cost initiatives, while simultaneously offering a differentiated service.

OPERATIONAL MATTERS

Perhaps the most obvious aspect of practice related to Blue Ocean Strategy is that pursuit of such uncontested market space requires innovative thinking and deep investigation on the part of healthcare marketers. Identifying blue oceans is challenging but highly rewarding upon discovery of such opportunities. As markets become increasingly saturated with competitors, the viability of healthcare entities rests with the discovery of new opportunities for growth. Blue Ocean Strategy represents an approach for identifying and pursuing pathways to growth and prosperity.

SUMMARY

Blue Ocean Strategy serves to remind healthcare marketers that they must look beyond the traditional boundaries of established markets for opportunities to achieve growth and prosperity. Certainly, healthcare marketers must not neglect established markets, as many gains and even marketplace dominance can be achieved in such markets, but significant attention must also be directed toward the uncontested market space afforded by blue oceans.

EXERCISES

1. Prepare a detailed essay comparing and contrasting Red Ocean Strategy and Blue Ocean Strategy. Based on your knowledge of healthcare establishments in your local market, do you perceive the entities to be competing primarily in red oceans, blue oceans, or both? Please justify your characterizations.
2. Select a healthcare entity in your local marketplace, choose a product offered by the entity, and study the associated target markets, characterizing them as either red oceans or blue oceans. What opportunities remain and are they red oceans or blue oceans? Report your findings in detail.

REFERENCE

Kim, W. Chan, and Renee Mauborgne. 2005. *Blue ocean strategy: How to create uncontested market space and make the competition irrelevant.* Boston: Harvard Business School Press.

CHAPTER 17

Philip Kotler's Segment-by-Segment Invasion Plan

LEARNING OBJECTIVES

After examining this chapter, readers will have the ability to:

- Understand that all market segments, if successfully pursued, will eventually be exhausted of growth opportunities.
- Realize the imperative of identifying not only those market segments that will be pursued in the present but also those segments that will be pursued in the future.
- Appreciate the value and utility afforded by Philip Kotler's Segment-by-Segment Invasion Plan as a tool for mapping current and future market segment pursuits.

INTRODUCTION

When progressive healthcare marketers engage in target marketing, they not only identify the market segments they wish to immediately pursue but also the market segments they might target in the future. In essence, they formulate plans that outline current and future market segment pursuits. This practice is beneficial due to the fact that all market segments, if successfully pursued, will eventually be exhausted of growth opportunities for given product offerings. By proactively identifying future market segments to pursue, marketers are better prepared to embark on a course of sustained growth.

The practice of identifying future market segment pursuits is greatly facilitated through the use of Philip Kotler's Segment-by-Segment Invasion Plan. As illustrated in Figure 17-1, the Invasion Plan consists of a vertical axis, representing product varieties, and a horizontal axis, representing customer groups. Each of the resulting cells in the matrix identifies market segments that are available to pursue, with the actual number of cells being dependent, of course, on the number of product varieties and customer groups identified.

To create an Invasion Plan, marketers simply (1) construct a matrix of sufficient size, (2) list product varieties on the vertical axis, (3) list customer groups on the horizontal axis, (4) identify, using unique hatch patterns, all of the organizations that are currently pursuing the market segments formed in the matrix, and (5) identify, using arrows, the market segments that represent desirable future pursuits for the evaluating entity. The resulting Segment-by-Segment Invasion Plan provides marketers with a concise

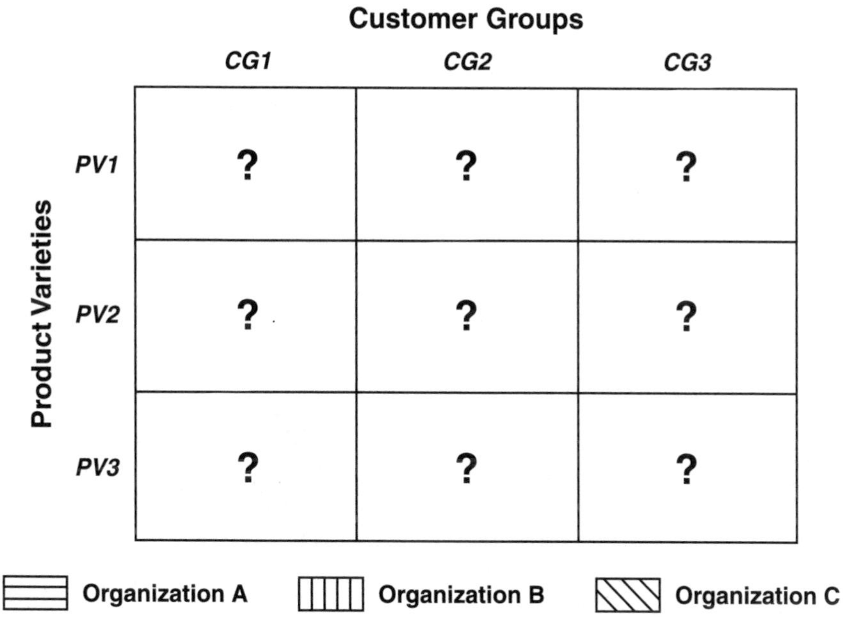

Adapted from Kotler, Philip, Marketing Management, 11th Edition, © 2003, Pg. 302.
Reprinted by permission of Pearson Education, Inc., Upper Saddle River, NJ.

FIGURE 17-1 Kotler's Segment-by-Segment Invasion Plan

self and competitive assessment of current market segment pursuits. It also illustrates the anticipated future market segment pursuits of the evaluating organization.

OPERATIONAL MATTERS

Figure 17-2 illustrates a Segment-by-Segment Invasion Plan that was developed for Madison Wellness, a physical therapy clinic. The diagram indicates that Madison Wellness is targeting the adult and senior markets for physical therapy services; Oakdale Clinic is targeting the youth market for speech therapy services; and Village Therapies is targeting the youth, adult, and senior markets for speech therapy services.

Seeking increased growth, Madison Wellness is planning to expand beyond its current physical therapy offering by first entering the occupational therapy market, targeting adults and seniors simultaneously, as indicated by the first series of arrows in Figure 17-2. If successful, Madison Wellness will later enter the speech therapy market, once again targeting both adults and

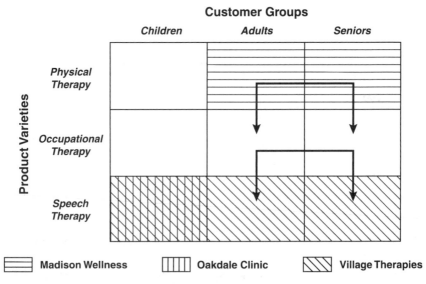

Constructed using design methodologies in Kotler, Philip. *Marketing Management.* 11th ed. Upper Saddle River, NJ: Prentice Hall, 2003.

FIGURE 17-2 A Physical Therapy Clinic's Invasion Plan

seniors, as indicated by the second series of arrows in Figure 17-2. With this information, marketers at Madison Wellness have a concise portrayal of the current market segment pursuits of identified competitors. These marketers also possess a useful depiction of the market segments that Madison Wellness might pursue in the future.

Beyond the depiction of current and future market segment pursuits, Kotler's Segment-by-Segment Invasion Plan affords marketers with opportunities to formulate marketing strategies and tactics associated with their growth pursuits. Marketers can, for example, assess barriers to entry, evaluate competitors, predict competitive responses to invasions, and assess segment limitations. By proactively addressing the requirements of upcoming segment invasions, marketers increase the likelihood that their pursuits will be successful.

It should be noted that marketers must ensure that their Segment-by-Segment Invasion Plans are kept strictly confidential. The element of surprise is essential for any segment invasion. If competitors gain access to this information, the element of surprise is, of course, eliminated. This allows competitors the opportunity to take preemptive actions to defend themselves against anticipated segment invasions, making invasions much more difficult or even impossible.

SUMMARY

Despite success in particular market segments, marketers must understand that every segment possesses growth boundaries. Therefore, if marketers and their organizations desire sustained growth, they must identify and pursue new markets and market segments—a task facilitated by Kotler's Segment-by-Segment Invasion Plan. Usefully, this tool forces marketers to identify future market segment pursuits that will yield sustained organizational performance.

EXERCISES

1. Provide a detailed account profiling Philip Kotler's Segment-by-Segment Invasion Plan, identifying and explaining its uses and steps of development, accompanied by an appropriate illustration. Share your thoughts on the degree to which modern healthcare organizations focus on future market segment pursuits.

2. Contact an area healthcare establishment (e.g., hospital, nursing home, retail pharmacy) and arrange an informational interview with its marketing director to learn about the facility's segmentation planning practices. Specifically, investigate the degree to which the institution has defined future segments for pursuit. Present Philip Kotler's Segment-by-Segment Invasion Plan and ask the executive for insights regarding the value of the tool for use in his or her particular workplace. Report your findings in detail.

REFERENCE

Kotler, Philip. 2003. *Marketing management.* 11th ed. Upper Saddle River, NJ: Prentice Hall.

CHAPTER 18

The Perceptual Map

LEARNING OBJECTIVES

After examining this chapter, readers will have the ability to:

- Realize the importance of product positioning, the determination and assignment of appropriate and effective images for products to convey to customers.
- Understand the necessity of monitoring consumer perceptions related to healthcare products to ensure that these offerings are perceived in the manner desired.
- Recognize the value of the Perceptual Map as a tool for effecting better product positioning outcomes in the healthcare industry.

INTRODUCTION

Target marketing is an essential practice involving three interrelated activities: market segmentation, targeting, and product positioning. Market segmentation is the process of dividing a market into groups (i.e., segments) of individuals who share common characteristics. When the market has been segmented, marketers engage in targeting where they select (i.e., target) attractive segments and focus their efforts on satisfying the wants and needs of these groups. After segmenting and targeting activities have been completed, marketers then position their products.

Product positioning involves the determination of an appropriate and effective image for products to convey to customers. An aspirin manufacturer, for example, might wish to portray its product as an instant pain reliever, while another might emphasize the affordability of its product. A medical clinic might wish to emphasize its prestigious medical staff, while another might convey its convenient service. A hospital might wish to convey an image of technological innovation, while another might desire an image of altruistic concern for patients. When determined, marketers formulate methods to convey the desired product imagery to target markets through advertising, personal selling, sales promotion, and other means.

When products have been positioned, marketers must monitor consumer perceptions related to the offerings to ensure that associated goods and services are perceived in the manner desired. A useful tool that provides guidance to marketers in this endeavor is known as the Perceptual (or Positioning) Map, which, as illustrated in Figure 18-1, consists of two intersected axes that represent different product-related attributes. When completed, a Perceptual Map demonstrates how consumers perceive products based on designated product attributes—information that is essential for the purpose of product positioning.

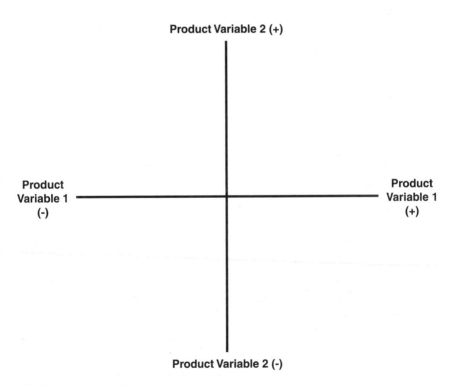

FIGURE 18-1 The Perceptual Map

To assess products using the Perceptual Map, marketers (1) identify the offerings to be evaluated, (2) construct the map diagram, as illustrated in Figure 18-1, (3) determine the product-related attributes that will compose the map's axes, labeling the diagram accordingly, (4) gather data pertaining to the consumer perceptions of products to be evaluated, and (5) plot the coordinates of each product on the Perceptual Map. This visual representation is then analyzed to determine if product offerings are perceived in the manner desired, allowing marketers to make adjustments as necessary to elicit desired perceptions. For increased insights into consumer perceptions, marketers can add competitive products to the Perceptual Map.

OPERATIONAL MATTERS

Figure 18-2 illustrates a Perceptual Map that was completed by a medical clinic. Here, the clinic sought to evaluate consumer perceptions regarding its medical services in relation to competitive offerings on the basis of

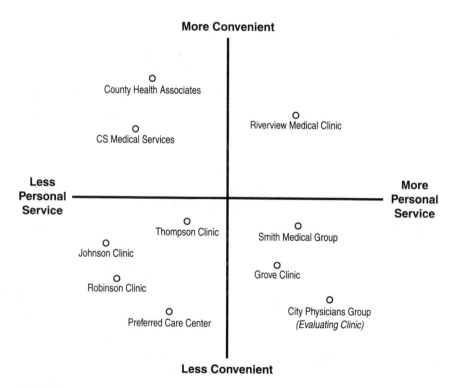

FIGURE 18-2 A Medical Clinic's Perceptual Map

personal service (more or less) and convenience (more or less). The diagram indicates that one clinic is perceived to offer more personal and more convenient service, three clinics—including the evaluating clinic—are perceived to offer more personal but less convenient service, four clinics are perceived to offer less personal and less convenient service, and two clinics are perceived to offer less personal but more convenient service. Of course, by examining each quadrant, more specific information can be obtained. The evaluating clinic is, for example, viewed as the most personal of the three clinics in the "more personal, less convenient" quadrant, but it is the least convenient of the three.

With the information provided by the Perceptual Map, the clinic can take steps to improve the manner in which it is perceived. Because the facility was viewed negatively in the area of convenient service, the clinic might consider introducing measures to increase convenience, such as better parking and extended hours. Of course, the clinic could gain even greater insights into its operation by completing additional Perceptual Maps to view consumer perceptions regarding other product attributes.

EXPLORATORY PERCEPTUAL MAPS

Beyond assessing current products, Perceptual Maps are also useful for positioning new and anticipated product offerings. Figure 18-3 identifies an Exploratory Perceptual Map that was completed by a long term care corporation seeking to assess expansion opportunities in a particular community. Here, the corporation assessed the community's existing assisted living centers based on amenities (many or few) and price (high or low). The completed Exploratory Perceptual Map indicates that three assisted living centers are perceived to offer many amenities at a high price, one center is perceived to offer few amenities at a low price, and one center is perceived to offer few amenities at a high price.

With this map, the corporation has an enhanced perspective of the assisted living market in the community, which can guide it in determining how it might possibly enter the market. Notably, the diagram illustrates that a void exists in the market's "many amenities, low price" quadrant. This void may represent an opportunity for the corporation to differentiate itself from existing competitors by establishing the community's only assisted living center that offers many amenities at a low price. The Exploratory

FIGURE 18-3 A Long Term Care Corporation's Exploratory Perceptual Map

Perceptual Map also allows the corporation to assess various competitive approaches to assisted living.

OTHER POINTS

It is important to remember that Perceptual Maps are only as accurate as the information that is used to complete them. In constructing these maps, some marketers simply use their own judgment regarding consumer perceptions related to the product offerings under examination. Others assemble groups consisting of members of their product management teams to discuss likely consumer perceptions, developing Perceptual Maps accordingly. Still other marketers use formal market research to construct these maps. Although Perceptual Maps remain useful even with informally collected data, the use of data derived from formal market research can greatly improve their accuracy.

It is also important to remember that Perceptual Maps do indeed deal with perceptions. Consumer perceptions, of course, change over time—a fact which necessitates that marketers routinely construct and analyze Perceptual Maps in an effort to stay abreast of the latest consumer perceptions regarding product offerings.

SUMMARY

The Perceptual Map provides marketers with a helpful tool for understanding consumer perceptions related to product offerings. Usefully, the Perceptual Map can be employed to assess consumer perceptions related to both current and anticipated product offerings. Such information greatly assists marketers in their ongoing product positioning responsibilities, making the Perceptual Map an indispensable marketing tool.

EXERCISES

1. Provide a comprehensive overview of the Perceptual Map, explaining its purpose, components, uses, and benefits, accompanied by an associated illustration. Be sure to indicate how the instrument can be used not only for current product offerings but also for potential product offerings in the marketplace. Share your views regarding how this instrument can be used to effect better product positioning outcomes in the healthcare industry.

2. Select a healthcare product of your choice for placement in your local market and envision its key features and benefits. Then, prepare an Exploratory Perceptual Map for the potential offering, selecting applicable product-related attributes for the axes and plotting all competitive products in the market on the diagram based on your views of how consumers might perceive the offerings. Provide a narrative assessing this new product offering in the context of existing competition.

CHAPTER 19

Ries & Trout's Product Ladder

LEARNING OBJECTIVES

After examining this chapter, readers will have the ability to:

- Realize that healthcare marketers must direct attention to the manner in which consumers perceive their product offerings relative to those of competitors.
- Understand that significant efforts are required to ensure that consumers view given healthcare products more favorably than competitive offerings.
- Recognize that consumers tend to rank products in their minds.
- Appreciate the value of Ries and Trout's Product Ladder as a tool for visualizing and understanding the product rankings formulated by consumers.

INTRODUCTION

Given that marketers ultimately seek to effect exchanges with target markets, they must constantly focus on the manner in which consumers perceive their products in relation to competitive offerings. Ideally, marketers would like for their goods and services, rather than those of competitors, to be viewed most favorably by consumers. Achieving such prominent positions in the minds of consumers is a difficult task, but if attained, yields significant benefits.

For insights into attaining such lofty positions in the minds of consumers, marketers frequently refer to the Product Ladder, a useful tool developed by Al Ries and Jack Trout. Illustrated in Figure 19-1, the Product
Ladder consists of an outline of a human head, representing a consumer's
mind, with a ladder situated inside, representing the consumer's rank order
of brands within a particular product category.

Ries and Trout developed the Product Ladder to illustrate that, given the
limitations of the human mind coupled with the proliferation of available
goods and services in the marketplace, consumers are forced to rank products in their minds.

These rankings can be depicted as a series of ladders in the minds of
consumers, with each ladder representing a different product category and
each step representing a different product brand. Products situated on

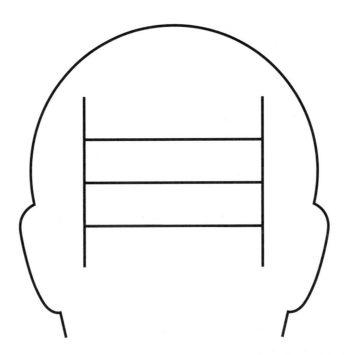

From *Positioning: The Battle for Your Mind*, 20th anniversary ed. by Al Ries and Jack Trout.
Copyright © 2001, 1981 by The McGraw-Hill Companies, Inc. Published by McGraw-Hill.
Reproduced with permission of The McGraw-Hill Companies.

FIGURE 19-1 Ries & Trout's Product Ladder

higher steps rank higher in the minds of consumers than products situated on lower steps.

Product Ladders may consist of as few as one step to many steps, although Product Ladders with seven or more steps are considered to be quite lengthy. Product Ladders are also consumer-specific—they are based on the particular views of given individuals.

Some consumers may not be aware of brands within particular product categories and would, therefore, not possess associated Product Ladders. Consumers who, for example, have never had a need for surgery may not possess a Product Ladder for surgical services. When consumers develop needs for unfamiliar goods and services, however, Product Ladders form rather quickly as consumers actively solicit information regarding given product offerings through both formal and informal channels.

OPERATIONAL MATTERS

To assess products using the Product Ladder, marketers simply (1) identify the product category to be evaluated, (2) gather data pertaining to the consumer perceptions of product brands within the identified category, and (3) construct a Product Ladder that is representative of the findings. This visual representation is then analyzed to gain product insights.

Figure 19-2 presents a series of Product Ladders illustrating a particular consumer's perceptions regarding a variety of healthcare offerings; namely, medical centers, medical clinics, and assisted living centers. The products occupying the top rungs of these Product Ladders represent those offerings that, in their respective product categories, the consumer views as most favorable. Products at lower levels, however, are not as highly regarded by the consumer.

Of course, these particular Product Ladders represent the perceptions of only one individual whose views may or may not coincide with prevailing perceptions in the market. Marketers seeking more extensive, and thus useful, perspectives of consumer perceptions would need to acquire representative samples of product rankings for given product categories from targeted consumers. The data could then be aggregated and used to construct "market representative" Product Ladders that marketers could, in turn, use to determine strategic and tactical priorities.

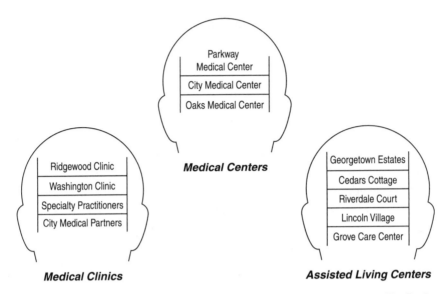

Constructed using design methodologies in Ries, Al, and Jack Trout. *Positioning: The Battle for Your Mind.* 20th anniversary ed. New York: McGraw-Hill, 2001.

FIGURE 19-2 A Series of Product Ladders for Health Offerings

MOVING UP THE PRODUCT LADDER

Marketers whose products occupy lower-level positions face an extremely difficult challenge as they pursue the top steps of Product Ladders. Although the outright dislodging of top-rung brands is usually impossible, marketers can make inroads toward these positions by relating their products to market leading offerings.

A newly established medical clinic, for example, might feature in its advertisements its enhanced scope of services in relation to the market's leading clinic. A pharmaceutical firm might tout in its advertisements that its pain reliever works faster than the leading product. Sales representatives for a durable medical equipment manufacturer might tout their product line's enhanced durability, better warranty, and more comprehensive customer support policy relative to the market leader's offerings. By relating lower-rung products to market leading offerings, marketers exploit consumer familiarity to leverage their own product positions.

NEW PRODUCTS & THE PRODUCT LADDER

It should be mentioned that when marketers introduce *new-to-the-world products*, those products that define entirely new product categories never before offered to the public, consumers must formulate new Product Ladders in their minds. Marketers can assist consumers in the construction of these new Product Ladders by relating totally new product offerings to existing products. Ries and Trout note that this approach was used with the introduction of the automobile, which was initially referred to as a "horseless" carriage, allowing consumers a familiar point of reference to understand and evaluate the new-to-the-world product offering. Once again, marketers exploit familiarity to gain a foothold in the minds of consumers.

SUMMARY

Ries and Trout's Product Ladder provides marketers with a useful tool for understanding the manner in which consumers perceive products in relation to competitive offerings. Notably, this tool directs attention to the fact that consumers rank products in their minds, with higher rankings indicating more favorable product offerings. The useful insights generated by the Product Ladder provide great assistance to marketers in their endeavors to achieve prominent positions for their product offerings in the minds of consumers.

EXERCISES

1. Define and comprehensively discuss Ries and Trout's Product Ladder, providing insights regarding its uses, features, meaning, and value, accompanied by an appropriate illustration. Be sure to include in your discussion an overview of the instrument's importance as a target marketing device in the healthcare industry.
2. Secure a copy of a telephone directory for a municipality of which you are familiar. Select a particular medical category (e.g., eye surgery centers, nursing homes, etc.) and view the listings provided in the directory. Then, based on your knowledge of the given establishments,

construct a Product Ladder for the particular medical category. If any of the listings are unfamiliar to you, seek information about the given entities in an effort to assign them an appropriate place on the Product Ladder. Provide a brief narrative explaining your illustration.

REFERENCE

Ries, Al, and Jack Trout. 2001. *Positioning: The battle for your mind.* 20th anniversary ed. New York: McGraw-Hill.

PART FOUR

Consumer Behavior & Product Promotions Tools

CHAPTER 20

Abraham Maslow's Hierarchy of Needs

LEARNING OBJECTIVES

After examining this chapter, readers will have the ability to:

- Understand that motivations to purchase and consume healthcare offerings are very complex and highly diverse.
- Realize that different healthcare issues, events, and circumstances spark different motivations that require different interventions.
- Recognize the necessity for healthcare marketers to possess an understanding of human motivation in an effort to better understand their customers.
- Appreciate the value of Maslow's Hierarchy of Needs as a device for understanding human motivation.

INTRODUCTION

Motivations to purchase and consume healthcare products are as complex and varied as the number of available goods and services in the marketplace. These motivations are fueled by an equally complex and varied array of human wants and needs, which marketers seek to address through the development and distribution of goods and services.

Different healthcare issues, events, and circumstances spark different motivations that require different interventions (i.e., goods and services).

137

Given this, it is essential for marketers to possess a thorough understanding of human motivation.

One leading theory of human motivation was developed by Abraham Maslow, who theorized that all human needs can be grouped into one of five hierarchical categories—physiological, safety, social, esteem, and self-actualization—and that needs at one level will not motivate a person until needs at the preceding level have been satisfied. In other words, physiological needs must be satisfied before safety needs will become motivators, safety needs must be satisfied before social needs will become motivators, social needs must be satisfied before esteem needs will become motivators, and so on.

Illustrated in Figure 20-1, Maslow's Hierarchy of Needs is depicted as a pyramid consisting of five hierarchical levels representing different cate-

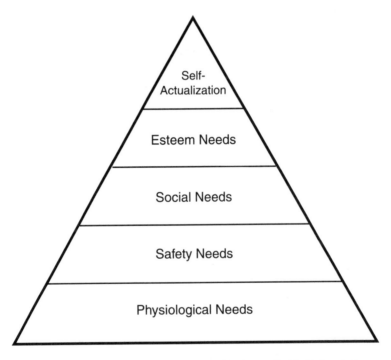

FIGURE 20-1 Maslow's Hierarchy of Needs

gories of human needs. These categories, accompanied by healthcare industry examples, are identified as follows.

PHYSIOLOGICAL NEEDS

Physiological needs represent basic human needs that are required for survival, including air, food, water, and health. Life-saving interventions, such as ambulance transportation and emergency department services, provide some of the best examples of healthcare offerings that satisfy physiological needs.

Other examples would include labor and delivery services for expectant mothers and well-baby checkups for infants. Without such services, medical complications are more likely to occur, possibly resulting in injury or death. Still another example would be that of radiological and chemotherapeutic interventions designed to extend the lives of patients suffering from cancer. Each of these interventions is conducted for physiological purposes.

SAFETY NEEDS

Safety needs represent human needs for security and protection. Health insurance is an excellent example of a healthcare product that addresses the safety and security needs of individuals. Assisted living centers also address safety needs by offering elderly individuals living accommodations that provide nursing assistance in secure environments. These products offer individuals the peace of mind of knowing that they are protected.

SOCIAL NEEDS

Social needs involve human needs for love, friendship, affiliation, and acceptance by others. Psychiatric therapies and medications are examples of healthcare goods and services that address the social needs of individuals. These interventions offer hope to those suffering from socially confining illnesses, such as anxiety and depression. Wheelchairs and prosthetic devices represent additional examples of healthcare products that address social needs. These product offerings enable the injured and disabled to engage society and interact more easily with others.

ESTEEM NEEDS

Esteem needs represent human needs for pride, prestige, and attention and recognition from others. Cosmetic surgery offers an excellent example of a medical service that addresses esteem needs. Face lifts, breast augmentation, and liposuction represent only a few of the many cosmetic procedures that individuals routinely undergo to enhance their appearance, often as a means of increasing their self-confidence, pride in themselves, and appeal to others.

SELF-ACTUALIZATION NEEDS

Self-actualization needs represent human needs for personal growth and fulfillment, and the healthcare marketplace offers rich opportunities for individuals to satisfy these desires. Donations of time (through volunteerism) and money (through financial contributions) to local medical centers, nursing homes, and health-related charitable organizations are examples of healthcare marketplace opportunities that allow individuals to fulfill self-actualization needs. When individuals reach this level, they are operating at their pinnacle.

OPERATIONAL MATTERS

Maslow's Hierarchy of Needs is perhaps most useful to marketers as a tool for conceptualizing the underlying wants and needs—collectively termed *needs* by Maslow—that drive consumption of goods and services. By possessing a better understanding of the wants and needs satisfied by particular products, the underlying associated motivations, and the hierarchical order of the corresponding needs categories, marketers are better prepared to formulate promotional campaigns and engage in ongoing product management responsibilities.

Although Maslow theorized that higher-level needs will not motivate individuals until lower-level needs have been satisfied, he acknowledged that variations are possible and do occur. One could easily envision a situation where a person might decide to use his or her resources to pay for elective cosmetic surgery (i.e., an esteem need) rather than to secure an adequate health insurance policy (i.e., a safety need). This example illustrates that, among individuals, priorities often differ and may lead to unique pursuits.

SUMMARY

Maslow's Hierarchy of Needs serves as a simple, yet highly effective, tool for understanding human motivation. This tool is particularly useful in the healthcare industry where motivations to consume the seemingly endless array of goods and services are driven by an equally intensive array of wants and needs.

Quite obviously, marketers can greatly improve marketing results if they understand how their product offerings fit into the overall scheme of human motivation. By understanding human motivation, marketers can better devise promotional campaigns that emphasize the attributes of associated product offerings in the context of the wants and needs that drive exchange, thus increasing the likelihood of marketing success.

EXERCISES

1. Provide a detailed overview of Maslow's Hierarchy of Needs, identifying and explaining its theoretical underpinnings, structure, and features and benefits. Support this overview by drawing an illustration of the hierarchy. Be sure to discuss the model's implications for healthcare marketing professionals and their associated institutions.
2. Select a local medical center and investigate its product offerings, making a comprehensive list of these offerings. Then, prepare a diagram identifying the five categories listed in Maslow's Hierarchy of Needs and place the listed products in their appropriate categories. Provide an overview of your rationale for placing the products in the diagram as you did and provide details as to how you might go about marketing products in each of the identified categories.

REFERENCE

Maslow, Abraham H. 2000. *The Maslow business reader*, ed. Deborah C. Stephens. New York: Wiley.

CHAPTER 21

Everett Rogers' Diffusion of Innovations Model

LEARNING OBJECTIVES

After examining this chapter, readers will have the ability to:

- Understand that consumers vary in their willingness to adopt new product offerings, with some being quicker to adopt than others.
- Recognize that earlier adopters possess characteristics that are different from later adopters.
- Understand the benefits that earlier adopters provide to marketers as hasteners of the innovation diffusion process. .
- Realize that personal issues, events, and circumstances often influence one's willingness to adopt new healthcare goods and services.
- Appreciate the value of Everett Rogers' Diffusion of Innovations Model as a tool for understanding the product adoption tendencies of consumers.

INTRODUCTION

Healthcare innovations—new goods and services that significantly improve health and extend life—are usually not adopted by all members of a target market simultaneously. Instead, acceptance of these new products occurs gradually over time—a process referred to as *diffusion*. Emergent situations aside, consumers vary in their willingness to adopt new products. Some are quick to embrace new offerings, while others are less inclined to do so. Those who eagerly accept new products possess characteristics that are different from those who delay adoption. To understand the unique characteristics of adopters and their levels of innovativeness, marketers frequently turn to Everett Rogers' Diffusion of Innovations Model.

Illustrated in Figure 21-1, Rogers' Diffusion of Innovations Model is depicted as a bell-shaped curve that represents the adoption of an innovation over time. The model categorizes individuals as innovators, early adopters, early majority, late majority, or laggards based on when they adopt an innovation. These adopter categories are described as follows.

INNOVATORS

Described as "venturesome," innovators represent the first 2.5% of adopters. These individuals are comfortable with risk and uncertainty and are also typically wealthy—a prerequisite given that they must have the ability to absorb losses in the event that innovations fail to meet expectations. Although they are rarely community opinion leaders, innovators are instrumental in the diffusion process because of their willingness to quickly adopt new goods and services. Their initial usage experiences indirectly promote innovations to other consumers in the market, building product awareness and ultimately hastening the diffusion process.

EARLY ADOPTERS

Early adopters are characterized by "respect" and make up the next 13.5% of adopters. They are community opinion leaders who command the respect of their peers—peers who look to these early adopters for advice on whether they, too, should adopt innovations. Early adopters serve as information disseminators in that, upon adoption of product offerings, they are quick to convey their experiences to others. Given these characteristics, it is quite obvious that early adopters play an essential role in the diffusion process.

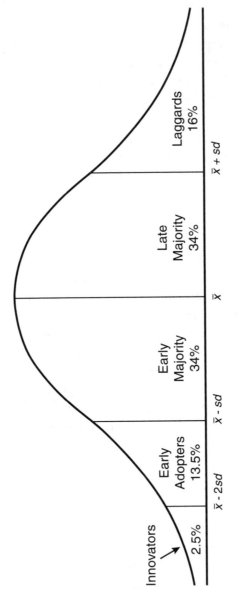

FIGURE 21-1 Rogers' Diffusion of Innovations Model

EARLY MAJORITY

Members of the early majority are described as "deliberate" and represent the next 34% of adopters. These individuals are rarely opinion leaders, but they do actively interact with their peers. They tend to deliberate for some time before they adopt new products. Early majority members do not want to be the first or the last to adopt innovations.

LATE MAJORITY

Members of the late majority are described as "skeptical" and make up the next 34% of adopters. These cautious individuals are leery of new ideas and often only adopt innovations under peer pressure. Their reluctance to adopt innovations is related to their relatively scarce resources—a factor which necessitates that late majority members delay adoption until new product uncertainties are removed.

LAGGARDS

Laggards are described as "traditional" and represent the last 16% of adopters. These individuals are suspicious of new products and are highly resistant to change of any kind. They are almost never opinion leaders and have very limited marketplace interactions. Like members of the late majority, laggards possess few resources—a factor that reduces their willingness to adopt innovations until new product uncertainties are eliminated.

OPERATIONAL MATTERS

Research suggests that differences between earlier and later adopters are quite pronounced, as illustrated in Table 21-1. By targeting earlier adopters, those who more quickly adopt innovations, significant new product publicity can be generated through their extensive informal networks. This increased—and free—publicity, of course, acts to hasten the innovation diffusion process, making earlier adopters very desirable targets for cost-conscious marketers seeking to maximize their promotions resources.

Table 21-1 Differences Between Earlier and Later Adopters

Earlier adopters have more years of formal education than later adopters.

Earlier adopters have higher social status than later adopters.

Earlier adopters have a greater degree of upward social mobility than later adopters.

Earlier adopters have greater intelligence than later adopters.

Earlier adopters have a more favorable attitude toward change than later adopters.

Earlier adopters are better able to cope with uncertainty and risk than later adopters.

Earlier adopters have a more favorable attitude toward science than later adopters.

Earlier adopters are more highly interconnected through interpersonal networks in their social system than later adopters.

Earlier adopters are more cosmopolite than later adopters.

Earlier adopters have greater exposure to mass media communications channels than later adopters.

Earlier adopters seek information about innovations more actively than later adopters.

Earlier adopters have a higher degree of opinion leadership than later adopters.

Derived from information in Rogers, Everett M. *Diffusion of Innovations*. 5th ed. New York: The Free Press, 2003: 287–292.

Of course, there are situations in the healthcare marketplace where instant, market-wide innovation adoption would be expected. Many healthcare innovations are consumed not out of desire but out of need, which tends to hasten the diffusion process. Individuals who have been severely injured in automobile accidents, for example, would hardly discourage the receipt of innovative emergency medical services. Likewise, individuals suffering from debilitating illnesses would likely immediately adopt any innovation that offered hope for recovery.

The same rapid innovation acceptance would occur during public health epidemics where it would be expected that available treatment options would immediately be adopted by affected populations. Clearly, emergent healthcare situations act as innovation adoption catalysts.

SUMMARY

The innovation-rich healthcare environment necessitates that marketers possess a thorough understanding of the innovation diffusion process. Rogers' Diffusion of Innovations Model yields significant insights into the unique characteristics of adopters and their levels of innovativeness. This tool allows marketers to better understand their customers and more effectively design promotional campaigns that expedite the innovation diffusion process.

EXERCISES

1. Prepare a detailed overview of Everett Rogers' Diffusion of Innovations Model, describing each of the five identified consumer groups and their innovation adoption tendencies. Share your thoughts regarding the tool's implications and uses in the healthcare industry.
2. Place yourself in the role of marketing director for a newly established healthcare entity promoting a product of your choice. Based on your knowledge of Everett Rogers' Diffusion of Innovations Model, develop a strategy for acquiring patronage. What group or groups would you target and why? How would you go about reaching these designated groups? What additional steps would you take to ensure maximum patronage?

REFERENCE

Rogers, Everett M. 2003. *Diffusion of innovations.* 5th ed. New York: The Free Press.

CHAPTER 22

The DAGMAR Marketing Communications Spectrum

INTRODUCTION

Society has become reliant on the seemingly endless array of innovations in health care. Not only have healthcare innovations become commonplace, they have also become expected and even demanded by the public. The extensive range of innovative healthcare goods and services is simply overwhelming, from life-saving emergency medical services to life-enhancing pharmaceutical products, with new innovations constantly entering the marketplace.

It might seem as though commercial success would be guaranteed simply by developing and providing new and improved healthcare goods and services. However, an equally important prerequisite for commercial success involves the successful communication of new offerings to potential customers. If customers are not aware of new and improved products, one could hardly expect the healthcare offerings to achieve commercial success. New and improved healthcare goods and services can and do fail, often as a result of failed communications efforts. Clearly, marketers must endeavor to use good communicative techniques in their attempts to build consumer awareness of their product offerings.

THE MECHANICS OF COMMUNICATION

The awareness-building process is a process of communication, an aspect of product management that falls under the promotions component of the marketing mix. Successes in promotion are the direct result of successes in communication. As illustrated in Figure 22-1, the communications process involves two parties: a sender and a receiver. The sender's objective is to deliver his or her intended message to the receiver. To do this, the sender encodes the message, which is sent via selected media—the communications channel or channels through which the message is delivered—to the receiver. The receiver then decodes the message and, if inclined to do so, encodes a response that is returned to the sender as feedback. Feedback from the receiver may take many forms, including requests for additional information, acceptances or rejections of sales proposals, and purchases of goods and services.

Throughout the communications process, message distortion and/or elimination may occur due to negative environmental influences, collectively referred to as *noise* (e.g., competitive messages, distractions). Although the communications process seems quite simple, in reality it is among the most complex of processes and must be mastered for marketing success. Clearly, the ability of marketers to successfully communicate with current and potential customers greatly improves the marketplace experiences of associated product offerings.

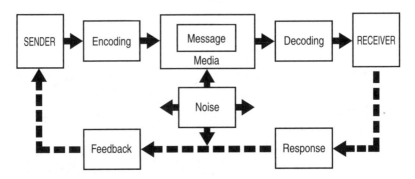

From KOTLER, PHILIP, MARKETING MANAGEMENT, 11th Edition, © 2003, Pg. 565.
Reprinted by permission of Pearson Education, Inc., Upper Saddle River, NJ.

FIGURE 22-1 The Communications Process

THE DAGMAR MARKETING COMMUNICATIONS SPECTRUM

Medical emergencies aside, when consumers adopt new products, the act of adoption is rarely a singular event. Singularity of the process would not be expected, of course, because consumers must minimally gain familiarity with new product offerings, determining, among other things, the potential benefits that might be offered by the associated goods and services. This is particularly true in the healthcare marketplace where increasingly complex innovations have become commonplace. Instead, adoption consists of a series of progressive steps leading up to the purchase and consumption of new products.

To understand the adoption process, marketers frequently turn to the DAGMAR Marketing Communications Spectrum. (DAGMAR is an acronym for *Defining Advertising Goals for Measured Advertising Results*, the title of the book that presents the spectrum.) Illustrated in Figure 22-2, the DAGMAR Marketing Communications Spectrum divides the adoption process into five sequential levels or stages: unawareness, awareness, comprehension, conviction, and action. Each of these stages is influenced by marketing forces and countervailing forces, which are depicted by arrows in the diagram. The stages of the DAGMAR Marketing Communications Spectrum are explained as follows.

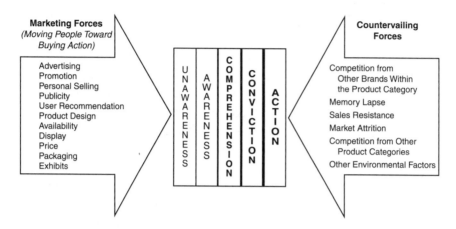

Marketing Forces
(Moving People Toward Buying Action)

Advertising
Promotion
Personal Selling
Publicity
User Recommendation
Product Design
Availability
Display
Price
Packaging
Exhibits

UNAWARENESS AWARENESS COMPREHENSION CONVICTION ACTION

Countervailing
Forces

Competition from
    Other Brands Within
    the Product Category
Memory Lapse
Sales Resistance
Market Attrition
Competition from Other
    Product Categories
Other Environmental Factors

From *DAGMAR: Defining Advertising Goals for Measured Advertising Results*, 2nd ed. by Solomon Dutka. (1st ed. by Russell Colley). Copyright © 1995 by NTC Publishing Group. Published by NTC Business Books.

FIGURE 22-2 The DAGMAR Marketing Communications Spectrum

STAGE I: UNAWARENESS

During the unawareness stage, consumers are oblivious to the existence of new goods and services. Any promotional messages that have been disseminated have not successfully reached consumers.

STAGE II: AWARENESS

Consumers first become aware of the existence of new products during the awareness stage. Here, they also gain a general understanding of the potential benefits associated with new offerings. At this point, consumers possess a base level of knowledge regarding new products but little more. They cannot recall, for example, the entities that produce and provide the offerings, associated locations of availability, and so on.

STAGE III: COMPREHENSION

During the comprehension stage, consumers gain a detailed understanding of new products. Consumers are able to recall, for example, the entities that produce and provide the offerings, associated features and benefits, locations of availability, packaging, brand names, and logos.

STAGE IV: CONVICTION

During the conviction stage, consumers develop strong beliefs regarding the virtues of new products. Here, preferences for new offerings are formulated. Consumers have filtered through the information gained from prior stages of the spectrum and have become reasonably confident that the associated products will meet or exceed their expectations.

STAGE V: ACTION

The DAGMAR Marketing Communications Spectrum concludes with the action stage where consumers decide to adopt—purchase and consume—new product offerings.

ENCOURAGING ACTION

Beyond identification of the stages of adoption, the DAGMAR Marketing Communications Spectrum illustrates the influences that marketing forces and countervailing forces have on consumers throughout the adoption process. Marketing forces (e.g., product design, pricing, advertising, personal selling, publicity) seek to move consumers toward action, while countervailing forces (e.g., competition, memory lapse, sales resistance, market attrition) seek to drive consumers away from action. Healthcare marketers must strive to develop promotional campaigns that will effectively neutralize countervailing forces and move consumers toward action in as expeditious a fashion as possible.

The exact composition of any promotional campaign is, of course, dependent on the specific nature of the products being marketed. In their quest to entice target markets to purchase and consume products, healthcare marketers normally promote goods and services using a variety of methods.

The array of methods used by marketers to communicate product information to customers is referred to as the *promotions mix*. Also termed the *communications mix*, this array is identified in Figure 22-3 and defined in Table 22-1. Advertising tends to be used universally by all types of healthcare entities (e.g., hospitals, pharmaceutical manufacturers, medical clinics, home health agencies). However, other forms of promotion tend

FIGURE 22-3 The Promotions Mix

to be used more heavily in certain industry segments, such as personal selling in the pharmaceutical and medical device areas. Each promotional method possesses strengths and weaknesses and must be studied carefully to ensure a goodness of fit with the given products to be marketed.

When promotional methods have been selected, marketers must make additional decisions, many of which are specific to particular promotions vehicles. Advertising, for example, involves a variety of unique points of consideration that Philip Kotler termed the *five Ms of advertising*, as illustrated in Figure 22-4. Regardless of the communicative tools utilized, the goal of any promotional campaign is to move consumers through the successive stages of the DAGMAR Marketing Communications Spectrum as swiftly as possible.

Table 22-1 Promotions Mix Definitions and Examples

ADVERTISING	A promotional method involving the paid use of mass media to deliver messages.
	Examples include newspaper, magazine, radio, television, and billboard advertisements.
PERSONAL SELLING	A promotional method involving the use of a sales force to convey messages.
	Examples include sales representatives and account executives.
SALES PROMOTION	A promotional method involving the use of incentives to stimulate consumer interest.
	Examples include discount coupons, free gifts, samples, and contests.
PUBLIC RELATIONS	A promotional method involving the use of publicity and other unpaid forms of promotion to deliver messages.
	Examples include press releases, open houses, facility tours, and educational seminars.
DIRECT MARKETING	A promotional method involving the delivery of messages directly to consumers.
	Examples include direct-mail marketing, telemarketing, and catalog marketing.

CONTINUED PRODUCT USE

It should be noted that although the DAGMAR Marketing Communications Spectrum concludes with product adoption, marketers must not neglect customers after the adoption decision. Continued use of product offerings by customers is as important as the initial adoption of the associated goods and services. Marketers must, therefore, strive to ensure that post-adoption attention is not neglected.

An assisted living center, for example, that provides poor service to a resident will likely lose the occupancy of this individual along with any personal referrals that would potentially be forwarded. A medical center's maternity services department that neglects the wants and needs of an expectant mother will almost certainly lose the trust and the future business of this new mother and possibly that of her network of friends. Clearly, post-adoption support is imperative for enduring marketing success.

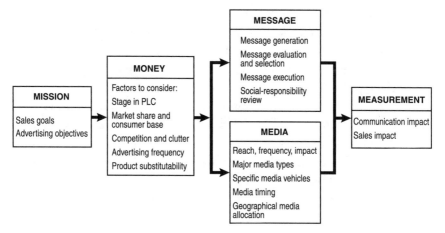

From KOTLER, PHILIP, MARKETING MANAGEMENT, 11th Edition, © 2003, Pg. 591.
Reprinted by permission of Pearson Education, Inc., Upper Saddle River, NJ.

FIGURE 22-4 Kotler's Five Ms of Advertising

SUMMARY

The DAGMAR Marketing Communications Spectrum clearly illustrates the successive steps that consumers pass through toward the purchase and consumption of new goods and services, giving attention to the influences forwarded by marketing forces and countervailing forces. Among other things, the spectrum serves as a useful reminder of the necessity to effectively communicate with target markets. Such effective communication acts to neutralize countervailing forces and move consumers toward action. The more expeditiously consumers move through the stages of the DAGMAR Marketing Communications Spectrum, the quicker the occurrence of exchange and resulting marketing success.

EXERCISES

  1. Define and comprehensively discuss the DAGMAR Marketing Communications Spectrum, its successive stages leading to action, and the marketing forces and countervailing forces that influence

movement through these stages. A diagram of the spectrum should be included to add value to your narrative. Be sure to include in your discussion details regarding the importance of communicating effectively with target audiences in the healthcare marketplace.

2. Place yourself in the role of marketing director for a newly established healthcare entity promoting a product of your choice. Develop a communications strategy for addressing target audiences during each of the stages of the DAGMAR Marketing Communications Spectrum, indicating how you plan to hasten the purchase and consumption of your given product offering. Also reflect on what actions you might take to ensure post-adoption attention and support.

REFERENCES

Dutka, Solomon. 1995. *DAGMAR: Defining advertising goals for measured advertising results*. 2nd ed. (1st ed. by Russell Colley). Lincolnwood, IL: NTC Business Books.

Kotler, Philip. 2003. *Marketing management*. 11th ed. Upper Saddle River, NJ: Prentice Hall.

23

Raphel & Raphel's Loyalty Ladder

LEARNING OBJECTIVES

After examining this chapter, readers will have the ability to:

- Understand that the patronage of customers is vital to institutional survival, growth, and prosperity.
- Realize that long-term relationships with customers yield lasting benefits for healthcare entities.
- Recognize that the pursuit of customer loyalty represents a worthwhile marketing practice.
- Appreciate Raphel and Raphel's Loyalty Ladder as a tool for understanding the loyalty-building process.

INTRODUCTION

Healthcare entities are ultimately dependent on customers and their continued patronage for survival, growth, and prosperity. Given this, marketers must focus significant attention on addressing the wants and needs of target markets through the provision of superior product solutions. When marketers select target markets, they must diligently pursue these groups in an effort to gain their patronage. Beyond individual transactions, however, marketers ideally seek to establish long-term relationships with their target audiences.

If marketers can gain a loyal following of customers, long-term success becomes a distinct possibility. Hence, marketers must possess a thorough understanding of loyalty and the methods for its attainment. To gain insight into the loyalty-building process, marketers frequently refer to Raphel and Raphel's Loyalty Ladder.

Illustrated in Figure 23-1, Raphel and Raphel's Loyalty Ladder is depicted as a series of five steps—prospects, shoppers, customers, clients, and advocates—representing progressive levels of customer loyalty. The steps of the Loyalty Ladder are explained as follows.

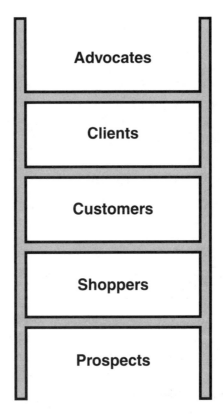

Adapted from *Up the Loyalty Ladder: Turning Sometime Customers into Full-Time Advocates of Your Business* by Murray Raphel and Neil Raphel. Copyright © 1995 by Neil Raphel and Murray Raphel. Published by HarperBusiness. Reprinted by permission of Neil Raphel.

FIGURE 23-1 Raphel & Raphel's Loyalty Ladder

PROSPECTS

Individuals who might potentially have wants and needs for the goods and services of particular entities are considered prospects. At this step, individuals may or may not be aware of given entities and products. Regardless of this, however, purchase activity has not occurred.

A medical clinic providing general medical services in a community is immersed within an environment of prospects. The same could be said of a local pharmacy that recently opened for business. Both of these entities must entice prospects to visit their establishments for current and future healthcare needs. To do this, marketers must convey the attributes of their various product offerings to consumers through the use of marketing communications (e.g., advertising, sales promotion, public relations).

SHOPPERS

Individuals who advance beyond the prospect stage and inquire about the goods and services offered by entities are considered to be shoppers. Shoppers have learned of organizations and associated product offerings and are debating about extending their patronage.

Even in the healthcare environment, people shop for goods and services. Shopping for healthcare goods is conducted in much the same fashion as shopping for any other consumer good. Individuals might, for example, visit a retail drugstore seeking particular pain relievers, the lowest priced prescription drugs, or even the friendliest service.

Individuals also shop for healthcare services, albeit in a different manner. Perhaps they noticed a billboard advertisement announcing the grand opening of a new medical clinic and decided to attend the event to learn more about the establishment. Perhaps they received a direct mail piece promoting a local pharmacy and decided to inquire about prescription prices. If shoppers believe that the products under consideration will meet or exceed their expectations, they will advance to the next rung of the Loyalty Ladder—they become customers.

CUSTOMERS

When individuals purchase and consume the goods and services offered by organizations, they become customers. Perhaps an individual unexpectedly becomes ill and visits a clinic that he or she has seen advertised in a local newspaper. With this person's visit, the clinic has gained a new customer. If the person has his or her prescriptions filled by a new drugstore in town, the drugstore, too, has gained a new customer. If these entities successfully meet and exceed the customer's expectations, the individual may become a repeat customer and graduate to the next rung of the Loyalty Ladder—the client.

CLIENTS

Clients are those individuals who *regularly* purchase goods and services from given organizations. An individual who annually visits a particular medical clinic for his or her physical examination would be considered a client. The same would be said of an individual who routinely has his or her prescriptions filled by a particular pharmacy.

Importantly, entities must not take the patronage of clients for granted. Organizations must ensure that they continue to offer the same quality and service that originally converted customers into clients. Clients are extremely valuable to the entities they frequent. They become even more valuable if they can be converted into advocates.

ADVOCATES

Advocates are individuals who have been so impressed with given establishments and associated product offerings that they openly encourage others to extend their patronage. If a client of a medical clinic openly communicates the virtues of the given establishment to coworkers, family members, and friends, the client becomes an advocate of the clinic.

Advocates stand at the top of the Loyalty Ladder. They are the most valuable patrons of establishments for an obvious reason: Through their testimonials to others, advocates generate new patrons for entities.

OPERATIONAL MATTERS

According to Raphel and Raphel, individuals are *always prospects, frequently shoppers, often customers, sometimes clients,* and *rarely advocates.* This statement succinctly illustrates that the more beneficial patrons, those occupying the top steps of the Loyalty Ladder, are not as common as their less valuable counterparts.

Fortunately, marketers can take steps to advance their customer base to higher levels of the Loyalty Ladder. This progression can be achieved by (1) producing and providing goods and services that meet and exceed the expectations of patrons and (2) embracing a customer service orientation that is championed by all employees.

Typical healthcare industry examples of activities that are likely to convert prospects ultimately into advocates include operating clean and well-organized facilities, providing the latest medical technologies, ensuring that staff members are helpful and courteous, ensuring that patients are seen by medical practitioners in a timely manner, and ensuring that patient information is kept strictly confidential.

By engaging in these activities, healthcare entities are communicating to visitors that they are committed to excellence. Healthcare entities that invest in institutional excellence will undoubtedly be rewarded by the resulting loyalty of valuable patrons occupying the upper levels of the Loyalty Ladder.

SUMMARY

Raphel and Raphel's Loyalty Ladder provides healthcare marketers with a useful method for visualizing the progressive levels of customer loyalty. This tool serves as a reminder of the need for healthcare entities to produce and provide top-quality goods and services, along with ever-increasing levels of customer service, in an effort to boost individuals to progressively higher and more prosperous rungs of the Loyalty Ladder.

EXERCISES

1. Define and comprehensively discuss Raphel and Raphel's Loyalty Ladder, identifying and explaining its theoretical underpinnings, structure, features, and benefits. Support this overview by drawing an illustration of the Loyalty Ladder. Share your thoughts regarding the tool's implications and uses in the healthcare industry.

2. Select a healthcare product of your choice for placement in your local market and envision its key features and benefits. Then, prepare a detailed list of innovative techniques for advancing consumers up the steps of Raphel and Raphel's Loyalty Ladder. How do you intend to keep patrons in and around the highest rung of the Loyalty Ladder?

REFERENCE

Raphel, Murray, and Neil Raphel. 1995. *Up the loyalty ladder: Turning sometime customers into full-time advocates of your business.* New York: HarperBusiness.

24

Bernd Schmitt's CEM Framework

LEARNING OBJECTIVES

After examining this chapter, readers will have the ability to:

- Understand the historical progression of marketing from a discipline initially focused on production, to one concentrating on sales, and finally, in present times, to one focused on customer wants and needs.
- Recognize the imperative of focusing on the wants and needs of customers, permitting such to guide marketing decisions.
- Realize that mutual benefits are afforded to healthcare entities and their respective customer populations by designing and managing all-encompassing customer experiences.
- Appreciate the innovative guidance for the assembly and management of customer experiences provided by Bernd Schmitt's CEM (Customer Experience Management) Framework.

INTRODUCTION

Proficiently addressing the wants and needs of customers stands as one of the greatest challenges facing healthcare marketers. Those who consistently meet and exceed customer expectations are rewarded with lasting patronage and the accompanying results of growth and prosperity. Those who fail in this regard, however, find themselves with a dwindling customer base and the accompanying results of institutional decline and, ultimately, failure.

The discipline of marketing has made great strides over time to place the customer first in all aspects of operation. Early efforts tended to focus on issues such as production (i.e., the production concept) and sales (i.e., the sales concept), viewing customer expectations as secondary matters. As the discipline progressed, however, marketers began to understand and appreciate the role of customers in marketing, realizing that focusing attention on meeting and exceeding the wants and needs of target audiences would yield significant mutual benefits—a philosophy referred to as the *marketing concept.*

Today, marketing efforts are clearly focused on customers, with robust initiatives in the areas of customer satisfaction (i.e., the marketing practice of meeting and, ideally, exceeding the wants and needs of customers), customer relationship management (i.e., the marketing practice of delivering personalized attention, service, and support to target audiences in an effort to establish lasting bonds with customers, ensuring their enduring patronage), and so on.

Such efforts have unquestionably improved the marketing performance of healthcare organizations, but future gains will require continued innovations. One particular innovation is offered by Bernd Schmitt, who advocates that marketers embrace an approach that completely envelopes their target audiences through the design and management of comprehensive customer experiences. This innovation, illustrated in Figure 24-1, is known as the CEM (Customer Experience Management) Framework.

Schmitt's CEM Framework consists of a series of five steps—analyzing the experiential world of the customer (an analysis step), building the experiential platform (a strategy step), designing the brand experience (an implementation step), structuring the customer interface (an implementation step), and engaging in continuous innovation (an implementation step)—which ultimately yields a complete and highly fulfilling customer experience.

As its name suggests, the CEM Framework focuses on *experience* rather than the traditional pursuit of *satisfaction.* A customer experience is multifaceted and, if well designed and managed, yields customer satisfaction, among other benefits. Hence, the development of productive and enjoyable customer experiences affords benefits to customers that eclipse those garnered via the traditional, but more limited, pursuit of customer satisfaction. The steps of Schmitt's CEM Framework are explained as follows.

From *Customer Experience Management: A Revolutionary Approach to Connecting with Your Customers* by Bernd H. Schmitt. Copyright © 2003 by Bernd H. Schmitt. Reprinted with permission of John Wiley & Sons, Inc.

FIGURE 24-1 Schmitt's CEM Framework

STEP 1: ANALYZING THE EXPERIENTIAL WORLD OF THE CUSTOMER

The first step of Schmitt's CEM Framework involves the investigation and analysis of the experiential world of the customer. During this step, healthcare marketers are essentially seeking to develop an intensive knowledge of their customer base with the intention of understanding the types of experiences that their target audiences are seeking through the purchase and consumption of given goods and services.

To achieve an accurate understanding of customers and the experiences they desire, healthcare marketers must ensure that they have accurately defined their target audiences. Then, they must study the meaning of their product offerings and desired characteristics of delivery from the perspective of these groups. How, for example, do customers view given healthcare entities and their products? What information requirements do customers have regarding given healthcare goods and services? What can be done to ensure that customers receiving given healthcare offerings have the most pleasing customer experience possible?

Coupling the information gained from customer-oriented inquiries with information regarding competitors and their customer experience initiatives yields significant insights. Such discoveries far eclipse those gained via traditional customer satisfaction assessment approaches, such as the customer satisfaction survey. Although traditional approaches remain valuable, enhanced details that yield comprehensive profiles of customers, their wants and needs, and their experiential preferences undoubtedly improve marketing outcomes.

STEP 2: BUILDING THE EXPERIENTIAL PLATFORM

The second step of Schmitt's CEM Framework involves the construction of experiential platforms for given product offerings based on discoveries identified in the previous step of the CEM Framework. Here, healthcare marketers take the information gained from customer analyses and formulate product delivery methods, known as *experiential platforms*, that are consistent with the experiences desired by their target audiences.

Importantly, experiential platforms must be thoroughly documented, as such platforms become the blueprints for delivering customer experiences. These platforms essentially stipulate the strategy that will be implemented through the remaining steps of the CEM Framework.

STEP 3: DESIGNING THE BRAND EXPERIENCE

Designing the brand experience represents the third step of Schmitt's CEM Framework. Here, healthcare marketers seek to convey the essence of their experiential platforms through the development of meaningful identity-related elements (e.g., logos, signage, packaging, advertisements) associated with given product offerings. Importantly, each element portraying these offerings must be formulated in a manner to convey, as richly as possible, defined experiential platforms. Conveyance of the experiences that customers can expect to receive as patrons is essential for marketing success under the CEM Framework, and branding initiatives offer immense opportunities to communicate such experiences.

STEP 4: STRUCTURING THE CUSTOMER INTERFACE

The fourth step of Schmitt's CEM Framework involves the design, development, and implementation of the infrastructure (i.e., the customer interface) that is instituted to ensure the exchange of information between organizations and their target audiences. Depending on the particular healthcare product under examination, the nature of the exchange of information can be face-to-face (e.g., a physician examining a patient, a pharmacist providing medication usage instructions to a customer) or at a distance (e.g., a postcard sent to remind a patient of a dental appointment, an email confirmation of an order placed via a retail pharmacy's Web site).

The customer interface is arguably the most important element associated with the delivery of experiential platforms. This is true for all healthcare products, but it is especially relevant in the healthcare service arena where customers are completely immersed within given healthcare institutions as they receive medical attention. As with designing brands, structuring customer interfaces requires that healthcare marketers ensure that selected information exchange vehicles support the experiential platforms that were defined earlier in the CEM Framework.

STEP 5: ENGAGING IN CONTINUOUS INNOVATION

The final step of Schmitt's CEM Framework involves the continual pursuit of innovation, with healthcare marketers striving to incorporate such advancements in a manner that will not only enhance their given product offerings but also the experiences afforded to customers, courtesy of the new discoveries.

New innovations in the healthcare industry can be quite varied. Some may directly pertain to healthcare product offerings (e.g., new imaging technologies, breakthrough pharmaceuticals, enhanced ambulance transportation technologies). Others may indirectly relate to healthcare goods and services (e.g., enhanced patient information systems, breakthrough leadership innovations, improved institutional heating and air conditioning systems). Regardless of the particular innovations at hand, healthcare marketers must ensure that they stay abreast of the latest advancements in an effort to deliver both product and experiential value to customers.

OPERATIONAL MATTERS

When healthcare marketers implement the CEM Framework, they must remind themselves that their primary task is to study, design, and continually improve customer experiences within their healthcare institutions. Crafting the customer experience is the element that differentiates the CEM Framework from other customer-focused marketing initiatives. By focusing on delivering a customer experience, rather than a static event of customer satisfaction, opportunities to meet and exceed the expectations of customers are greatly enhanced. Clearly, healthcare entities that incorporate the CEM Framework are well positioned to deliver enhanced value to customers, resulting in enduring patronage and its associated benefits.

SUMMARY

Schmitt's CEM Framework provides healthcare marketers with an innovative formula for advancing beyond static customer satisfaction initiatives and into the dynamic realm of delivering comprehensive customer experiences that completely immerse target audiences. Clearly, the CEM Framework can assist healthcare marketers in their endeavors to proficiently address the wants and needs of their target audiences.

EXERCISES

1. Provide a detailed overview of Bernd Schmitt's CEM (Customer Experience Management) Framework, noting facets regarding its purpose, use, and value in healthcare organizations. Share your thoughts and ideas regarding the degree to which modern healthcare organizations arrange excellent customer experiences.

2. Place yourself in the role of marketing director for a soon-to-be-launched healthcare establishment of your choice in your local market. Briefly define the entity's mission and product array. Then, prepare a detailed plan of how you might go about delivering comprehensive customer experiences that completely immerse your target audiences. Be sure to indicate how your plan represents an improve-

ment over standard customer service practices in today's healthcare organizations.

REFERENCE

Schmitt, Bernd H. 2003. *Customer experience management: A revolutionary approach to connecting with your customers.* Hoboken, NJ: Wiley.

25

Osgood, Suci, & Tannenbaum's Semantic Differential

LEARNING OBJECTIVES

After examining this chapter, readers will have the ability to:

- Realize that a chief responsibility of healthcare marketers involves ensuring that products effectively address and satisfy customer wants and needs.
- Understand that to effectively monitor prowess at addressing and satisfying customer wants and needs, healthcare marketers must understand customers and their perceptions of product offerings.
- Recognize the value of Osgood, Suci, and Tannenbaum's Semantic Differential as a mechanism for collecting and understanding customer perceptions of product offerings.

INTRODUCTION

Despite the multitude of activities that marketers perform, they are ultimately charged with satisfying the wants and needs of their target markets through the provision of effective product solutions. Given this, marketers must thoroughly understand customers and their perceptions regarding product offerings.

A useful tool for assessing customer perceptions related to healthcare offerings is known as the Semantic Differential, an objective method for measurement developed by Charles Osgood, George Suci, and Percy Tannenbaum. The Semantic Differential is a broad-based measurement tool that can be implemented in a wide variety of fashions depending on the associated research inquiries at hand. The broad-based nature of the Semantic Differential gives the tool enormous flexibility but requires that it be adapted to given situations.

The Semantic Differential is best explained by viewing an example, such as the one identified in Figure 25-1 that seeks customer perceptions regarding a medical clinic. As depicted in Figure 25-1, the Semantic Differential is essentially a survey that presents a series of descriptive scales pertaining to perceptions associated with a particular good or service. The survey is distributed to customers or other applicable parties who are asked to judge the particular product based on the associated scales. Completed surveys are then averaged to reveal a single line, such as the one illustrated in Figure 25-2, which depicts the product perspectives of those who completed the survey.

The results of the medical clinic's survey, as depicted in Figure 25-2, clearly illustrate that the clinic is viewed very positively by its customer base in all areas except in regard to admitting and waiting time. With this information, the clinic can work to improve its performance in these areas. Admissions convenience might be increased by introducing an enhanced patient information system. Waiting room delays might be reduced by increasing the clinic's staff of medical practitioners or by scheduling appointments more appropriately.

OPERATIONAL MATTERS

Clearly, the Semantic Differential offers marketers a convenient method for assessing customer perceptions related to given healthcare offerings. As illustrated in the previous example, this tool requires that marketers simply (1) formulate a series of scales related to a given offering, (2) prepare a survey depicting these scales, (3) distribute the survey to customers, and (4) average and illustrate survey results. The results of the Semantic Differential survey are then analyzed to determine the strengths and weaknesses associated with the product under evaluation.

What do you think?   **Jackson Medical Clinic**

For each of the following scales, place an "X" in the blank that best reflects your views
regarding the given attribute. When completed, please return the survey to our front
desk receptionist.

Convenient parking ____:____:____:____:____:____:____ Inconvenient parking

Convenient hours ____:____:____:____:____:____:____ Inconvenient hours

Convenient admitting ____:____:____:____:____:____:____ Inconvenient admitting

Short waiting times ____:____:____:____:____:____:____ Long waiting times

Clean facilities ____:____:____:____:____:____:____ Dirty facilities

Modern technology ____:____:____:____:____:____:____ Dated technology

Friendly staff members ____:____:____:____:____:____:____ Unfriendly staff members

Excellent patient care ____:____:____:____:____:____:____ Poor patient care

Excellent customer service ____:____:____:____:____:____:____ Poor customer service

Thank you for your participation!

Constructed using design methodologies in Osgood, Charles E., George J. Suci, and Percy
H. Tannenbaum. *The Measurement of Meaning.* Urbana, IL: University of Illinois Press, 1957.

FIGURE 25-1 A Medical Clinic's Semantic Differential Survey

In addition to its use as an assessment tool for the products held by entities, the Semantic Differential can also provide valuable insights into
competitive offerings. Gaining this knowledge simply requires that marketers circulate an expanded survey that includes a section for respondents
to complete concerning competitive products. If used in this manner, the
results can be respectively averaged and displayed on a single diagram, such

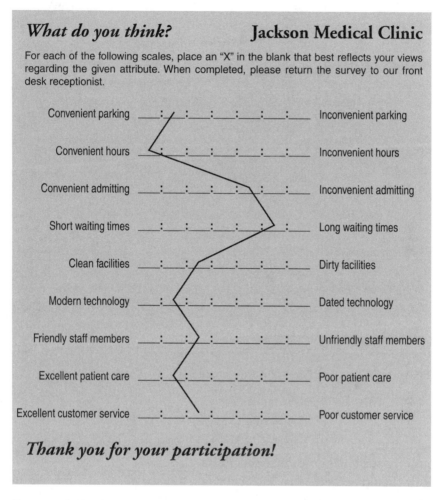

Constructed using design methodologies in Osgood, Charles E., George J. Suci, and Percy H. Tannenbaum. *The Measurement of Meaning*. Urbana, IL: University of Illinois Press, 1957.

FIGURE 25-2 A Medical Clinic's Semantic Differential Survey Results

as the one illustrated in Figure 25-3, that was developed to assess competing retail pharmacies in a community.

The results clearly indicate that City Pharmacy, the evaluating entity, is perceived by survey respondents to be superior to Village Pharmacy in all areas with the exception of the price category, where it is viewed to charge higher prices. With this information, City Pharmacy can concentrate on

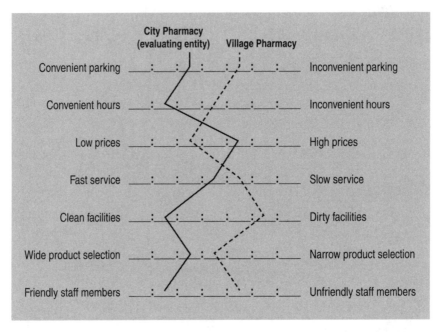

Constructed using design methodologies in Osgood, Charles E., George J. Suci, and Percy H. Tannenbaum. *The Measurement of Meaning.* Urbana, IL: University of Illinois Press, 1957.

FIGURE 25-3 Survey Results for Competing Retail Pharmacies

addressing the "high price" issue while maintaining the overwhelmingly positive attributes noted by respondents.

It should be noted that the Semantic Differential can also be used to monitor institutional progress. This is accomplished by circulating identical Semantic Differential surveys over time and comparing the results. By using the Semantic Differential in this manner, marketers gain even greater insights into marketing operations.

SUMMARY

The Semantic Differential provides marketers with a highly flexible tool for understanding how customers perceive product offerings. With this information, marketers can take steps to build upon product strengths and reduce or eliminate associated weaknesses. By gaining a better understanding of consumer perceptions regarding products, marketers are better equipped to offer goods and services that satisfy the wants and needs of target markets.

EXERCISES

1. Provide a detailed overview of Osgood, Suci, and Tannenbaum's Semantic Differential, illustrating its use and value as a device for collecting and understanding customer perceptions of product offerings. Share your perspectives regarding the degree to which healthcare organizations in your local community actively assess customer perceptions of their product offerings.

2. Select a local healthcare organization and arrange to meet its marketing director for the purpose of discussing the entity's techniques for the assessment of customer perceptions. Be sure to note any techniques that are employed, along with their frequency of deployment. Present Osgood, Suci, and Tannenbaum's Semantic Differential to the marketing director and ask about variables deemed critical for measurement in his or her organization. Construct an instrument incorporating these variables and prepare a written account of insights gained from speaking with the institution's marketing director.

REFERENCE

Osgood, Charles E., George J. Suci, and Percy H. Tannenbaum. 1957. *The measurement of meaning.* Urbana, IL: University of Illinois Press.

PART FIVE

Environmental Analysis & Competitive Assessment Tools

26

The PEST Analysis

LEARNING OBJECTIVES

After examining this chapter, readers will have the ability to:

- Understand that healthcare entities exist in a larger macroenvironment that consists of opportunities and threats that have the potential to positively, neutrally, or negatively impact operations.
- Realize that environmental forces must actively be monitored and evaluated in an effort to best position healthcare organizations to respond to such forces.
- Appreciate the value of the PEST Analysis as a tool for monitoring and evaluating the macroenvironment.

INTRODUCTION

Healthcare entities exist in a much larger macroenvironment teeming with opportunities and threats capable of bolstering or destroying institutional progress. Although these environmental forces are beyond the control of those responsible for managing entities, it is essential for marketers to actively monitor and evaluate these elements in an effort to capitalize on opportunities and avoid or eliminate threats.

A useful tool for performing this evaluative task is known as the PEST Analysis. This analysis, illustrated in Figure 26-1, involves the assessment

Political Forces	Economic Forces	Social Forces	Technological Forces
1. _____	1. _____	1. _____	1. _____
2. _____	2. _____	2. _____	2. _____
3. _____	3. _____	3. _____	3. _____
4. _____	4. _____	4. _____	4. _____
5. _____	5. _____	5. _____	5. _____
6. _____	6. _____	6. _____	6. _____
7. _____	7. _____	7. _____	7. _____
8. _____	8. _____	8. _____	8. _____
9. _____	9. _____	9. _____	9. _____
10. _____	10. _____	10. _____	10. _____

FIGURE 26-1 The PEST Analysis

of a series of macroenvironmental variables—political, economic, social, and technological—that can potentially influence organizations. Political, economic, social, and technological forces are defined as follows.

POLITICAL FORCES

Political forces involve all aspects associated with the legal and political framework of the environment. Although the political environment influences all industries, it has an even more profound impact on the healthcare industry. This increased political attention is due to the unique role of health care in society. First, the health status of a nation influences national prosperity and is, therefore, of significant concern to political leaders. Second, health care is very expensive and thus draws government scrutiny, especially given the fact that the US government pays for a significant portion of national healthcare expenditures. Third, the healthcare industry deals with life and death issues and must be monitored and, in some cases, regulated by the government to protect the public. Medicare and Medicaid insurance programs; certificate of need legislation; and regulatory oversight by the Food and Drug Administration, state licensure boards, and other entities all serve as examples of political and politically driven forces impacting the healthcare marketplace.

ECONOMIC FORCES

Economic forces involve all aspects associated with the economy of a society, notably including factors related to economic health (e.g., inflation, unemployment, income). The economic climate exerts a powerful influence on both organizations and individuals. In weak economies, healthcare entities might scale back or even eliminate product offerings. Rising costs might deter facilities from introducing new services or upgrading technologies. Poor economies might even result in the closure of facilities.

An environment of company layoffs and closures often reduces the number of individuals covered by health insurance. Laid off individuals lose their eligibility for company-sponsored health plans and often lack the funds necessary to obtain private coverage. Declining income levels can destroy demand for elective procedures. Individuals will often bypass even medically necessary services when they have been negatively impacted by economic downturns. Alternatively, strong economies can stimulate consumption of healthcare offerings and positively impact the depth and breadth of goods and services offered by healthcare entities.

SOCIAL FORCES

The social climate of a society impacts virtually every organization operating within the particular environment. Social forces include such aspects as the demographic composition and system of values and beliefs of a society. Demographic factors (e.g., age, gender, race, family size, education) heavily influence the healthcare industry. An aging population, for example, will likely increase the demand for long term care services, such as home health, assisted living, and nursing home care, whereas a youthful population heavily composed of women of childbearing age will likely drive the demand for labor and delivery services in the area.

Values and beliefs also impact the environment of healthcare entities. These lifestyle factors can positively or negatively influence the health status of a society. Healthy eating habits, for example, positively impact the health status of a population in that these practices contribute to an increased level of community health and wellness.

Promiscuous sexual behavior, on the other hand, negatively impacts the health of a society in that it increases the likelihood of unwanted pregnancies and sexually transmitted diseases. Healthcare entities, of course, must be prepared to deal with the health-related wants and needs of their communities, whether driven by positive or negative social forces.

TECHNOLOGICAL FORCES

Technological forces significantly influence broad society, including the healthcare industry. Both the healthcare industry and the individuals it serves have greatly benefited from technological innovations, which have become frequent and expected in society. Noninvasive medical technologies, advanced surgical techniques and procedures, and therapeutic and curative pharmaceuticals represent only a few of the many healthcare innovations that significantly improve the health of a population.

Healthcare innovations are likely to become all the more spectacular with promising new developments in biotechnology and other scientific frontiers. As more healthcare innovations enter the market, demand will undoubtedly increase, positively impacting the health status of society.

OPERATIONAL MATTERS

Formulating a PEST Analysis requires that marketers (1) construct the PEST diagram, as illustrated in Figure 26-1, (2) identify relevant macroenvironmental forces, and (3) describe how these forces are expected to impact given healthcare entities. The resulting diagram is then analyzed to gain macroenvironmental insights.

Figure 26-2 presents a PEST Analysis that was developed for a rural hospital. This diagram clearly and concisely identifies relevant macroenvironmental forces. With this tool, the hospital can quickly assess macroenvironmental influences and formulate strategies and tactics to address pressing issues. Opportunities can be identified and exploited, while threats can be assessed and avoided or eliminated. The PEST Analysis allows organizations to proactively, rather than reactively, address macroenvironmental forces.

Importantly, the PEST Analysis should be conducted in an inclusive fashion where input from all organizational members involved in the development and management of associated goods and services is actively encouraged. The multiple perspectives offered by this extended group of individuals can greatly enhance resulting PEST Analyses.

Political Forces	Economic Forces	Social Forces	Technological Forces
Recent election placed "friends" of quality health care in office *...expected to...* Improve government support for healthcare facilities and services	**Robust economy: rising income, low unemployment** *...expected to...* Increase percentage of insured patients; increase demand for elective medical procedures	**Growth of newly married couples and young families** *...expected to...* Increase demand for OB/GYN and pediatric medical services	**New Emergency 911 automated system** *...expected to...* Improve ambulance response times and ER efficiencies
State lawmakers recognize looming long term care crisis *...expected to...* Increase nursing home beds; offer incentives to build assisted living centers	**Significant industrial growth** *...expected to...* Increase demand for general medical services; increase demand for occupational health services	**Growth of senior citizen population** *...expected to...* Increase demand for geriatric services	**Improved imaging technologies** *...expected to...* Improve hospital's diagnostic capabilities
Legislation pending regarding rural health improvement initiative *...expected to...* Increase reimbursement rates for rural health entities		**Teen smoking on the rise** *...expected to...* Increase demand for substance abuse and smoking cessation programs	**More efficacious pharmaceuticals** *...expected to...* Reduce number of inpatient days

FIGURE 26-2 A Rural Hospital's PEST Analysis

It should be noted that the information derived from the PEST Analysis should ideally be combined with microenvironmental information (e.g., information regarding suppliers, competitors, customers, and so on). When this is accomplished, organizations possess a complete environmental assessment—invaluable information for planning marketing strategies and tactics.

SUMMARY

With its external focus, the PEST Analysis provides healthcare marketers with a useful method for monitoring the macroenvironment. By routinely conducting this analysis, healthcare marketers can proactively respond to opportunities and threats that exist in the larger environment, allowing their organizations the increased opportunity to achieve growth and prosperity.

EXERCISES

1. Define and comprehensively discuss the PEST Analysis, the four forces that the tool acts to monitor, and methodology associated with effecting this instrument. A diagram of the PEST Analysis should be included in your narrative. Share your thoughts regarding the tool's implications and uses in the healthcare industry. Do you believe that marketing departments in modern healthcare organizations are effectively monitoring their macroenvironments? Please justify your response.

2. Over the course of a 1-month period, monitor national, regional, and local news sources, noting elements of the macroenvironment that have the potential to impact local healthcare entities. Then, develop a PEST Analysis incorporating these elements. In this exercise, the PEST Analysis need not be tied to a specific healthcare institution but can instead be assembled as a general guide to macroenvironmental issues that might impact any area healthcare entity. Provide a brief narrative explaining overall discoveries and implications.

CHAPTER 27

The SWOT Analysis

LEARNING OBJECTIVES

After examining this chapter, readers will have the ability to:

- Realize the importance of routinely engaging in the systematic evaluation of product offerings in the healthcare marketplace.
- Understand the importance of identifying strengths, weaknesses, opportunities, and threats associated with healthcare institutions and their associated product offerings.
- Appreciate the value of the SWOT Analysis as a tool for analyzing the state of affairs associated with healthcare organizations and the various goods and services they provide to customers.

INTRODUCTION

Progressive healthcare marketers routinely engage in the systematic evaluation of their product offerings and associated target markets. For assistance in this evaluative process, marketers often rely on a tool known as the SWOT Analysis. Illustrated in Figure 27-1, the SWOT Analysis involves the identification of institutional strengths, weaknesses, opportunities, and threats. As indicated in the diagram, strengths and weaknesses relate to internal environmental factors, while opportunities and threats pertain to external environmental factors. The SWOT Analysis is also known as a *situation analysis* because it focuses on the state of affairs of an organization.

Although the SWOT Analysis has traditionally been used for institutional assessment purposes, it also serves as a highly effective tool for

	Strengths	Weaknesses
INTERNAL	1. _____ 2. _____ 3. _____ 4. _____ 5. _____	1. _____ 2. _____ 3. _____ 4. _____ 5. _____
	Opportunities	**Threats**
EXTERNAL	1. _____ 2. _____ 3. _____ 4. _____ 5. _____	1. _____ 2. _____ 3. _____ 4. _____ 5. _____

FIGURE 27-1 The SWOT Analysis

marketers when the focal point of the analysis is shifted from the organization to its product offerings. Instead of assessing the organization (e.g., City Hospital), marketers analyze the strengths, weaknesses, opportunities, and threats of associated product offerings (e.g., City Hospital's labor and delivery unit, emergency department, clinic, wellness center, and so on). Strengths, weaknesses, opportunities, and threats are defined as follows.

STRENGTHS

Strengths are positive product and product-related attributes that facilitate exchange. Outstanding quality, excellent brand identity, rising market share, excellent marketing management, superior research and development, world-class customer service, and patent protection are all examples of product and product-related strengths. Through exploitation of strengths, marketers can make great progress in the realization of marketing goals.

WEAKNESSES

Weaknesses are negative product and product-related attributes that adversely impact exchange. Weaknesses might include poor customer service, inconvenient access to offerings, inferior product quality, outdated technology, declining market share, inadequate advertising funds, and so on. Weaknesses undermine product performance and, ultimately, exchange in the marketplace. Therefore, positive steps must be taken to eliminate these negative attributes.

OPPORTUNITIES

Opportunities are external events and circumstances that have the potential to positively impact products. Opportunities might include newly discovered product uses, substantial market growth, newly developed technologies, anticipated favorable government legislation, and so on. Marketers must vigorously pursue and capitalize on opportunities to increase the likelihood of institutional survival, growth, and prosperity.

THREATS

Threats are external events and circumstances that have the potential to negatively impact products. Threats might include new competitors, market attrition, anticipated adverse government legislation, changing customer preferences, competitors equipped with superior technologies, and superior substitute products. Marketers must endeavor to develop strategies and tactics that will reduce or eliminate the potentially detrimental impact of threats.

OPERATIONAL MATTERS

Formulating a SWOT Analysis requires that marketers (1) construct the SWOT diagram, as illustrated in Figure 27-1, (2) determine the particular product that will be evaluated, and (3) identify associated strengths, weaknesses, opportunities, and threats. The resulting diagram is then analyzed to gain product insights.

Figure 27-2 presents a SWOT Analysis that was developed for a hospital's labor and delivery unit. This diagram illustrates the concise information portrayal offered by this simple, yet highly effective, marketing tool. With this tool, marketers can quickly assess internal and external product and product-related characteristics and influences—information that is essential for monitoring current performance and determining future strategic and tactical pursuits.

Not only can the SWOT Analysis be used to assess the products held by evaluating entities; it can also be used to analyze the offerings held by competitors. This method simply requires that marketers gain information regarding competitive offerings and then perform related SWOT Analyses. By using the SWOT Analysis in this fashion, many useful insights can be gained that can assist marketers in formulating marketing strategies and tactics.

	Strengths	Weaknesses
INTERNAL	Newly renovated unit Located in city's premier hospital Reputable physicians and nurses Large advertising budget Modern patient information system Greater capacity than competitors Best technology in community	Inadequate customer care delivered by some staff members High nurse employment turnover Inconvenient patient admit/discharge process Patient rooms not as elaborate as competitors
	Opportunities	**Threats**
EXTERNAL	Increasing number of women of childbearing age in the community Possible closure of one competing unit New and improved technologies available soon	Three competing units One new unit to open in 6 months Growing interest in midwifery Road construction hampering access to facility

FIGURE 27-2 A Labor & Delivery Unit's SWOT Analysis

Although marketers will be most concerned with the strengths, weaknesses, opportunities, and threats associated with the products they are responsible for managing, they must not neglect the value of performing the traditional, organization-focused SWOT Analysis. Goods and services are products of the organizations that produce and provide them. Coupling product-focused SWOT Analyses with organization-focused assessments will undoubtedly provide a higher degree of insight into marketing operations.

It should be noted that while multiple SWOT Analyses are virtually required for organizations with multiple product offerings, such detail may not be necessary in organizations with very few products. A small, independent medical clinic, for example, would likely require only one SWOT Analysis. Here, the organization and its product offerings are virtually one and the same. A single SWOT Analysis would, therefore, be sufficient.

Importantly, the SWOT Analysis should be conducted in an inclusive fashion where input from all organizational members involved in the development and management of associated goods and services is actively encouraged. The multiple perspectives offered by this extended group of individuals can greatly enhance resulting SWOT Analyses.

SUMMARY

The SWOT Analysis provides a simple, convenient, and effective method for quickly assessing the internal and external factors associated with products and the organizations that produce and provide them. Knowledge of this information allows marketers to formulate success-generating strategies and tactics that will yield positive marketing outcomes.

EXERCISES

1. Provide a comprehensive overview of the SWOT Analysis, explaining its purpose, components, uses, and benefits, accompanied by an associated illustration. Be sure to indicate how the tool can be used not only for one's own product offerings, but also for the product offerings of competitors. Share your views regarding how this instrument can be used to effect success-generating strategies in the healthcare industry.

2. Within your local marketplace, select a healthcare entity and investigate its mission, product offerings, etc. using publicly available information, such as annual reports, the Internet, and so on. With this information, prepare a SWOT Analysis. Provide a narrative offering an overview of this assessment, your methods for its assembly, sources of information called upon for the analysis, and the resulting outlook for the healthcare entity.

Michael Porter's Five Forces Model

INTRODUCTION

The healthcare marketplace is characterized by intense competition and rivalry—elements that will only intensify as healthcare entities of all kinds vie for the opportunity to serve target markets. Those entities that can

191

successfully navigate the complex healthcare environment will be handsomely rewarded with increased market share and prosperity.

Successful navigation of this environment, of course, requires a deep understanding of marketplace competitors. All too often, however, entities view their competitive environment in an overly narrow fashion that fails to acknowledge the true depth and breadth of competitive forces in the marketplace. Competition is multidimensional, and its vastness must be clearly understood if marketing success is to be achieved. The critical task of accurately identifying the competitive elements in a market is greatly facilitated by Michael Porter's Five Forces Model.

Illustrated in Figure 28-1, Porter's Five Forces Model provides useful insights into the multifaceted nature of competition. According to Porter, the nature of competition in any industry is based on five forces: existing competitors, potential entrants, substitutes, suppliers, and buyers.

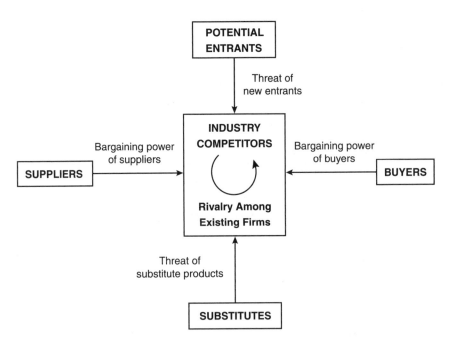

FIGURE 28-1 Porter's Five Forces Model

These forces are unique to each industry—and industry segment—and combine to determine the competitive intensity and ultimate potential of associated markets. These five forces are explained as follows.

EXISTING COMPETITORS

Existing competitors are the most obvious competitive force, jockeying for position through new product development, innovative promotional campaigns, and so on. Rivalry among existing competitors is especially intense when competitors are numerous and fairly equivalent in terms of size and power, when exit barriers are high, and when industry growth is slow resulting in struggles for market share. These characteristics are frequently observed in the healthcare marketplace, illustrating the intense rivalry within the industry.

POTENTIAL ENTRANTS

Entities that might potentially enter the market represent significant threats to existing competitors. New entrants bring new capacity and resources to the market along with desires for market share. The magnitude of the threat posed by new entrants is largely based on the particular barriers to entry that exist. Typical examples of entry barriers include capital requirements, proprietary product differences, government policy, and the market dominance and brand identity of existing competitors. Significant entry barriers yield significant protection from the threat of new entrants, while few barriers increase the competitive nature of the market. Certificates of need possessed by hospitals and patent protection possessed by pharmaceutical firms are examples of barriers that offer substantial protection in the healthcare marketplace.

SUBSTITUTES

Substitutes are products that differ from particular offerings but largely, and sometimes completely, fill equivalent wants and needs. As a result, substitute offerings can greatly impact the performance of healthcare entities and even threaten their very existence. Laser vision correction could be viewed as a substitute for eyeglasses and contact lenses. The services of a chiropractor could be viewed as a substitute for the services of an orthopedic surgeon. The seriousness of the threat of substitutes is predominantly based on their performance and price characteristics. Substitutes that offer equal or better performance pose significant threats, especially when price advantages exist.

SUPPLIERS

Suppliers provide the components necessary for healthcare organizations to offer goods and services to their customers. Surgery scalpels, pharmaceuticals, hospital beds, and diagnostic imaging equipment represent just a few of the many products that healthcare entities purchase from suppliers. Without these "raw materials," healthcare entities could not function. This dependence on suppliers poses a significant threat to healthcare entities.

Suppliers can raise their prices, lower the quality of the components that they provide, or simply go out of business—all situations that can yield potentially devastating effects. Suppliers are particularly powerful if they are few in number, if few substitutes exist, and if entities are not key customers.

BUYERS

Porter's term *buyers* is equivalent to the term *customers*, which is better suited for the healthcare marketplace. Quite obviously, customers possess significant bargaining power over healthcare entities because their patronage ultimately determines institutional survival, growth, and prosperity. The array of customers in the healthcare marketplace is quite varied, including residents in nursing home beds, patients in hospital beds, patrons at local pharmacies, recipients of home health services, and even health insurance companies and other third-party payer entities that pay for medical services on behalf of clients. Without customers, operations cease. For this reason, marketers must ensure that all marketing efforts are customer focused. Importantly, marketers must strive to accurately assess the wants and needs of customers and serve them in a manner that will meet and exceed their expectations.

OPERATIONAL MATTERS

Porter's Five Forces Model is highly useful in that it clearly illustrates the multidimensional nature of marketplace competition. Its use, however, can greatly be extended through the assembly and completion of a Five Forces Worksheet. Marketers simply (1) identify the product offering to be evaluated, (2) construct the Five Forces Worksheet, as illustrated in Figure 28-2, (3) identify existing competitors, potential entrants, substitutes, suppliers, and buyers, and (4) place the identified current and potential competitors on the diagram accordingly. When completed, the Five Forces Worksheet clearly identifies all five competitive forces that entities currently face or could potentially face, as illustrated in Figure 28-3. Completion of this simple, yet highly effective, device yields considerable insights into the current

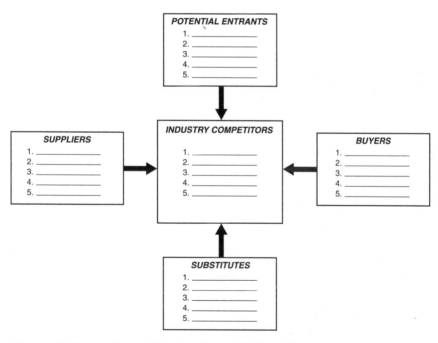

FIGURE 28-2 A Five Forces Worksheet

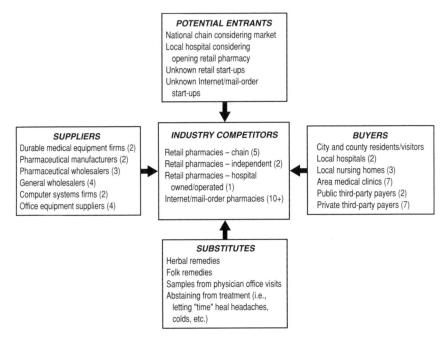

FIGURE 28-3 A Retail Pharmacy's Five Forces Worksheet

and future competitive marketplace and hence serves as an essential marketing planning tool.

SUMMARY

By clearly illustrating the true depth and breadth of the competitive environment, Porter's Five Forces Model serves as an indispensable resource for marketers. With this information, healthcare marketers can establish strategic and tactical priorities and position their organizations to capitalize on opportunities and avoid or eliminate threats. Ideally, healthcare marketers will address each of the five forces. By properly addressing the complete competitive environment, healthcare marketers are better prepared to meet and exceed market share and related performance objectives.

EXERCISES

1. Define and comprehensively discuss Michael Porter's Five Forces Model, providing insights regarding its uses, features, methods of interpretation, and value, accompanied by an appropriate illustration. Be sure to include in your discussion an overview of the instrument's importance as a strategic marketing device in the healthcare industry.
2. Select a healthcare entity of your choice for placement in your local market and assign the hypothetical establishment an appropriate brand name. Consult a variety of information sources (e.g., telephone directories, the Internet, industry databases) in an effort to identify entities occupying associated categories of competition listed in Michael Porter's Five Forces Model, preparing an appropriate illustration accordingly. Based on your Five Forces Model, what have you learned about the depth and breadth of competition in the marketplace?

REFERENCE

Porter, Michael E. 1998. *Competitive strategy: Techniques for analyzing industries and competitors.* New York: The Free Press.

Lehmann & Winer's Levels of Competition Model

LEARNING OBJECTIVES

After examining this chapter, readers will have the ability to:

- Recognize that every competitor represents a potential threat to the business operations of healthcare institutions.
- Understand that the actions of rivals must closely be monitored to proactively address developing issues, events, and circumstances.
- Recognize that healthcare marketers often define their competitive field too narrowly, failing to realize the true extent of competition in the marketplace.
- Appreciate the value afforded by Lehmann and Winer's Levels of Competition Model as an instrument for accurately identifying and understanding competition.

INTRODUCTION

Progressive healthcare marketers understand that it is essential to accurately identify and assess their competition because every competitor represents a threat. Although marketers cannot control their competitors, they can closely monitor the actions of rivals and proactively address developing issues.

When marketers fail to identify competitors, they inadvertently afford the unidentified rivals with the strategic advantage of operational secrecy. This gives competitors the element of surprise and, along with it, valuable time to secure market share.

Possibly the most common competitive assessment error committed by marketers is that of defining the competitive field too narrowly. To assist marketers in understanding the true extent of the competitive environment, Donald Lehmann and Russell Winer developed a diagram that depicts levels of market competition.

Illustrated in Figure 29-1, Lehmann and Winer's Levels of Competition Model identifies four competitive levels—product form, product category, generic, and budget—that are depicted by four concentric circles that

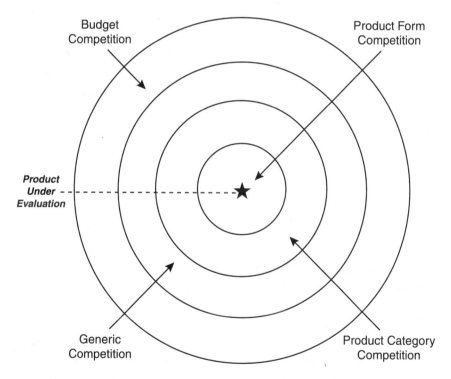

Adapted from *Analysis for Marketing Planning*, 6th ed. by Donald R. Lehmann and Russell S. Winer. Copyright © 2005, 2002, 1997, 1994, 1991, 1988 by The McGraw-Hill Companies, Inc. Published by McGraw-Hill. Reproduced with permission of The McGraw-Hill Companies.

FIGURE 29-1 Lehmann & Winer's Levels of Competition Model

surround the product under evaluation. Competitive offerings are placed on the diagram based on how they compare to the product under evaluation. Competitive products that occupy inner levels of the diagram are more comparable to the product under evaluation than those that occupy outer levels. The four competitive levels are defined as follows.

PRODUCT FORM COMPETITION

Product form competition is the narrowest view that can be taken of competition. Identified by the innermost circle on the Levels of Competition Model, product form competition includes all competitive products that have roughly equivalent product features and compete in the same market segments. At this level, competitive entities include direct, head-to-head rivals that offer similar goods and services and compete for the same "turf."

PRODUCT CATEGORY COMPETITION

The level just beyond product form competition is known as product category competition. Here, competition expands to include all competitive products that possess similar features, regardless of the market segments targeted. Competition at this level represents what marketing managers have traditionally viewed as their competitive set.

GENERIC COMPETITION

The third level of competition is known as generic competition. Generic competition includes all competing products that, although unrelated to given product offerings, fill equivalent wants and needs. Whereas product form and product category levels are inward focused (i.e., focused on products similar to those produced and provided by given entities), generic competition is outward focused (i.e., focused on potential alternatives or substitutes for associated product offerings). Marketers wishing to capitalize on opportunities and avoid threats must be certain that their view of competition includes the generic level. Such a focus will ensure that marketers avoid what Theodore Levitt termed *marketing myopia*—a detrimental practice where entities define their businesses too narrowly.

BUDGET COMPETITION

Budget competition, the outermost level of competition, involves all products that compete for the same customer dollar. Budget competition represents the broadest view of competition. Although budget competition is useful from a conceptual perspective, it is of very little strategic value because the number of potential competitive offerings is so immense.

OPERATIONAL MATTERS

To assess product competition using Lehmann and Winer's Levels of Competition Model, marketers simply (1) identify the product offering to be evaluated, (2) construct the Levels of Competition diagram, as illustrated in Figure 29-1, (3) identify product form, product category, generic, and budget competitors, and (4) place the identified competitors on the diagram accordingly. The resulting Levels of Competition diagram is then analyzed to gain insights into product competition.

Figure 29-2 presents a Levels of Competition Model that was developed for an urban medical center that primarily serves an affluent, privately insured customer population. At the product form level, the medical center would view its competition as other area medical centers that provide the same services to the same affluent, insured customer population. The product category level represents a broadened competitive scope that would include all medical centers in the marketplace, regardless of the clientele served. Here, the medical center would include facilities that serve low-income customers, along with all other medical centers in the marketplace, regardless of their particular target markets.

At the generic level, the competitive scope increases significantly to include facilities that address similar wants and needs. Here, the medical center would add area clinics, health departments, and other health service providers to its competitive framework. Although these entities do not directly compete with the medical center, they do offer alternatives in many clinical areas for prospective customers.

Lastly, budget competition could be anything and everything, health care-related or not, that might divert customer resources away from the medical center. An individual might, for example, forgo an elective medical procedure—or even one that is medically necessary—to pay for his or her

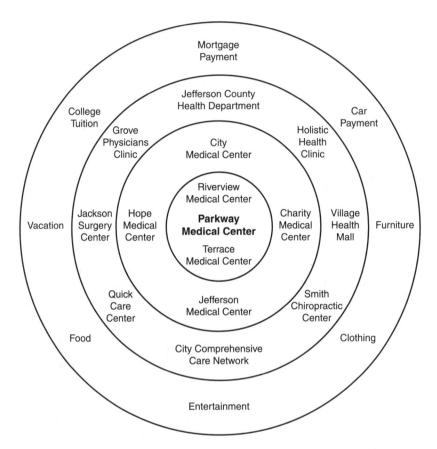

Constructed using design methodologies in Lehmann, Donald R., and Russell S. Winer. *Analysis for Marketing Planning.* 6th ed. New York: McGraw-Hill, 2005.

FIGURE 29-2 A Medical Center's Levels of Competition Model

child's college tuition, to take a vacation, to buy a new car, to purchase furniture, etc.

Figure 29-3 presents a Levels of Competition Model that was developed for a cosmetic surgery center. At the product form level, the cosmetic surgery center would view its competition as other area cosmetic surgery centers that provide the same services to the same clientele. At the product category level, the clinic would view its competition as all area cosmetic surgery centers, regardless of the clientele served.

At the generic level, the clinic's competition would increase to include medical centers and hospitals that provide cosmetic surgery services, pre-

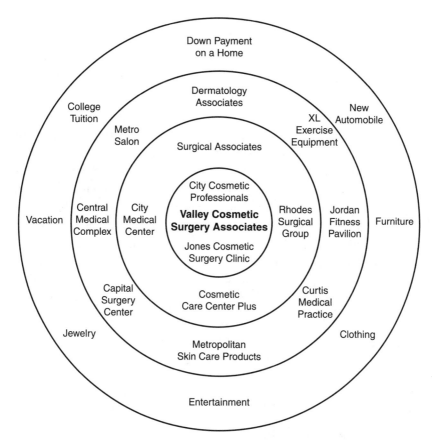

Constructed using design methodologies in Lehmann, Donald R., and Russell S. Winer. *Analysis for Marketing Planning.* 6th ed. New York: McGraw-Hill, 2005.

FIGURE 29-3 A Cosmetic Surgery Center's Levels of Competition Model

scription and over-the-counter beautification ointments and creams, beautifying cosmetic make-up, exercise equipment and other devices that can enhance one's body, and so on. All of these products, to some degree, satisfy wants and needs that are similar to those satisfied by the clinic under evaluation. Lastly, at the budget level, competition would include anything that would compete for the cosmetic surgery dollars of customers—a down payment on a house, a computer, clothing, jewelry, etc.

It is important to remember that in the healthcare marketplace, some product offerings do not have appropriate substitutes. A hospital emergency department would certainly compete with other area emergency departments, potentially at both the product form and product category levels. However, as providers of potentially life-saving services for the ill and injured, they stand alone and, as a result, do not have any competition of note at the generic level. Given that patients receiving such services are fighting for their lives, budget competition would also be of little concern to any emergency department.

It is also important to note that the Levels of Competition Model does not assess the threat potential forwarded by competitive elements. For example, in Figure 29-2, it might be very likely that a generic competitor, such as a medical clinic, would pose more of a threat to the medical center under evaluation than a product category competitor, such as a charity hospital. Instead, the model identifies competitive elements based on their characteristics in relation to the product under evaluation. It categorizes competition by *type* of competitor, which does not necessarily equate with threat intensity. Given this, it might be useful to indicate on the Levels of Competition diagram those offerings, regardless of their competitive level, that are believed to pose the most significant threat to the product under evaluation. This information greatly assists marketers in determining strategic and tactical priorities, particularly in the area of product promotion.

SUMMARY

Given the dangers associated with defining the competitive field too narrowly, healthcare marketers must diligently seek to identify all current and potential rivals in the market. Lehmann and Winer's Levels of Competition Model serves as a useful guide for marketers to consult in this pursuit, reminding them of the true extent of competitive elements in the marketplace.

EXERCISES

1. Provide a detailed overview of Lehmann and Winer's Levels of Competition Model, noting facets regarding its purpose, use, implementation, and value in healthcare organizations. Preface your work by discussing the competitive nature of the healthcare industry and the need for monitoring the activities of rivals. Be sure to share your perspectives regarding the degree to which modern healthcare organizations actively and accurately define their competitive fields.

2. Within your local marketplace, identify a healthcare product offering. Then, study the offering, seeking information on its features and benefits, position in the marketplace, and competitive field. Based on this assessment, construct a Levels of Competition Model for the product, identifying product form, product category, generic, and budget competitors. Be sure to indicate on the diagram those offerings that are believed to pose the most significant threat to the product under evaluation. Provide a narrative explaining your illustration.

REFERENCES

Lehmann, Donald R., and Russell S. Winer. 2005. *Analysis for marketing planning.* 6th ed. New York: McGraw-Hill.

Levitt, Theodore. 1960. Marketing myopia. *Harvard Business Review* (July–August): 45–56.

Mintzberg & Van der Heyden's Organigraph

LEARNING OBJECTIVES

After examining this chapter, readers will have the ability to:

- Realize that progressive healthcare marketers must possess an intuitive knowledge of their organizations, product offerings, sought markets, and associated environmental relationships.
- Recognize that visualizing inter- and intraorganizational relationships increases the understanding of such relationships, permitting healthcare marketers to formulate productive strategies.
- Appreciate the value afforded by Mintzberg and Van der Heyden's Organigraph as a tool for shedding light on the inter- and intraorganizational relationships of healthcare institutions.

INTRODUCTION

Progressive marketers clearly understand that to achieve marketing success, they must possess an intricate knowledge of their organizations, the products offered, the markets sought, and associated environmental relationships. With such knowledge, marketers are able to formulate productive strategies that yield positive marketing results.

Gaining this extensive insight into inter- and intraorganizational relationships, however, is not a simple activity because these facets are typically quite complex. Achieving this understanding can be hastened, however, by assembling and analyzing an Organigraph, an evaluative tool developed by Henry Mintzberg and Ludo Van der Heyden.

In essence, an Organigraph is a diagram that depicts the activities and operations of organizations. Mintzberg and Van der Heyden developed the Organigraph to shed light on the often complex inter- and intraorganizational relationships of institutions—a feat that the traditional organizational chart cannot accomplish. The Organigraph derives its name from the word *organigramme*, the French term for organizational chart.

Rather than using the series of boxes and lines that are common in organizational charts, the Organigraph uses a series of shapes to illustrate the actual relationships that exist inside and outside of organizations. This feature greatly increases the level of detail that can be incorporated into these diagrams.

Although the construction and use of Organigraphs is typically associated with strategic management, these tools also have marketing applications. By depicting inter- and intraorganizational relationships, most notably those dealing with suppliers and target markets, Organigraphs can be quite helpful to marketers seeking an overall view of their entities and associated interrelationships, many of which directly impact marketing.

CONSTRUCTING AN ORGANIGRAPH

Constructing an Organigraph requires imagination. Unlike organizational charts, which have strict rules governing their assembly, Organigraphs do not possess such guidelines. To construct an Organigraph, marketers must (1) think about their organizations, the products offered, the markets sought, and associated environmental relationships and (2) map this vision using a series of shapes that accurately illustrates associated activities and operations.

As illustrated in Figure 30-1, Organigraphs are typically assembled using some combination of four primary components: sets, chains, hubs, and webs. A set indicates an independent relationship; a chain indicates the progressive development or assembly of something; a hub indicates a coordinating center that links activities; and a web indicates a series of nodes depicting relationships among components that do not possess a

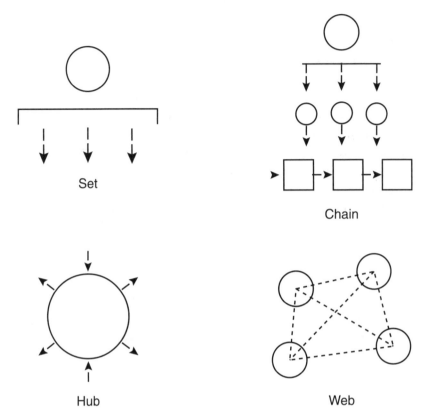

FIGURE 30-1 Common Components of Organigraphs

coordinating center. Other shapes can, of course, be used to assemble Organigraphs, provided that the shapes accurately convey relationships.

OPERATIONAL MATTERS

Figure 30-2 illustrates an Organigraph that was constructed for a multispecialty clinic. Quite noticeably, the Organigraph is shaped as a web, indicating the presence of relationships among the multispecialty clinic's four units: family medicine, internal medicine, cardiology, and gastroenterology.

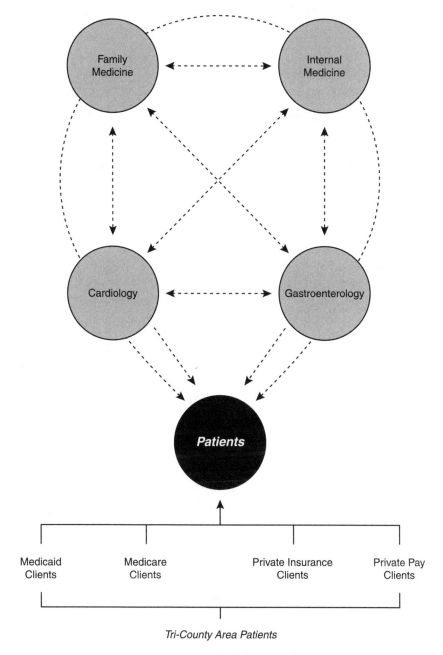

Constructed using design methodologies in Mintzberg, Henry, and Ludo Van der Heyden. "Organigraphs: Drawing How Companies Really Work." *Harvard Business Review* (September–October) 1999: 87–94.

FIGURE 30-2 A Multispecialty Clinic's Organigraph

As indicated in the diagram, each of these specialty units interacts with one another but operates in a largely autonomous fashion in the course of serving patients. These units, for example, independently schedule patient appointments, coordinate internal activities, and manage patient account information. Also of note in the Organigraph is the depiction of the clinic's customer base, identified by payer category, for the geographic region served by the entity.

If desired, the clinic could create a more detailed Organigraph that illustrates suppliers, competitors, internal support departments (e.g., patient accounts, human resources), and so on. With this additional detail, the Organigraph easily becomes a strategic tool that possesses value for all administrative units within the entity.

Figure 30-3 depicts an Organigraph that was constructed for a home health agency. This diagram clearly and concisely illustrates the central coordinating role of the agency's corporate office—as depicted by its hub shape—which distributes supplies and provides direction to its five regions that ultimately deliver home health services to clients. In illustrating the supplier role in this diagram, the agency used a funnel shape to indicate the collection of multiple elements—raw materials from suppliers—that are directed in a coordinated fashion into the entity for use throughout the organization. If desired, of course, more detail could be added to the diagram, increasing its value and use within the home health agency.

SUMMARY

Mintzberg and Van der Heyden's Organigraph provides marketers with a powerful tool for achieving a thorough understanding of their organizations, the products offered, the markets sought, and associated environmental relationships. The diagram's flexibility allows marketers to illustrate virtually any institutional relationship. By understanding the many inter- and intraorganizational relationships of entities, marketers are better prepared to develop appropriate, success-generating marketing strategies.

EXERCISES

1. Prepare a detailed overview of Mintzberg and Van der Heyden's Organigraph, describing its foundations, uses, methods of construction, and practical applications. What are the implications of

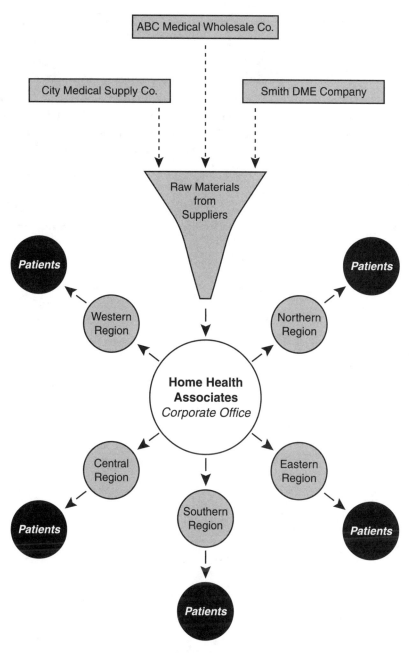

Constructed using design methodologies in Mintzberg, Henry, and Ludo Van der Heyden. "Organigraphs: Drawing How Companies Really Work." *Harvard Business Review* (September–October) 1999: 87–94.

FIGURE 30-3 A Home Health Agency's Organigraph

this tool for the healthcare industry? Why do you view this to be the case?

2. Contact an area healthcare establishment (e.g., medical center, nursing home, cosmetic surgery clinic) and arrange an informational interview with a member of the executive management team to learn about the institution's inter- and intraorganizational relationships. At the conclusion of the interview, develop an Organigraph to illustrate the various relationships. Provide a narrative explaining your Organigraph.

REFERENCE

Mintzberg, Henry, and Ludo Van der Heyden. 1999. Organigraphs: Drawing how companies really work. *Harvard Business Review* (September–October): 87–94.

PART SIX

Marketing Management Tools

31

Leonard Berry's Success Sustainability Model

LEARNING OBJECTIVES

After examining this chapter, readers will have the ability to:

- Understand the importance of establishing core values that serve to guide healthcare organizations in their strategic and tactical pursuits.
- Realize that sustained success requires the formulation and implementation of strategies and tactics based on core values that facilitate excellence.
- Recognize the value offered by Leonard Berry's Success Sustainability Model as a device for communicating drivers of excellence that will yield sustained success.

INTRODUCTION

Administrative excellence does not arise out of luck or chance but rather through the development and implementation of appropriate institutional systems that guide entities to prosperity. Numerous systems must be incorporated, but possibly none is as important as the underlying array of principles embraced by organizations. The composition of these principles ultimately determines the potential of organizations to achieve and sustain success.

215

To understand the prerequisites for sustained operational excellence, marketers often refer to Leonard Berry's Success Sustainability Model, which was developed from Berry's research inquiries into the practices of top-performing service organizations.

Illustrated in Figure 31-1, Berry's Success Sustainability Model is depicted as a circular diagram containing nine boxes that denote drivers of excellence. Eight of these drivers—strategic focus, executional excellence, control of destiny, trust-based relationships, investment in employee success, acting small, brand cultivation, and generosity—occupy boxes that en-

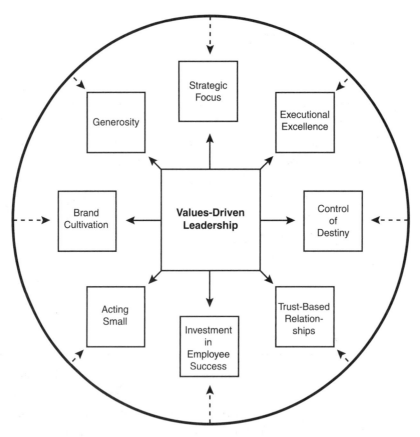

FIGURE 31-1 Berry's Success Sustainability Model

compass the perimeter of the diagram, each extending from the primary driver (i.e., values-driven leadership) situated in the center of the diagram.

Arrows drawn with solid lines denote primary relationships, while those drawn with dotted lines indicate interrelationships among success drivers. The nine drivers of excellence are defined as follows.

VALUES-DRIVEN LEADERSHIP

Values-driven leadership serves as the foundation or root of all other drivers of excellence. Values represent the core beliefs held by organizations. If these values are not strong, sustainable success cannot be achieved. Importantly, entities seeking sustained success must possess seven core values: excellence (i.e., striving for high performance in all areas), innovation (i.e., striving to make current offerings better), joy (i.e., working to uplift the human spirit and celebrate achievement), teamwork (i.e., collaborating to achieve common goals), respect (i.e., concern for employees, customers, suppliers, and others), integrity (i.e., conducting operations in an ethical fashion), and social profit (i.e., giving back to the community).

These values must actively be communicated by leaders, demonstrated through value-laden actions, and cultivated to achieve excellence. By embracing these values, healthcare organizations establish solid institutional foundations that foster excellence.

STRATEGIC FOCUS

Organizations seeking sustained success must formulate strategies that embody their embraced values. This specifically requires that entities clearly define their businesses and develop specialized systems of activities to implement their missions. Strategies should reflect the dynamic and innovative nature of organizations. Importantly, organizations must strive to ensure that their strategies remain mission focused because deviations hamper the attainment of excellence.

A hospital, for example, that embraces a mission of providing comprehensive services to a rural population must formulate an array of strategies that focuses exclusively on the delivery of quality health services to its rural target market. If the hospital deviates from its mission by formulating divergent strategies that target, say, urban populations, the establishment has obviously lost sight of its mission and will ultimately suffer the perils associated with a failed strategic focus, notably institutional decline and, possibly, failure.

EXECUTIONAL EXCELLENCE

Not only must organizations formulate well-planned strategies, but they also must ensure that these strategies are appropriately and successfully executed through sound tactics. Execution is as important as the strategy itself, and progressive entities place a significant emphasis on excellence in this area. Tactical pursuits must flow directly from the strategies embraced by entities for excellence to be achieved. Through well-executed tactics, strategic goals and objectives are accomplished, thus fulfilling associated missions. The best developed missions and accompanying strategies are pointless if they are not executed appropriately through sound tactics, hence the importance of excellence in this area.

CONTROL OF DESTINY

Control of destiny is largely an attitudinal mindset, which holds that by taking appropriate actions, entities can control the future. Such actions taken by healthcare entities in an effort to control their destiny might include the continuous enhancement of medical technologies, the recruitment and retention of highly skilled administrative and clinical employees, the delivery of products that possess greater value than competitive offerings, and the establishment of world-class customer service.

Entities that possess a control of destiny mindset are prepared to positively address the rigorous healthcare environment and its associated challenges. This positive mindset undoubtedly motivates organizations to take success-generating actions that enhance prosperity.

TRUST-BASED RELATIONSHIPS

Entities cannot attain success without conducting all operations in a genuine fashion. This involves honoring obligations and commitments, treating all parties fairly and respectfully, maintaining confidentiality, and so on. When a medical clinic takes steps to ensure that its providers see patients in a timely and courteous manner, it establishes trust with its clients.

When an emergency department purchases the latest medical technologies for its patient base, it establishes trust with the community members that it serves. When a hospital meets financial obligations with its vendors in a timely fashion, it establishes trust with its various suppliers. When healthcare entities of all kinds ensure that patient confidentiality is maintained, they establish trust with their patient populations. Trust allows the formation of lasting, commitment-laden relationships with customers, employees, suppliers, and communities.

INVESTMENT IN EMPLOYEE SUCCESS

A talented labor force represents a key source of competitive advantage. The ability to recruit and retain the best employees requires an investment in their professional growth and development that indirectly represents an investment in the organizations that sponsor such assistance. The healthcare industry is continuously changing, requiring that entities ensure that their employees, both administrative and clinical, possess the tools necessary for enduring success.

Mechanisms for providing such tools include funding continuing education coursework, sponsoring college tuition reimbursement programs, and providing on-site educational seminars for personnel. Employees who receive such institutional assistance will have both the ability and the desire to return the investment through service excellence.

ACTING SMALL

Large and small organizations each possess advantages and disadvantages associated with scale. Large entities have the luxury of economies of scale, more notoriety, and a larger customer base. Smaller entities, however, possess their share of advantages, too. These include nimbleness, less bureaucracy, and more personal service.

Given the ever-changing nature of the healthcare environment, coupled with increasing customer demands for personal service and attention, healthcare entities would do well to remember the positive attributes associated with small entities and ensure that these characteristics are incorporated into their operations.

BRAND CULTIVATION

Through branding, healthcare entities give their products *identity*. Brand identity greatly assists customers in the process of product differentiation and, therefore, represents a key source of competitive advantage. Upstanding entities that successfully brand themselves and their products afford customers with assurances of quality that facilitate lasting patronage. Given the importance of branding, entities must strive to develop—cultivate—their brands in an effort to capitalize on the many associated benefits.

In some situations, particular healthcare entities represent, in and of themselves, the brands to be cultivated. In other situations, units within healthcare establishments may each represent brands to be cultivated. A large medical center, for example, might seek to brand its multiple divisions (e.g., labor and delivery, emergency medical services, oncology), as well as itself. Similarly, goods-producing firms, like pharmaceutical companies, often brand individual products, as well as themselves, in an effort to capitalize on the benefits of branding.

GENEROSITY

Institutional generosity acts as a catalyst to all things good within organizations and even beyond. Acts of kindness (e.g., sponsoring student education programs, awarding scholarships to members of the community, supporting charitable foundations) inspire customers, employees, suppliers, and communities. Through generosity, healthcare entities become more than producers and providers of products; they become true members of the greater community—an appropriate place for healthcare organizations.

OPERATIONAL MATTERS

Clearly, healthcare entities that incorporate the nine drivers of excellence identified by Berry are well on their way to achieving success in the marketplace. All too often, however, the change-rich environment of the healthcare industry directs attention away from these important drivers of sustainable success, which is the reason many entities fail to meet and exceed the expectations of their target markets. Indeed, ensuring the presence of these drivers requires significant effort. Those entities that are willing to incorporate the success drivers into their daily operations position themselves for enduring growth and prosperity.

SUMMARY

Berry's Success Sustainability Model clearly illustrates the drivers of excellence that entities must possess if they desire sustained growth and prosperity. Given the competitive nature of the healthcare industry, along with its environmental complexities, healthcare entities would do well to incorporate the nine drivers of excellence into their operations to reap the many benefits of sustained success.

EXERCISES

1. Provide a detailed overview of Leonard Berry's Success Sustainability Model, identifying and explaining its components, features and benefits, and value to healthcare organizations. Add value to your discussion by including an illustration of this instrument, and be sure to preface your work by describing why excellence is an absolute necessity in the healthcare industry.

2. Conduct a review of trade journals, Web sites, and other sources in an effort to identify articles profiling various healthcare entities. From these profiles, seek to identify a specific healthcare organization that appears to embrace the philosophy that underlies Leonard Berry's Success Sustainability Model. Provide specific details as to how this organization measures up with the various components of the Success Sustainability Model. Be sure also to identify any areas where the organization appears to fall short or where information is insufficient to make a determination.

REFERENCE

Berry, Leonard L. 1999. *Discovering the soul of service: The nine drivers of sustainable business success.* New York: The Free Press.

George Day's Market Orientation Model

LEARNING OBJECTIVES

After examining this chapter, readers will have the ability to:

- Understand the importance of embracing a market-driven mindset in the healthcare industry.
- Realize that the proactive, externally focused stance taken by market-driven organizations positions them to capitalize on opportunities and avoid or eliminate threats.
- Appreciate George Day's Market Orientation Model as a tool for providing guidance in the assembly of market-driven work environments, focused externally, rather than internally.

INTRODUCTION

Progressive marketers understand that marketing success is largely based on how well they assess and address the markets they serve. This requires, among other things, the accurate assessment of customer wants and needs, the provision of products that effectively address those wants and needs, and the proactive assessment and management of competitive threats in the environment. Simply stated, these marketers understand the importance of being market driven.

When marketers adopt a market-driven mindset, they are perfectly positioned to capitalize on opportunities and avoid or eliminate threats in the environment. Through this proactive, externally focused stance, marketers are able to thoroughly understand their target markets and deliver product solutions that will earn confidence and trust, ultimately resulting in the enduring, valuable patronage of customers.

Despite the benefits associated with being market driven, many marketers fail to successfully incorporate this mindset, largely because of institutional systems that support inside-out, rather than outside-in, approaches. Organizations embracing such inside-out approaches allow internal factors (e.g., prior histories and traditions, existing internal capabilities), rather than the externally based wants and needs of target markets, to guide operational decisions. Only by being market driven, an outside-in approach, can organizations deliver superior customer value and reap the many benefits associated with this philosophy.

Organizations seeking to become market driven must shift their focus to the market. To assist organizations in this transformation, George Day developed the Market Orientation Model, a diagram that presents the components of a market-driven organization. Illustrated in Figure 32-1, Day's

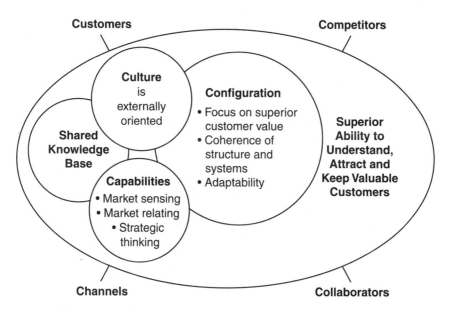

FIGURE 32-1 Day's Market Orientation Model

Market Orientation Model consists of an oval, representing the internal environment of an organization, which encompasses a series of four circles, representing the entity's shared knowledge base and the three elements of a market orientation: culture, capabilities, and configuration. These three elements are defined as follows.

CULTURE

Culture, specifically one that is externally oriented, represents the first element of Day's Market Orientation Model. Culture can broadly be defined as the group of values, beliefs, and behaviors embraced by an organization. Every organization possesses a culture that is unique to that particular entity. Depending on the composition of values, beliefs, and behaviors embraced, culture can positively or negatively influence operations and, when established, culture can be very difficult to change. Market-driven organizations must possess an externally oriented, participative culture that heavily emphasizes the delivery of superior customer value and continually strives to secure new sources of competitive advantage.

A hospital, for example, that seeks to establish an externally oriented culture must ensure that the appropriate constructs are in place to allow the culture to develop. One such construct is the hospital's mission statement. As an openly circulated document, the mission statement is available for internal parties (e.g., administrators, physicians, nurses), as well as external parties (e.g., stockholders, stakeholders, customers, suppliers), to view and quickly understand the institution's purpose.

When used appropriately, the mission statement serves as a guide for executives and employees to follow in their many operational pursuits. It, therefore, is an excellent starting point for building an externally oriented culture. Hospital officials would simply (1) develop a mission statement that incorporates the elements of an externally oriented culture (i.e., an external, participative orientation emphasizing customer value and the continual search for competitive advantage) and (2) take steps to ensure that they, along with other institutional members, base their actions on this statement. Such a mission statement greatly facilitates the establishment of an externally oriented culture.

CAPABILITIES

Capabilities represents the second element of Day's Market Orientation Model. Specifically, market-driven organizations must possess distinctive capabilities in the areas of *market sensing* (i.e., the ability to accurately assess and understand markets), *market relating* (i.e., the ability to create and maintain relationships with customers), and *strategic thinking* (i.e., the ability to devise successful strategies that proactively, rather than reactively, address marketplace opportunities and threats). With this set of capabilities, marketers are able to gain a thorough understanding of the customers and markets they serve. They also are able to strategically address associated environmental issues.

Possession of these capabilities is all the more essential in the healthcare industry, which is characterized by innovation, intense competition, and uncertainty. Given this turbulent environment, healthcare marketers, in particular, must ensure that they acquire and develop market sensing, market relating, and strategic thinking capabilities because they are ultimately the individuals looked to by others in their organizations to provide leadership in the areas of environmental analysis and strategic management.

CONFIGURATION

Configuration represents the third and final element of Day's Market Orientation Model. This specifically involves the establishment of an organization-wide structure that allows all units within entities to proactively address changing customer requirements and marketplace conditions. In keeping with the attributes associated with market-driven organizations, the particular configuration must emphasize the delivery of superior customer value, incorporate coherence between institutional structures and systems, and be adaptable to meet environmental challenges.

The configuration element of Day's Market Orientation Model essentially involves the creation of an institution-wide environment that fosters the development of a market orientation within every departmental unit. This is most beneficial in the healthcare marketplace where institutions, particularly comprehensive medical centers, typically incorporate extensive functional arrays (e.g., marketing, finance, nursing, radiology, dietary services, environmental services) not seen within any other type of entity. Given the scope and diversity of these functions, complex entities could never hope to become market driven without creating a configuration that fosters such a mindset across all organizational units.

OPERATIONAL MATTERS

It is important to understand that to be market driven, the three elements of culture, capabilities, and configuration must be supported by a shared knowledge base. This essentially requires that entities ensure that information is openly shared interorganizationally in an effort to improve overall institutional performance.

All too often, information is poorly disseminated within organizations. This is caused by a variety of factors, including poor communications systems, interorganizational conflict, and so on. Regardless of the reasons for poor information dissemination, organizations must take steps to open communications channels so that information can freely flow throughout entities, providing the requisite shared knowledge base that supports the three elements of culture, capabilities, and configuration.

SUMMARY

Day's Market Orientation Model provides guidance in the assembly of work environments that are externally, rather than internally, focused. By incorporating this philosophy, marketers and their organizations become market driven and are perfectly positioned to capitalize on opportunities and avoid or eliminate threats in the environment, increasing the likelihood of successful commercial endeavors.

EXERCISES

1. Define and comprehensively discuss George Day's Market Orientation Model, its components, and value as an instrument for the assembly of market-driven mindsets in healthcare institutions. A diagram of the Market Orientation Model should be included to add value to your narrative. Do you believe healthcare institutions

have become more or less market driven over the past several decades? Why do you believe this to be the case?

2. Place yourself in the role of marketing director for a hypothetical, soon-to-be-launched retail pharmacy in your local community. Using George Day's Market Orientation Model, craft a mini business plan that addresses each of the Model's elements, ultimately in an effort to develop and sustain a market-driven mindset within the pharmacy.

REFERENCE

Day, George S. 1999. *The market driven organization: Understanding, attracting, and keeping valuable customers*. New York: The Free Press.

Blake & Mouton's Sales Grid

LEARNING OBJECTIVES

After examining this chapter, readers will have the ability to:

- Understand the value of personal selling in both traditional and nontraditional capacities within the healthcare industry.
- Realize that sales quotas are effective for assessing sales outcomes, but they offer little in the way of assessing sales approaches.
- Recognize the importance of understanding the particular approaches used by healthcare sales representatives.
- Appreciate the value offered by Blake and Mouton's Sales Grid as a device for assessing the approaches used by healthcare sales representatives.

INTRODUCTION

Personal selling is a promotional method involving the use of a sales force to convey messages. This promotional method is used extensively in the healthcare industry, most notably in the pharmaceutical, medical device, and health insurance segments. Personal selling, however, is also used in segments that are not traditionally associated with this promotional method, such as assisted living, where sales agents visit potential occupants seeking to encourage them to lease assisted living dwellings.

Sales representatives are often evaluated using some sort of quota, where performance is measured by comparing actual sales with prior-conceived sales goals for a given time period. This practice accurately assesses sales outcomes but does little to assess the techniques that sales representatives use in carrying out their assigned duties and responsibilities. The sales approaches used by representatives are certainly of great importance to entities. Sales agents do, after all, represent organizations. With the introduction of the Sales Grid, an evaluative tool developed by Robert Blake and Jane Mouton, the process of assessing the techniques used by sales representatives was greatly enhanced.

Illustrated in Figure 33-1, Blake and Mouton's Sales Grid consists of a nine-point horizontal scale that measures "concern for the sale" and a nine-point vertical scale that measures "concern for the customer." On these scales, 9 represents maximum concern and 1 represents minimum concern. A sales representative is evaluated first on his or her concern for the sale and then on his or her concern for the customer. This evaluation yields a two-number score that describes the sales representative's approach to selling. Of the 81 possible "concern for the sale" and "concern for the customer" combinations on the Sales Grid, Blake and Mouton specifically identify and describe five that are explained as follows.

LOCATION 9,1 (PUSH-THE-PRODUCT ORIENTATION)

The 9,1 strategy, located in the lower right corner of the Sales Grid, involves a complete concern for making the sale with little or no regard for the customer. Due to its total focus on making the sale, this strategy is termed the push-the-product orientation. Sales agents with such orientations use hard sell, pressure-oriented tactics to generate sales. Their concern for the sale is so pronounced that it is to the detriment of customers. Quite obviously, customers resent this approach. Here, there is virtually no concern for the needs, preferences, or feelings of customers.

LOCATION 1,9 (PEOPLE ORIENTATION)

The 1,9 strategy, located in the upper left corner of the Sales Grid, involves little or no concern for the sale and maximum concern for the customer and is thus termed the people orientation. Sales representatives who practice

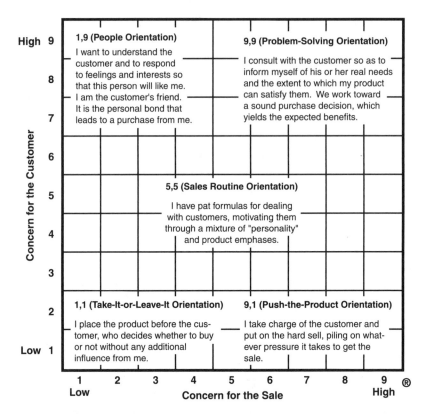

FIGURE 33-1   Blake & Mouton's Sales Grid

this strategy seek to develop bonds with customers in hopes that sales will be generated through these relationships. Very little direct persuasion is used in their sales pitches. To the detriment of themselves and their organizations, salespersons become dependent on friendships, rather than effective sales techniques, for success.

LOCATION 1,1 (TAKE-IT-OR-LEAVE-IT ORIENTATION)

The 1,1 strategy, located in the Sales Grid's lower left corner, is termed the take-it-or-leave-it orientation. This approach involves little or no concern for both the sale and the customer. These sales representatives operate in a passive manner, doing nothing to develop customer relationships or communicate product features and benefits. Products are simply placed before customers who make purchase decisions without any assistance or influence from sales agents. With complete disregard for both sales and customers, these sales representatives serve to the detriment of all parties involved—themselves, their organizations, and their customers.

LOCATION 5,5 (SALES ROUTINE ORIENTATION)

The 5,5 strategy, located in the center of the Sales Grid, represents a middle-of-the-road approach. Termed the sales routine orientation, this approach involves a moderate amount of concern for both the sale and the customer. Here, sales representatives seek to make customers comfortable through light conversation and "small talk" as they present their pat formulas for generating sales. Their pat formulas are well-rehearsed sales presentations that come across rather mechanically. Although their performance is not stellar, sales representatives using this approach do achieve adequate results.

LOCATION 9,9 (PROBLEM-SOLVING ORIENTATION)

The 9,9 strategy, located in the Sales Grid's upper right corner, is termed the problem-solving orientation. This approach involves maximum concern for both the sale and the customer. Sales representatives using this strategy possess a highly detailed knowledge of both the products they sell and the specific needs of their customers. Here, sales agents work closely with customers to assist them in making sound purchase decisions that meet and exceed expectations, yielding desired benefits.

These sales representatives provide solutions for customers. Given its maximum concern for both the sale and the customer, the 9,9 strategy yields superior results. Sales representatives who practice this strategy are assets to both their organizations and the customers they serve. Clearly, the 9,9 strategy is the most desirable sales approach.

OPERATIONAL MATTERS

Healthcare entities can greatly benefit by using Blake and Mouton's Sales Grid to assess the techniques embraced by their sales representatives. By evaluating these techniques, entities can identify strengths and weaknesses within their sales operations, taking corrective actions when necessary to ensure superior performance.

Figure 33-2 illustrates the usefulness of the Sales Grid. Here, a pharmaceutical manufacturer has evaluated each of its 12 sales representatives and plotted the resulting scores on the Sales Grid using an "X" accompanied by each sales agent's initials. This grid reveals that the company's sales

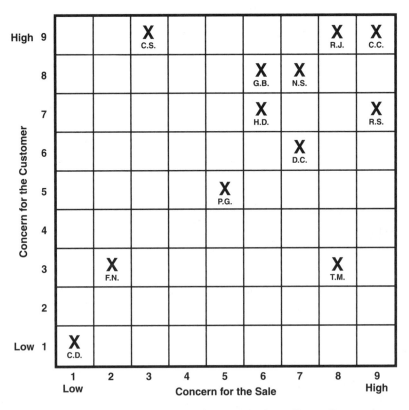

Adapted from *The Grid for Sales Excellence: New Insights into a Proven System of Effective Sales*, 2nd ed. by Robert R. Blake and Jane Srygley Mouton. Copyright © 1980, 1970 by Robert R. Blake and Jane Srygley Mouton. Published by McGraw-Hill. Sales Grid Copyright © Grid International, Inc. Reprinted by permission of Grid International, Inc.

FIGURE 33-2 A Sales Force Assessment Using the Sales Grid

force primarily uses sales techniques that are pitched toward the 9,9 problem-solving orientation. Notably, it also identifies a few sales agents whose techniques warrant alteration.

Not only is the Sales Grid useful as an assessment tool, it is also useful as a training tool—particularly for new sales representatives. By instilling the 9,9 approach in sales trainees, these new recruits will be fully aware of the importance of carrying out their duties and responsibilities in a problem-solving fashion. The Sales Grid can also be employed as a self-assessment tool for sales representatives. When used in this manner, sales representatives are reminded of desirable and undesirable approaches to selling and can alter their techniques accordingly.

Although the Sales Grid is primarily designed as a tool for the evaluation of sales representatives, it can productively be used to assess any occupation that involves customer contact. Whenever employees come into contact with customers, they become sales representatives for their organizations and the Sales Grid applies. When viewed in this manner, the Sales Grid becomes a helpful tool for evaluating the customer service techniques of virtually any healthcare employee—administrators, physicians, nurses, patient accounts representatives, and so on.

SUMMARY

Blake and Mouton's Sales Grid serves as an effective tool for evaluating the techniques used by sales representatives in carrying out their duties and responsibilities. It can also productively assess the approaches of all other employees who come into contact with customers. By using the Sales Grid, healthcare entities can ensure that all employees charged with engaging customers are performing at optimal levels.

EXERCISES

1. Provide a detailed overview of Blake and Mouton's Sales Grid, discussing its design, structure, value, and use as an evaluative tool in the healthcare industry. Be sure to include in your discussion insights as to how the Sales Grid can complement traditional sales outcomes assessments and serve as a training tool. Also provide insights into how the Sales Grid can be used to evaluate healthcare personnel who are serving in roles outside of formal sales positions.

2. Contact an area healthcare entity primarily involved in sales, such as a pharmaceutical company or medical device manufacturer. Arrange an interview with the firm's sales manager to discuss sales force assessment approaches. During the interview, present the manager with Blake and Mouton's Sales Grid and request completion of the instrument. Looking at the aggregate results, how would you characterize the firm's sales force? Prepare a narrative of insights gained from your interview and associated findings.

REFERENCE

Blake, Robert R., and Jane Srygley Mouton. 1980. *The grid for sales excellence: New insights into a proven system of effective sales.* 2nd ed. New York: McGraw-Hill.

PART SEVEN

Marketing Strategy & Planning Tools

CHAPTER 34

Michael Porter's Value Chain

LEARNING OBJECTIVES

After examining this chapter, readers will have the ability to:

- Realize that healthcare entities must strive to obtain competitive advantages across all areas of business operation in an effort to maximize their potential for marketplace success.
- Understand that a key source of competitive advantage is value because customers often seek and base their decisions on value.
- Recognize that value results from excellence across multiple, varying activities carried out by healthcare entities.
- Appreciate Michael Porter's Value Chain as an instrument for understanding value-producing activities within healthcare organizations.

INTRODUCTION

The term *competitive advantage* refers to anything possessed by an organization that gives it an edge over its competitors. One key source of competitive advantage is value. Customers seek and base their purchase decisions on value, and those entities that can deliver it will be rewarded.

Given the importance of value, its meaning to customers, and its ability to create a competitive advantage, marketers must possess a detailed understanding of this concept and the methods through which value is created—a task greatly facilitated by Michael Porter's Value Chain.

Illustrated in Figure 34-1, Porter's Value Chain is depicted as an arrow-shaped diagram that identifies value-producing activities that are common to all organizations. These value-producing activities are divided into two groups: primary activities (i.e., inbound logistics, operations, outbound logistics, marketing and sales, and service) and support activities (i.e., firm infrastructure, human resource management, technology development, and procurement).

Each of these activities represents a building block of value and has associated costs. The difference between the total value produced and the collective costs of performing value activities represents the available margin, which varies depending on the skills demonstrated by entities at performing value activities. Primary and support activities are described as follows.

PRIMARY ACTIVITIES

Primary activities consist of those pursuits that *directly* contribute to the production of specific goods and services. There are five primary activities

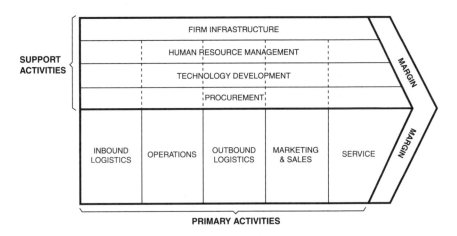

Reprinted with the permission of The Free Press, a Division of Simon & Schuster Adult Publishing Group, from COMPETITIVE ADVANTAGE: Creating and Sustaining Superior Performance by Michael E. Porter. Copyright © 1985, 1998 by Michael E. Porter. All rights reserved.

FIGURE 34-1 Porter's Value Chain

that are common to all entities: inbound logistics, operations, outbound logistics, marketing and sales, and service. These five activities are identified as follows.

Inbound Logistics

Inbound logistics activities involve all pursuits associated with the management of raw materials necessary to produce goods and services. Typical inbound logistics concerns include materials delivery, materials handling, inventory control, and warehousing. Pharmaceutical manufacturers, for example, must coordinate deliveries of raw materials to produce their therapeutic and curative offerings. Medical centers, too, must coordinate deliveries of raw materials (e.g., medical equipment and supplies, pharmaceuticals, environmental service equipment and supplies, food products for patient meals) to deliver care to patients. Not only must entities secure these products, but they also must effectively manage them through appropriate inventory control systems and warehousing techniques.

Operations

Operations activities involve all pursuits associated with the development and assembly of the goods and services that are to be offered to target markets. Goods-producing firms, such as durable medical equipment manufacturers, must assemble, test, and package their products. Likewise, pharmaceutical firms must produce their various therapeutic and curative offerings and package these goods.

Service-producing entities, such as hospitals, clinics, and nursing homes, must assemble and maintain diagnostic equipment, fixtures, and other service implements and ensure that their facilities are organized for effective service delivery. Operations activities essentially ready products for future purchase and consumption by customers.

Outbound Logistics

Outbound logistics activities involve all pursuits associated with making goods and services available to customers. Pharmaceutical firms and durable medical equipment manufacturers must, for example, determine inventory levels, warehouse finished goods, identify distribution channels, and coordinate product deliveries to distributors. Medical clinics must determine hours of operation and coordinate the schedules of practitioners and other staff members accordingly. Home health agencies must determine appropriate geographic service delivery areas and coordinate the schedules of caregivers. Each of these activities focuses on making product offerings readily available to customers for purchase and consumption.

Marketing & Sales

Marketing and sales activities involve all pursuits associated with encouraging customers to purchase and consume product offerings. Such activities include pricing products and promoting these offerings through advertising, personal selling, sales promotion, and other means. Ultimately, these activities seek to encourage exchange between entities and their target markets.

Service

Service activities involve those pursuits that support postpurchase/postconsumption needs. Pharmaceutical firms might offer toll-free product information hotlines to address customer inquiries. Durable medical equipment manufacturers might supply replacement parts for their products and repair damaged items.

Hospitals and medical clinics might provide follow-up inquiries to check the status of patients who were recently treated. These follow-up activities greatly influence customer perceptions regarding the quality of delivered goods and services and are, therefore, critical to the success of any organization.

SUPPORT ACTIVITIES

Support activities consist of those pursuits that *indirectly* contribute to the production of specific goods and services. These are broad-based activities that influence all departments within organizations, regardless of role or function.

There are four support activities that are common to all organizations: firm infrastructure, human resource management, technology development, and procurement. These four support activities are identified as follows.

Firm Infrastructure

Firm infrastructure activities involve general administration pursuits (e.g., management, accounting). Instead of benefiting single departments or small groups of departments, these activities impact organizations in their entirety.

Human Resource Management

Human resource management activities involve all employee and employment-related pursuits of organizations, including staffing, training, employee and labor relations, and compensation. These activities focus on the numerous workforce management issues and concerns that impact organizations.

Technology Development

Technology development activities involve all pursuits associated with the discovery and implementation of technologies that benefit organizations. Technology takes many forms, including know-how, product design, servicing procedures, and innovative equipment. These activities seek to incorporate innovations into organizations to reap associated benefits.

Procurement

Procurement activities involve all pursuits related to the acquisition of goods and services from suppliers. Examples include purchases of raw materials, buildings, furniture and fixtures, machinery, office equipment and supplies (e.g., copiers, fax machines, computers, paper, pens), and so on. These acquisitions activities supply entities with the wealth of components necessary to pursue their missions.

OPERATIONAL MATTERS

Each of the nine value activities identified by Porter represents an opportunity to create value. The more proficiently entities perform these value activities, the greater the value of their final products and resulting margins.

A key strength of Porter's Value Chain is that it forces entities to view the value-creation process on an activity level. Value is the product of multiple activities performed by entities. High performance in one value activity can be neutralized by low performance in another. Entities must, therefore, work to ensure that each of the nine value activities is performed at optimal levels. By performing these activities better than competitors, entities create more value in the goods and services that they produce and provide—a key source of competitive advantage.

SUMMARY

By identifying the nine value-producing activities that are common to all organizations, Porter's Value Chain provides useful insights into value and the value-creation process. By understanding Porter's Value Chain, marketers and their organizations are better prepared to deliver goods and services that possess value, increasing the likelihood of commercial success.

EXERCISES

1. Provide a comprehensive overview of Michael Porter's Value Chain, explaining its purpose, components, uses, and benefits, accompanied by an associated illustration. Be sure to discuss how the model reminds healthcare marketers to focus on the big picture because value is derived from excellence across multiple activities. Share your views regarding the degree to which healthcare marketers are actively involved in observing and influencing the value-creation process in healthcare organizations.

2. Place yourself in the role of marketing director for a hypothetical healthcare entity. Knowing the benefits afforded to those entities that successfully achieve and deliver value, describe how you would go about instilling a value-producing orientation across your organization. Because value requires a concerted effort from multiple parties within organizations, what actions would you take to ensure collaboration?

REFERENCE

Porter, Michael E. 1998. *Competitive advantage: Creating and sustaining superior performance*. New York: The Free Press.

35

Michael Porter's Generic Strategies

INTRODUCTION

Characterized by intense competition and rivalry, the healthcare environment poses extreme challenges for marketers seeking to successfully address the wants and needs of their target markets and ultimately achieve growth and prosperity. In addressing this turbulent environment, marketers must be armed with appropriate strategies that will allow them to outperform industry competitors. The process of formulating such strategies, however, is quite complex. Fortunately, marketers can turn to the work of Michael Porter for guidance in determining appropriate marketing strategies.

In an effort to assist marketers in determining appropriate strategies to pursue, Michael Porter developed a diagram that illustrates three strategies that can be employed to outperform industry competitors. Porter termed these alternatives *generic strategies* because of their applicability across industries. These strategies, which are illustrated in Figure 35-1, include overall cost leadership, differentiation, and focus. The particular strategy selected by entities depends on their strategic advantages and target markets. Porter's Generic Strategies are defined as follows.

OVERALL COST LEADERSHIP

The first strategy that organizations can employ to outperform industry competitors is termed overall cost leadership. This strategy, which entails targeting broad markets, is based on organizations achieving efficiencies of greater magnitude than those achieved by their competitors. These entities essentially incorporate every available cost-saving feature into their opera-

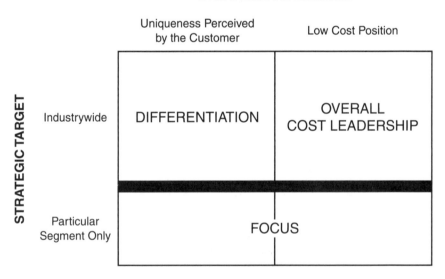

Reprinted with the permission of The Free Press, a Division of Simon & Schuster Adult Publishing Group, from COMPETITIVE STRATEGY: Techniques for Analyzing Industries and Competitors by Michael E. Porter. Copyright © 1980, 1998 by The Free Press. All rights reserved.

FIGURE 35-1 Porter's Generic Strategies

tions to gain strategic advantages over their competitors. Such cost savings can be derived from building efficient facilities; incorporating cost-saving technologies; maintaining strict overhead expenditure controls; and minimizing expenditures in the areas of research and development, advertising, and so on. By achieving operational efficiencies that are greater than those of competitors, organizations can produce and provide goods and services at reduced costs, thus allowing them to garner above average returns in comparison to their competitors.

DIFFERENTIATION

Another strategy that can be employed by organizations to outperform industry competitors is known as differentiation. This strategy, which involves targeting broad markets, is based on producing and providing goods and services that are perceived by customers to be unique. Entities can differentiate their products through such methods as technology leadership, product design and functionality, product efficiency and effectiveness, and customer service.

The exclusivity associated with these unique offerings grants entities a degree of leverage over customers. After all, customers cannot purchase these differentiated offerings from any other entity. This aspect also reduces customer price sensitivity, allowing for enhanced pricing latitude and greater possible returns.

FOCUS

A final strategy that organizations can employ to outperform industry competitors is termed focus. Organizations using this strategy focus exclusively on particular market segments in an effort to serve those segments better than any other entity. By concentrating on serving the wants and needs of particular market segments, entities can potentially achieve success through cost leadership, differentiation, or both.

OPERATIONAL MATTERS

Each of Porter's Generic Strategies can be used successfully in the healthcare industry. The particular strategy selected, however, is dependent on the strategic advantages possessed by entities and the particular markets sought.

Ideally, healthcare marketers should assess the strategic capabilities of their organizations, determine the markets sought, and then select appropriate strategies from Porter's framework. A pharmaceutical firm that exclusively sells, for example, diabetic care products would do well to adopt the focus strategy, whereas a firm offering broad-based pharmaceutical products to a national audience would fare better with a cost leadership or differentiation strategy.

Hospitals, medical clinics, home health agencies, and other entities involved in the direct delivery of patient care services are primarily segment oriented, often limiting service delivery to defined geographic markets and sometimes further segmenting those markets by addressing only certain populations, medical conditions, and so on. These entities would do well to adopt the focus strategy, where they could potentially achieve success through cost leadership, differentiation, or both. As these examples clearly illustrate, the strategy selected is dependent on institutional capabilities and markets sought.

It should be noted that entities rarely achieve success through the use of multiple strategies. The pursuit of markets using multiple strategies places a significant burden on institutional resources, increasing the likelihood of decline and failure. Therefore, it is highly recommended that given establishments select only one of Porter's Generic Strategies to pursue, thus avoiding potential resource allocation dilemmas.

SUMMARY

Through his identification and explanation of the three strategies that can be employed to outperform industry competitors, Michael Porter has provided a useful reference for marketers seeking guidance in formulating marketing strategy. With this information, marketers are better prepared to select appropriate strategies that will yield enduring marketing success.

EXERCISES

1. Provide a detailed account profiling Michael Porter's Generic Strategies, identifying and explaining each of the three strategy options, their characteristics, and rationale for deployment, accompanied by an appropriate illustration. Preface your work by discussing the importance of formulating appropriate strategies in the healthcare

industry. Also give insights regarding the risks associated with deploying multiple strategies within the same healthcare entity.

2. Visit a local retail pharmacy and spend time exploring aisles containing over-the-counter pharmaceuticals. Select a particular brand for more intensive investigation, noting its price, packaging, features and benefits, etc., in the context of competitive offerings on store shelves. Expand your investigation by visiting the Web site of the pharmaceutical company that produces the given brand and any specific Web pages dedicated to the product. Then, render an opinion as to which of Michael Porter's Generic Strategies, or possibly some combination of them, is employed by the brand. Report your findings in detail.

REFERENCE

Porter, Michael E. 1998. *Competitive strategy: Techniques for analyzing industries and competitors.* New York: The Free Press.

36

Kaplan & Norton's Balanced Scorecard

LEARNING OBJECTIVES

After examining this chapter, readers will have the ability to:

- Understand that healthcare marketers are perfectly positioned to gain internal and external perspectives of their organizations, making them invaluable as strategic resources within healthcare institutions.
- Realize that healthcare entities often look to their marketing professionals for strategic leadership because the intricate knowledge gained via managing marketing operations yields superior strategic insights.
- Appreciate the guidance provided by Kaplan and Norton's Balanced Scorecard as a device for guiding healthcare marketers in carrying out strategic management duties and responsibilities.

INTRODUCTION

Healthcare marketers are often called upon by their employers to provide strategic leadership within their given healthcare institutions, making strategic management one of the most important areas of study for healthcare marketers. This assignment of responsibility makes sense because, through their daily work endeavors, healthcare marketers gain an excellent understanding of their organizations from both internal and external perspectives. Such acquired insights include knowledge related to customer wants and needs, institutional capabilities, opportunities for growth, competitive elements in the environment, and so on.

Strategic management requires significant efforts on the part of healthcare marketers because the focus of such matters concerns organizations in their entirety. Because such endeavors set the strategic direction for healthcare entities, marketers charged with marshaling the process must not only call upon their own knowledge resources but also the knowledge resources of interdisciplinary teams of executives and employees within their particular healthcare establishments.

Given the importance of strategic management and the complexity associated with formulating, implementing, and monitoring such endeavors, healthcare marketers often look for guidance in carrying out these duties and responsibilities. This guidance can largely be found in the Balanced Scorecard, an innovative framework for strategic management that was developed by Robert Kaplan and David Norton.

Illustrated in Figure 36-1, the Balanced Scorecard depicts strategic management as a four-perspective framework—financial, customer, internal business process, and learning and growth—derived from the vision and strategy of a given organization. Importantly, the Balanced Scorecard—so termed because of its balanced treatment of the included perspectives—treats strategic management as a fluid process, rather than a static event, as indicated by arrows running from one perspective to another. The elements of the Balanced Scorecard are explained as follows.

VISION & STRATEGY

The center element of the Balanced Scorecard identifies the vision and strategy of the healthcare entity upon which the Balanced Scorecard is based. The four perspectives of the Balanced Scorecard—financial, customer, internal business process, and learning and growth—are crafted to achieve the designated strategy, thus fulfilling the vision of the given entity.

THE FINANCIAL PERSPECTIVE

The financial perspective identifies the financial goals and objectives of healthcare entities. Such goals and objectives can be quite diverse, but

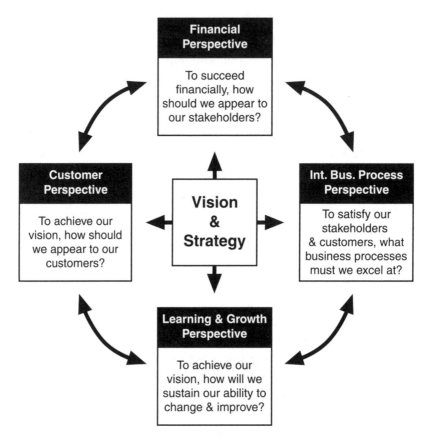

FIGURE 36-1 Kaplan & Norton's Balanced Scorecard

typical pursuits include growth (e.g., introducing new and profitable product offerings, altering product pricing structures to maximize revenue) and productivity (e.g., reducing costs, sharing resources interorganizationally, ensuring that assets are utilized to capacity, disposing of assets that are not generating adequate returns).

THE CUSTOMER PERSPECTIVE

The customer perspective identifies goals and objectives associated with the target audiences of healthcare institutions. Of the many potential goals and objectives associated with customer populations, common endeavors focus on product attributes (e.g., embedding the latest customer-desired features and benefits into product offerings, enhancing product quality), customer relationships (e.g., enhancing customer satisfaction, improving customer retention, increasing market share), and image (e.g., increasing customer awareness of products in the marketplace).

THE INTERNAL BUSINESS PROCESS PERSPECTIVE

The internal business process perspective identifies goals and objectives associated with the internal efforts of healthcare entities to ensure that product offerings meet and, ideally, exceed acceptable marketplace standards. Common internal business process goals and objectives pertain to innovation (e.g., enhancing research and development endeavors) and operations (e.g., improving product delivery and distribution systems, enhancing quality assurance practices).

THE LEARNING & GROWTH PERSPECTIVE

The learning and growth perspective identifies goals and objectives associated with the knowledge and development resources of healthcare organizations. Typical learning and growth goals and objectives are centered on employee capabilities (e.g., enhancing employee skill sets), information systems (e.g., improving information acquisition, retrieval, and dissemination capabilities), and motivation (e.g., improving employee morale, enhancing employee satisfaction).

OPERATIONAL MATTERS

Kaplan and Norton's Balanced Scorecard is highly useful in that it clearly illustrates the synergies required among various organizational elements to achieve the overall strategy and vision of associated institutions. To formulate a Balanced Scorecard, marketers (1) construct the Balanced Scorecard diagram, as illustrated in Figure 36-1, (2) identify the vision of the given institution, together with the strategy that will allow the vision to become a reality, placing these items in the center of the diagram accordingly, and (3) identify goals and objectives for each of the four perspectives—financial, customer, internal business process, and learning and growth—listing the items in their respective positions on the Balanced Scorecard. The resulting Balanced Scorecard is then utilized to facilitate strategic management endeavors.

Figure 36-2 illustrates a Balanced Scorecard that was developed for a retail pharmacy. This diagram clearly demonstrates the concise information portrayal offered by this strategic management tool. Additional insights, if desired, can be gained by tying measures (i.e., appropriate methods for determining progress), targets (i.e., particular sought results based on designated measures), and initiatives (i.e., specific tactics designed to achieve targets) to each goal and objective identified in the Balanced Scorecard, allowing the diagram to serve as a road map for vision and strategy fulfillment.

When preparing Balanced Scorecards, it is important for healthcare marketers to ensure that linkages exist across the four perspectives of the instrument. This practice ensures that perspectives are not viewed in isolation, hence fostering the formulation of a unified organizational strategy.

It is also important to understand that the Balanced Scorecard is intended to be a fluid, rather than static, document. Usefully, it affords opportunities for healthcare marketers to productively design, implement, and monitor strategy, altering pursuits as necessary to ensure vision and strategy fulfillment. Hence, the Balanced Scorecard serves as a strategic management system.

Given the broad scope of the Balanced Scorecard, it is very obvious that its success as a strategic management tool is largely based on the degree of collaboration and consensus achieved in its development. Input from multiple parties within given institutions is, therefore, essential for successful applications of the Balanced Scorecard.

SUMMARY

Kaplan and Norton's Balanced Scorecard provides a useful framework for designing, implementing, and monitoring the strategic pursuits of health-

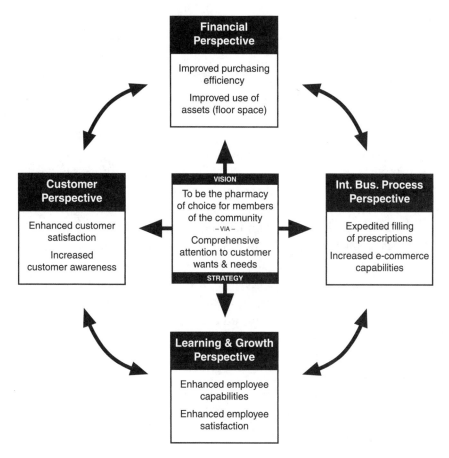

Constructed using design methodologies in Kaplan, Robert S., and David P. Norton. *The Balanced Scorecard: Translating Strategy into Action.* Boston: Harvard Business School Press, 1996.

FIGURE 36-2 A Retail Pharmacy's Balanced Scorecard

care organizations. With its focus on linkages among the elements that must appropriately be addressed for institutional success, the tool serves as an essential strategic management resource. Because healthcare marketers are frequently called upon to provide strategic leadership, the Balanced Scorecard remains an important resource for those engaged in marketing pursuits.

EXERCISES

1. Provide a detailed account profiling Kaplan and Norton's Balanced Scorecard, identifying and explaining its components, purposes, steps of implementation, and practical applications, accompanied by an appropriate illustration. Preface your discussion by offering insights as to how marketing professionals, courtesy of their training, experience, and internal and external perspectives of organizations, serve as ideal leaders of the strategic management process in healthcare entities. Share your thoughts on the degree to which healthcare marketing professionals are maximizing their value as strategic thought leaders in modern healthcare organizations.

2. Select a hypothetical healthcare entity of your choice and prepare a Balanced Scorecard depicting your vision and strategy for the entity, along with goals and objectives for the four perspectives identified in the instrument. Provide details as to why you fashioned the Balanced Scorecard as you did and what you expect your entity to achieve through implementation of such a strategic framework.

REFERENCES

Kaplan, Robert S., and David P. Norton. 1996a. *The balanced scorecard: Translating strategy into action.* Boston: Harvard Business School Press.

———. 1996b. Using the balanced scorecard as a strategic management system. *Harvard Business Review* (January–February): 75–85.

CHAPTER 37

Kaplan & Norton's Strategy Map

LEARNING OBJECTIVES

After examining this chapter, readers will have the ability to:

- Understand that the healthcare marketplace is among the most complex of operational environments, placing a premium on excellence in strategic planning and management.
- Realize that the global perspectives of the marketplace possessed by healthcare marketing professionals affords strategic insights not possessed by others in their respective organizations.
- Recognize that the process of illustrating strategy pursuits has immense value in formalizing such pursuits and communicating them to others.
- Appreciate Kaplan and Norton's Strategy Map as a tool for assembling illustrations depicting strategy pursuits.

INTRODUCTION

Due to their global perspective of the healthcare marketplace and its vast array of components, healthcare marketers are frequently charged with strategic management responsibilities. Such responsibilities are important in any institution, but they are especially vital in those that operate within environments of great complexity. Indeed, the complexity associated with the healthcare environment places a premium on excellence in strategic management. Such visionary leadership affords healthcare organizations with the opportunity to position themselves for long-term growth and prosperity.

When healthcare marketers are called upon to engage in strategic endeavors, it is very helpful for them to possess a range of tools that can assist them in the formulation, implementation, management, and assessment of strategy. Importantly, healthcare marketers must also be able to communicate designated strategic pursuits to organizational members—an essential ingredient for strategic success. One tool that can provide assistance to healthcare marketers in carrying out strategic management responsibilities is known as the Strategy Map, a useful instrument developed by Robert Kaplan and David Norton.

Kaplan and Norton's Strategy Map is essentially an enhanced illustration of the Balanced Scorecard, a tool also developed by Kaplan and Norton that depicts the vision and strategy of an organization along with accompanying financial, customer, internal business process, and learning and growth perspectives.

Specifically, the Strategy Map depicts the strategic perspectives of organizations—financial (i.e., financial-related goals and objectives, such as efforts to reduce costs or alter product pricing policies to maximize revenue), customer (i.e., customer-related goals and objectives, such as efforts to increase customer satisfaction or customer awareness of products in the marketplace), internal business process (i.e., internal operations-related goals and objectives to ensure that products meet and exceed marketplace standards, such as efforts to improve product delivery and distribution systems or enhance quality assurance practices), and learning and growth (i.e., knowledge and development-related goals and objectives, such as efforts to enhance employee skill sets or increase employee morale)—and their impact and influence on the achievement of the overall vision and strategy of associated entities.

OPERATIONAL MATTERS

To design a Strategy Map, marketers (1) identify, ideally with the assistance of other institutional parties, the vision of the associated entity and the overall strategy for achieving the vision, placing these items at the top of the Strategy Map, (2) formulate applicable goals and objectives for financial, customer, internal business process, and learning and growth perspectives, placing this information on descending levels of the Strategy Map, and (3) draw arrows indicating appropriate linkages to demonstrate the cause-and-effect relationships leading to the achievement of the identified institutional strategy and, ultimately, vision fulfillment. The resulting Strategy Map is then utilized to facilitate strategic management endeavors.

Figure 37-1 illustrates a Strategy Map that was developed for an assisted living center. This diagram clearly identifies the cause-and-effect relationships among the center's financial, customer, internal business process, and learning and growth perspectives that ultimately influence the achievement of the institution's overall vision and strategy. The assisted living center could gain even further strategic insights by completing an accompanying Balanced Scorecard to capitalize on the synergies between these two related tools.

Importantly, the success of the Strategy Map as a strategic management tool is largely based on the degree of collaboration and consensus achieved in its development, necessitating that healthcare marketers seek input from multiple parties within their institutions as they formulate these diagrams. The multiple perspectives offered by this extended group of individuals can greatly enhance resulting Strategy Maps.

SUMMARY

Kaplan and Norton's Strategy Map offers healthcare marketers a useful strategic management resource, greatly enhancing strategic pursuits through its visual depiction of designated endeavors. By clearly identifying strategic pursuits, the Strategy Map serves as a useful guide for charting a course to achieve overall organizational strategies and associated visions, ultimately resulting in institutional growth and prosperity.

EXERCISES

1. Define and comprehensively discuss Kaplan and Norton's Strategy Map and provide insights regarding its use and value in the healthcare industry. Be sure to include in your discussion an overview of the importance of strategic planning and management in the healthcare

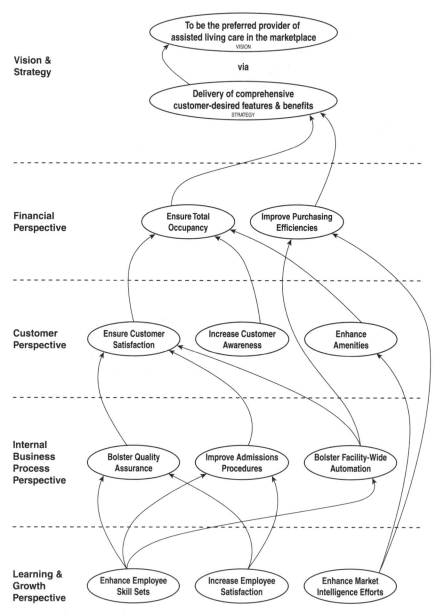

Constructed using design methodologies in Kaplan, Robert S., and David P. Norton. *Strategy Maps: Converting Intangible Assets into Tangible Outcomes*. Boston: Harvard Business School Press, 2004.

FIGURE 37-1 An Assisted Living Center's Strategy Map

industry. Also discuss the role of healthcare marketers as strategic thought leaders in the healthcare marketplace.

2. Prepare a Strategy Map for a hypothetical healthcare entity of your choice, identifying your vision and strategy for the entity, along with goals and objectives for the four perspectives, placed on descending levels of the diagram. Illustrate the cause-and-effect relationships among the various components using arrows, as specified in the instrument. Provide details as to why you arranged the Strategy Map as you did and what you expect your entity to achieve through implementation of such a strategic framework.

REFERENCES

Kaplan, Robert S., and David P. Norton. 1996a. *The balanced scorecard: Translating strategy into action.* Boston: Harvard Business School Press.

———. 1996b. Using the balanced scorecard as a strategic management system. *Harvard Business Review* (January–February): 75–85.

———. 2004. *Strategy maps: Converting intangible assets into tangible outcomes.* Boston: Harvard Business School Press.

38

Ries & Trout's Marketing Warfare Strategies

LEARNING OBJECTIVES

After examining this chapter, readers will have the ability to:

- Understand that the healthcare industry easily can be considered the most competitive of industries.
- Realize that competition represents one of the most significant obstacles to capturing and retaining market share.
- Recognize that healthcare marketers must not only be customer oriented but also competitor oriented to gain market share and achieve lasting success.
- Recognize the value offered by Ries and Trout's Marketing Warfare Strategies for assistance in understanding and implementing competitor-oriented marketing strategies that can be employed to increase market share.

INTRODUCTION

Hospitals, medical clinics, and other healthcare entities must attract and retain customers to achieve growth and prosperity. Success at attracting and retaining customers ultimately determines the share of the market—the market share—held by entities.

Market share is defined as an entity's portion, expressed as a percentage, of the total sales generated by a given product in a given market. The entity that possesses the greatest market share is known as the market leader—an enviable position to hold.

One of the most significant obstacles to gaining market share is that of competition. Healthcare entities compete in what might be considered the most competitive of industries. In their given markets, these organizations vie against one another for the valuable patronage of customers.

The term *competition* brings to mind images of contests, challenges, and so on and is a quite fitting descriptor for the healthcare environment. However, two authors view the marketing process as so intensely competitive that it is deserving of a most intense analogy—war.

In their book entitled *Marketing Warfare*, Al Ries and Jack Trout contend that "marketing is war" and apply warfare strategies and tactics to the marketing process. Ries and Trout specifically note that being customer oriented alone is not enough to achieve marketing success. Entities must also be competitor oriented, directing attention to the identification of competitors and the analysis of their strengths and weaknesses in an effort to wage marketing war.

To be successful, marketing campaigns must be planned like military campaigns. Marketers must, therefore, understand warfare principles and be able to implement these strategies and tactics effectively. For example, they must actively engage in the strategic planning process, seeking to formulate organizational goals and the action plans necessary for achieving these initiatives. They, too, must be skilled at anticipating competitive responses to various actions. Additionally, marketers must be proficient at gaining marketplace intelligence to plan and launch successful attacks. Importantly, marketers must also possess characteristics often associated with military leaders—character, perseverance, discipline, loyalty, and the like—to effectively wage marketing war.

According to Ries and Trout, marketing warfare can be waged using four different strategies: defensive warfare, offensive warfare, flanking warfare, and guerrilla warfare. As illustrated in Table 38-1, each strategy involves a number of basic, defining principles. The particular warfare strategy selected is dependent on the market position held by an entity. Accompanied by medical clinic examples, these four marketing warfare strategies are explained as follows.

Table 38-1 Ries and Trout's Marketing Warfare Strategies

DEFENSIVE WARFARE

Principle 1: Only the market leader should consider playing defense.

Principle 2: The best defensive strategy is the courage to attack yourself.

Principle 3: Strong competitive moves should always be blocked.

OFFENSIVE WARFARE

Principle 1: The main consideration is the strength of the leader's position.

Principle 2: Find a weakness in the leader's strength and attack at that point.

Principle 3: Launch the attack on as narrow a front as possible.

FLANKING WARFARE

Principle 1: A good flanking move must be made into an uncontested area.

Principle 2: Tactical surprise ought to be an important element of the plan.

Principle 3: The pursuit is just as critical as the attack itself.

GUERRILLA WARFARE

Principle 1: Find a segment of the market small enough to defend.

Principle 2: No matter how successful you become, never act like the leader.

Principle 3: Be prepared to bug out at a moment's notice.

Derived from information in Ries, Al, and Jack Trout. *Marketing Warfare.* New York: McGraw-Hill, 1986: 55–58, 68–72, 84–87, 101–107.

DEFENSIVE WARFARE

The defensive form of warfare should only be used by market leaders. Entities that possess such enviable positions should not, however, enter a hold-and-maintain mode. Instead, they should seek continuous improvement by attacking themselves. This involves the routine introduction of new and enhanced offerings that render existing products obsolete. Such offerings ultimately improve the already positive market positions held by market leaders.

It should be noted that when rivals orchestrate strong competitive moves, market leaders must block these actions. One useful blocking technique involves copying the particular competitor's move. By copying a competitor's move, a tit-for-tat philosophy, entities can maintain their market leadership positions by leveraging their market dominance. Blocking ensures that market leadership does not erode.

The leading medical clinic in a community occupies the most powerful position in the minds of consumers. Obviously, the entity would like to maintain its leadership status. This, however, is not accomplished by complacency. Instead, the clinic must actively seek to attack itself by enhancing existing services and adding new services. The clinic might offer extended hours, a "no waiting" policy, or any other feature that improves its existing service array. If the clinic's market position is threatened by a rival, the establishment must vigorously counter the threat by copying the competitor's move. If, for example, a rival clinic seeks to increase its market share by opening a women's health division, the market leader should block the move by opening a similar unit. The leader's powerful market position gives it the upper hand even if it follows the move of a competitor.

OFFENSIVE WARFARE

Offensive warfare should be used by those entities falling just behind market leaders. These entities must target leaders, seeking to shift market share away from their powerful positions, preferably at points of weakness. Here, attacks should be initiated on very narrow fronts, perhaps on single products or small groups of offerings rather than entire product lines.

A clinic that finds itself trailing the market leader in a community has a much more difficult task at hand than that of the leader. The trailing clinic must, in essence, find ways to reduce the leader's market share, gathering the fallout to better its own market position. The clinic would do well to study the leader and select a front to charge. Perhaps the clinic could challenge the leader for its senior citizen patient base by emphasizing geriatric services. The leader, of course, could block the move, illustrating the difficult position of trailing entities in the battle for market share.

FLANKING WARFARE

The flanking warfare strategy is useful for any entity seeking to gain market share. This strategy involves the identification and occupation of new market segments. Although difficult to discover and develop, new segments offer open, uncontested terrain for flankers to occupy. The success of a flanking attack is largely related to the degree of surprise achieved. The element of surprise provides valuable time for flankers to establish beachheads within these new segments, making competitive responses much more difficult or even impossible. It is important to remember that after flanking attacks, marketers must diligently pursue the targeted market segments. All too often, entities fail to maintain the intensity of campaigns after initial marketing success. Attack and pursuit are of equally critical importance in the achievement of marketing success.

Newly discovered market segments offer growth opportunities for any clinic, regardless of its size or market position. The difficulty is in the discovery of these new segments. Increasing industrialization in a community might lead a clinic to address the increasing occupational health needs associated with this development. This new opportunity could be exploited for significant gains, resulting in control of the new segment. The more quickly the clinic targets and serves the new segment, the more likely its success as its rivals struggle to mount competitive responses. If success is achieved in the occupational health segment, marketers must be sure to maintain the intensity demonstrated during the flanking attack to ensure the entity's enduring dominance in the new segment.

GUERRILLA WARFARE

Guerrilla warfare is most appropriately used by smaller entities competing in a market of larger competitors. These smaller entities do not possess the resources to compete directly with market leaders. Instead, they must identify small market segments where they can maintain leadership positions. Small entities must understand and appreciate their status and never be lulled by success into behaving like market leaders. These small entities must be quick in every regard, entering segments when they become desirable and exiting segments when they become undesirable.

A small clinic in a community should select a target appropriate to its scale by pursuing a narrow segment within the larger market. The clinic might, for example, seek to be the preferred healthcare provider for individuals residing in a certain geographic area of the community. Importantly, this small clinic should respect its position in the broad market. Regardless of its success, the clinic must avoid acting like the market leader. It must emphasize rapidity, which will enable it to capitalize on emerging opportunities.

SUMMARY

With their contention that "marketing is war," Ries and Trout provide a very useful, militaristic analogy for the marketing process. Their work is quite beneficial in that it introduces and advocates a competitor orientation to marketing and provides an array of strategies that can be employed to increase market share.

Given the competitive nature of the healthcare industry and the necessity for entities to attract and retain customers, marketers would do well to remember the useful guidelines offered by Ries and Trout. The authors have accurately identified successful strategies for waging marketing war.

EXERCISES

1. Provide a detailed overview of Ries and Trout's Marketing Warfare Strategies, identifying and explaining each of the identified strategies, their criteria for use, and associated implications for the healthcare industry. What are your thoughts on the accuracy and viability of the war analogy that Ries and Trout use to describe marketing?
2. Conduct a review of trade journals, Web sites, and other sources in an effort to identify articles profiling various healthcare entities. For each of the four Marketing Warfare Strategies, identify at least one healthcare entity that could be considered to be using such a strategy. If your research reveals entities that appear to be going against the strategy advice provided by Ries and Trout, feel free to identify these, as well. Describe your findings in detail.

REFERENCE

Ries, Al, and Jack Trout. 1986. *Marketing warfare*. New York: McGraw-Hill.

39

Philip Kotler's Marketing Plan

INTRODUCTION

Given the scope and diversity of marketing activities, it is essential for marketers to formalize their pursuits on at least an annual basis through the development of comprehensive marketing plans. By reducing marketing pursuits to writing, marketers are forced to think through upcoming periods, perform routine marketing analyses, and set marketing goals and objectives that are properly aligned with institutional goals and objectives.

When completed, marketing plans act as road maps, allowing marketers to assess their progress over time, making adjustments as necessary.

Without formal marketing plans, marketers will likely find themselves managing marketing pursuits in a reactive fashion, lacking insight, direction, and control—a formula for disaster.

Developing marketing plans requires significant effort and attention. Among other things, these plans require accurate product, market, and competitor information, as well as insightful and creative thinking on the part of plan authors and contributors. Marketing plans also must be well written and presented in an orderly fashion—aspects that greatly enhance the usefulness of these documents.

Although there are no mandatory guidelines for the format of marketing plans, a quite useful outline for such plans has been offered by Philip Kotler. Illustrated in Figure 39-1, Kotler's Marketing Plan consists of eight sections: an executive summary and table of contents, an overview of the

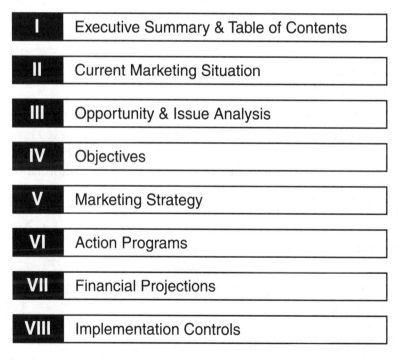

I	Executive Summary & Table of Contents
II	Current Marketing Situation
III	Opportunity & Issue Analysis
IV	Objectives
V	Marketing Strategy
VI	Action Programs
VII	Financial Projections
VIII	Implementation Controls

Derived from information in Kotler, Philip. *Marketing Management*. 11th ed. Upper Saddle River, NJ: Prentice Hall, 2003: 115–116.

FIGURE 39-1 Components of Kotler's Marketing Plan

current marketing situation, an opportunity and issue analysis, the identification of marketing objectives, the identification of the marketing strategies to be employed, the stipulation of action programs for attaining strategic objectives, the presentation of financial projections, and the identification of implementation controls for monitoring plan performance.

SECTION I: EXECUTIVE SUMMARY & TABLE OF CONTENTS

Kotler's Marketing Plan begins with an executive summary and table of contents. The executive summary specifically provides a concise overview of plan contents, emphasizing main goals and recommendations. This summary allows readers to quickly review the major facets of associated marketing plans. The executive summary is followed by a table of contents, which outlines given marketing plans and provides a page numbering system to assist readers in locating major plan components. Although this section is listed first, it is by necessity, of course, developed last.

SECTION II: CURRENT MARKETING SITUATION

The executive summary and table of contents section is followed by a review of the current marketing situation. Here, an overview of current marketing pursuits is presented, providing background information as necessary. This section includes information and analyses regarding customers, markets, and competitors, along with relevant performance data (e.g., sales, cost, and profit information), providing readers with a comprehensive snapshot of current marketing efforts.

SECTION III: OPPORTUNITY & ISSUE ANALYSIS

After identifying the current marketing situation, an opportunity and issue analysis is presented. In this section, the strengths, weaknesses, opportunities, and threats associated with product offerings are identified. Methods for capitalizing on the identified strengths and opportunities are noted, as are methods for avoiding or eliminating weaknesses and threats.

After this information has been presented and addressed, relevant issues and concerns are identified. Such issues and concerns might include whether particular markets should be pursued; whether promotional expenditures should be increased or decreased; whether given products should continue to be offered, be discontinued, or be modified; and so on.

SECTION IV: OBJECTIVES

When opportunities and issues have been identified and addressed, broad marketing objectives for the upcoming period are presented. A medical clinic, for example, might seek to increase its patient volume by 10% over the next 6 months. An antitobacco foundation might seek to reduce teen smoking by 20% over the next 2 years. A pharmaceutical company might wish to increase sales by $15 million over the next year. Depending on the particular organization, the number of identified objectives might be as few as one or quite numerous.

SECTION V: MARKETING STRATEGY

The objectives section of Kotler's Marketing Plan is followed by the identification of broad marketing strategies that will be used to achieve identified objectives. This section essentially presents the broad marketing game plan. The medical clinic seeking to increase patient volume might designate a strategy of increasing public awareness of its service offerings, hours of operation, and well-trained staff. The antitobacco foundation seeking to reduce teen smoking might devise a strategy involving the increased dissemination of its message in schools.

The pharmaceutical firm seeking to increase sales might formulate a strategy that involves increasing consumer awareness of its products, increasing the size of its sales force, and improving its product presence in retail establishments. These broad strategies are operationalized through the implementation of action programs identified in the following section.

SECTION VI: ACTION PROGRAMS

The marketing strategy section of Kotler's Marketing Plan is followed by the identification of action programs that specify how organizations plan to accomplish their broad marketing goals. The medical clinic would list how it plans to increase consumer awareness, possibly through the development of a new advertising campaign. It would also identify the nature of the campaign, the advertising media to be used, the scheduling pattern for associated advertisements, and related data. The antitobacco foundation would identify the particular schools targeted by its campaign, the nature of the educational programs to be conveyed to students, the individuals responsible for conveyance of these programs, and the associated program delivery schedule.

The pharmaceutical firm would discuss its specific plans for increasing sales, providing detailed information related to a possible new advertising campaign, the hiring and training of new sales agents, and methods for improving its product presence in retail establishments. Action programs are very specific and itemize the tactical operations necessary to carry out identified marketing strategies.

SECTION VII: FINANCIAL PROJECTIONS

After action programs have been identified, financial projections are presented, which stipulate expected financial outcomes and accompanying budgets. The revenue side of associated budgets presents anticipated cash inflows resulting from marketing efforts, while the expense side lists associated marketing costs (e.g., costs associated with advertising and distribution). The difference between the revenue side and the expense side of associated budgets reflects projected profit.

SECTION VIII: IMPLEMENTATION CONTROLS

The final section of Kotler's Marketing Plan identifies mechanisms for monitoring the progress of marketing pursuits. Importantly, this section includes a timeline for implementing stipulated marketing activities and for reviewing associated results. (Marketers should formally monitor marketing progress on either a monthly or a quarterly basis.) This section also includes contingency plans for use in the event that undesirable results occur.

SUMMARY

The complex and varied array of marketing activities within healthcare organizations necessitates the development and assembly of formal marketing plans. These plans force marketers to think through upcoming periods, perform routine marketing analyses, and set appropriate marketing goals and objectives. When completed, marketing plans serve as road maps that guide marketers, allowing them to proactively, rather than reactively, address and manage marketing pursuits.

Given the importance of marketing plans, marketers must take great care in preparation of these documents. Kotler's Marketing Plan provides marketers with a useful framework for presenting these documents in an orderly fashion. By using Kotler's framework, marketers are assured that their marketing plans contain necessary plan components and that these elements are presented appropriately. When content is added to this framework, marketers gain an invaluable marketing resource.

EXERCISES

1. Provide a detailed account profiling Philip Kotler's Marketing Plan, identifying and explaining each of its eight steps. Share your thoughts on the degree to which modern healthcare organizations adequately plan marketing pursuits via the development of formal marketing plans.

2. Contact an area healthcare establishment and arrange an informational interview with its marketing director to gain insights into the entity's marketing planning process. Specifically request information regarding the frequency of plan development, chief participants in plan design, methods for formulating goals and objectives, mechanisms for monitoring progress, and procedures for handling unforeseen circumstances that hamper original marketing plan designs. Report your findings in detail.

REFERENCE

Kotler, Philip. 2003. *Marketing management.* 11th ed. Upper Saddle River, NJ: Prentice Hall.

Appendix
An Introduction to Marketing

INTRODUCTION

Healthcare entities compete in what might be considered the most competitive of industries in an environment of immense complexity. On an ongoing basis, hospitals, medical clinics, pharmaceutical manufacturers, and other healthcare establishments vie against one another in their respective markets for the opportunity to serve customers. Each of these healthcare organizations ultimately is in search of growth and prosperity, and the best managed of these entities will indeed realize this goal.

Marketing is possibly the most critical management responsibility associated with the pursuit and realization of growth and prosperity. Marketing can broadly be defined as *a management process that involves the assessment of customer wants and needs, and the performance of all activities associated with the development, pricing, provision, and promotion of product solutions that satisfy those wants and needs.* Although most often associated with advertising and sales, marketing is much more encompassing, as its definition implies. Aside from promotions activities, marketing includes such critical functions as environmental scanning, wants and needs assessment, new product development, target marketing, product pricing, product distribution, and market research.

WANTS & NEEDS

Marketing pursuits normally begin with assessing the wants and needs of customers. The terms *want* and *need* are often used interchangeably in society; however, these words are actually quite distinct, particularly when

273

used in the healthcare environment. A *need* is something that a person requires for well-being and possibly survival, while a *want* is something that a person simply desires. Coronary artery bypass surgery, for example, is performed out of medical necessity and, therefore, represents a need. Elective cosmetic surgery, however, represents a want because the surgery is not medically necessary.

PRODUCTS: GOODS & SERVICES

The marketplace is filled with countless wants and needs with handsome rewards being offered to organizations that can satisfy those wants and needs with product solutions. The term *product* refers to any offering provided by an entity for purchase and consumption. A product can be a *good* (i.e., a tangible item), a *service* (i.e., an intangible item), or a *hybrid* (i.e., an item with tangible and intangible characteristics). This array of product variants can be illustrated on a continuum with tangible items at one end and intangible items at the other end. Figure A-1 illustrates this continuum along with several example products that have been placed on the continuum based on their tangibility or lack thereof.

Pure goods, such as over-the-counter pharmaceutical products and durable medical equipment, can be viewed in reasonable isolation from any intangible offering, while pure services, such as physical examinations and surgical procedures, can be viewed in reasonable isolation from any tangible offering. Orthodontic braces and prosthetic devices, however, represent hybrid products in that a service (i.e., fitting the patient) must accompany the delivery of the good that is provided (i.e., the particular appliance or device).

Beyond goods and services, it is important to note that ideas and philosophies can also be considered products—intangible, of course. The numerous cause-related healthcare organizations, such as those that dis-

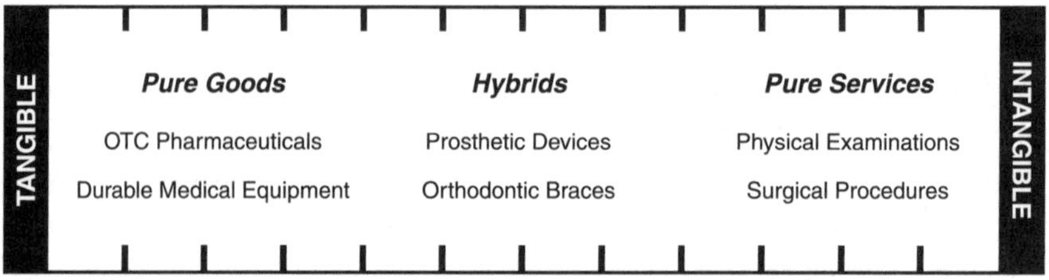

TANGIBLE	**Pure Goods**	**Hybrids**	**Pure Services**	INTANGIBLE
	OTC Pharmaceuticals	Prosthetic Devices	Physical Examinations	
	Durable Medical Equipment	Orthodontic Braces	Surgical Procedures	

FIGURE A-1 The Product Continuum

courage the use of tobacco and illegal drugs, are, in essence, attempting to sell products to designated populations.

Regardless of their tangibility or lack thereof, products that ineffectively address the wants and needs of customers will surely fail. By appropriately addressing customer wants and needs, marketers increase the likelihood that their goods and services will achieve commercial success.

TARGET MARKETING

When organizations develop new products, marketers must determine which customer groups they wish to pursue and how they wish to present their products to these groups—a practice known as target marketing. Through target marketing, marketers customize product offerings and associated marketing activities in an effort to address the wants and needs of specific customer groups.

Target marketing involves three interrelated activities: market segmentation, targeting, and product positioning. Market segmentation is the process of dividing a market into groups (i.e., segments) of individuals who share common characteristics. When the market has been segmented, marketers engage in targeting where they select (i.e., target) attractive segments and focus their efforts on satisfying the wants and needs of these groups. These targeted segments are known as an entity's target market. Product positioning follows targeting and involves the determination of an appropriate and effective image for products to convey to customers. Here, marketers seek to influence customer perceptions related to particular goods and services.

Usefully, target marketing allows marketers to craft customized promotional campaigns designed to appeal to given segments. This customization increases the likelihood that target markets will respond favorably to product offerings. Target marketing also allows marketers to make better use of their promotions resources in that marketing efforts can be directed toward specific audiences rather than entire markets.

THE MARKETING MIX

Upon identification of the particular segment or segments to pursue, marketers formulate the marketing mix for each customer group that is sought. Illustrated in Figure A-2, the marketing mix includes four interdependent

FIGURE A-2 The Marketing Mix

components: product, price, place, and promotion. It is often referred to as the *four Ps of marketing* for obvious reasons. For each product offering, marketers must design each component of the marketing mix in a manner that will entice target markets. The components of the marketing mix are explained as follows.

Product

The product component of the marketing mix involves the development of goods and services that will meet and, ideally, exceed the wants and needs of target markets. For goods, product development involves, among other things, the actual physical assembly of the offerings. For services, product development involves the assembly of all components required for the services to be offered, such as office space, equipment, operating permits, and personnel.

Marketers must take great care in assembling product attributes for targeted customer segments. An appropriate fit between given product offerings and the wants and needs of target audiences is an essential requirement for marketing success.

Price

The price component of the marketing mix involves all elements associated with pricing products in a manner that will be attractive to target markets. Price is defined as the amount of money that must be paid by customers to acquire particular goods and services.

The more features embedded into products, the greater they cost organizations to produce and provide. These costs, of course, are ultimately passed on to customers in the form of higher prices. Plush waiting rooms, the latest medical technologies, the community's most reputable practitioners, and so on all add to the costs associated with providing healthcare offerings. Some consumers have the means and the desire for enhanced healthcare offerings, while others do not.

Even with the support of third-party payer entities, there are limits to what individuals can and will pay for healthcare goods and services. Broadly speaking, a balance must be struck between the attributes of particular products and the prices charged for the offerings. This balance must meet the financial requirements of healthcare entities and the financial means of prospective customers—items that must be thoroughly addressed prior to bringing products to market.

Place

The place component of the marketing mix, which is sometimes termed *distribution*, refers to all elements involved in making products available to customers. These activities include such tasks as the identification of distribution channels, the determination of inventory levels, and the management of warehousing issues. Other place activities include the determination of locations of availability and hours of operation.

Different products often require different place considerations. Medical clinics would be concerned with such place matters as the physical location and hours of operation of their establishments. Home health agencies would focus heavily on their geographic service delivery areas. Mobile MRI services would be concerned with negotiating agreements with area hospitals to offer their services "on location" in accordance with agreed upon schedules.

Pharmaceutical firms would be concerned with creating and maintaining complex distribution linkages extending from their manufacturing plants to the various establishments that dispense pharmaceuticals to patients. Ambulance companies would be concerned with ambulance placements, dispatch protocols, and linkages with area emergency departments.

Consumption cannot occur if product offerings are not accessible to target markets, with ease of access positively influencing consumption. The place component of the marketing mix focuses on hastening the purchase process by making goods and services readily available to customers.

Promotion

The promotion component of the marketing mix involves all activities associated with communicating product attributes to target markets. Advertising is perhaps the best known promotional method; however, other forms exist, including personal selling, sales promotion, public relations, and direct marketing. These five promotional methods combine to form what is referred to as the promotions, or communications, mix.

Healthcare entities normally promote themselves using a variety of methods in their quest to entice customers to purchase and consume products. These communicative techniques build product awareness by engaging potential customers and encouraging their patronage through the conveyance of product attributes—the domain of the promotion component of the marketing mix.

ONGOING MARKETING SURVEILLANCE

Throughout the marketing process, marketers must maintain a keen awareness of the environment by engaging in ongoing marketing surveillance. Marketing surveillance activities include assessing customer wants and needs, assessing the potential of markets, identifying market trends, monitoring product performance in given markets, monitoring the activities of competitors, and determining future marketing pursuits. Importantly, marketers must ensure that surveillance activities are sustained over time—an absolute necessity given the ever-changing nature of the healthcare environment.

SUMMARY

Marketing is possibly the most critical management responsibility associated with the pursuit and realization of growth and prosperity. The essential role of marketing is even more pronounced in the intensely competitive healthcare industry where entities vie against one another in their respective markets for the opportunity to serve customers.

Given the importance of marketing, healthcare entities must ensure that they devote sufficient resources to marketing and its many activities. The success of an organization is directly linked to its success in marketing.

GLOSSARY

Adoption Process A series of progressive steps leading up to the purchase and consumption of new products.

Advertisement A verbal and/or visual message, forwarded to others via paid mass media, that is designed to inform potential customers of product offerings and attract their patronage.

Advertising A promotional method involving the paid use of mass media to deliver messages. Examples include newspaper, magazine, radio, television, and billboard advertisements.

Advertising Agency An organization that exists for the purpose of developing and placing advertisements, and typically other forms of promotion, on behalf of paying clients.

Advocacy Advertising Advertising that promotes a political, economic, social, or technological perspective of an entity, often calling for audiences to modify their behavior to adhere to given points of view.

All-You-Can-Afford Budgeting Method An advertising budgeting method where operational expenditures are identified and funded across given organizations, with the remaining resources (i.e., that which is left over after all other expenses have been paid) being assigned to fund advertising initiatives in the forthcoming period.

Antitrust Laws Laws designed and developed to promote competition by forbidding monopolies.

Atmosphere The aesthetic qualities of the environment of a particular establishment that combine to form an ambiance that has the ability to positively or negatively influence customers.

Audience   (1) The population that has been selected (i.e., targeted) by an organization for pursuit as customers. Also referred to as a target audience, target market, or target population. (2) The population that is exposed to a given mass media vehicle and is thus exposed to associated promotional messages.

Audience Fragmentation   A term used to characterize the dispersion of broad audiences resulting from the proliferation of various media sources that divide audiences into increasingly smaller groups, making it more difficult for marketers to conveniently reach target populations.

Availabilities   Units of advertising (e.g., space in outdoor advertising, air time in television advertising) that are available for purchase on a given date. In practice, the term is more commonly used in its abbreviated form—avails.

Bait and Switch Advertising   A form of deceptive advertising involving the promotion of a particular product, often at a very attractive price, as a means of generating customer traffic. When interested customers inquire about the advertised product, they are instead offered another item— typically carrying a higher price than the advertised offering—under the guise that the advertised product is of poor quality, has sold out, or is otherwise unavailable or inappropriate for their needs.

Barriers to Entry   Anything that blocks or otherwise prohibits an entity from entering and competing in a given market (e.g., regulations, capital requirements, superior competition).

Benchmarking   The practice of comparing the marketing performance of an organization and/or its product offerings to established standards of excellence known as benchmarks.

Billboard   A stationary advertising structure that is placed along transit pathways to display promotional messages to passersby.

Billboard Advertising   A form of outdoor advertising involving the use of stationary structures that are placed along transit pathways to display promotional messages to passersby. Standard billboard advertising products include the 8-Sheet Poster ($6' \times 12'$), the 30-Sheet Poster ($12'3'' \times 24'6''$), and the Bulletin ($10'6'' \times 36'$, $14' \times 48'$, and other sizes).

Black Market   An illegal market that develops when goods and services are exchanged in violation of governmental restrictions prohibiting such transactions.

Brainstorming   An activity involving intensive discussion and thought regarding a particular matter of concern for the purpose of generating applicable ideas, solutions, and so on.

Brand   A name, logo, slogan, or other reference that identifies goods and services, thus allowing consumers to differentiate product offerings.

Brand Equity   The value of a brand.

Brand Extension   The application of an established product's brand name to a new product in an effort to capitalize on existing brand awareness.

Brand Loyalty   An intense commitment to a particular brand resulting from a customer's prior positive experiences with the given brand.

Brand Portfolio   The overall collection of brands held by an organization.

Branding   The process of developing, assigning, and managing names, logos, slogans, and other identifiers associated with products.

Buyer   (1) An individual who purchases a product either for his or her own use or on behalf of another party. (2) An individual who, as part of his or her formal employment duties, purchases designated products on behalf of an organization for use in accomplishing a given mission.

Call to Action   A request, forwarded by an advertisement, calling on audience members to respond in some desired manner (e.g., to purchase a product).

Cannibalism   The introduction of a product that either partially or completely serves as a substitute for an existing product held by the same organization, thus diminishing the sales associated with the existing item.

Caveat Emptor   A Latin phrase meaning "let the buyer beware," which serves to remind consumers of the need to investigate given products and the entities that provide them prior to completing a purchase in the marketplace.

Channel of Distribution   A pathway through which products are routed from their producers ultimately to the end users of associated offerings. This pathway can be direct, with products flowing directly from producer to consumer, or indirect, with products flowing from producer to consumer through one or more intermediaries (e.g., wholesalers, retailers).

Clutter   A term used to describe elements in the environment (e.g., competing advertising messages, distractions) that compete with the marketing communications of given establishments for the attention of target audiences. Also termed noise.

Cobranding   The practice of applying two brand names, each held by different organizations, to a given product offering in an effort to capitalize on the synergies afforded by combined brand identity.

Commercialization   The full-scale marketplace introduction of newly developed product offerings.

Communications Mix   The five promotional methods used by marketers to reach target audiences: advertising, personal selling, sales promotion, public relations, and direct marketing. Also referred to as the promotions mix.

Comparative Advertisement   An advertisement that presents the features and benefits of a product in relation to competitive offerings in an effort to demonstrate product superiority for the purpose of encouraging exchange.

Competitive Advantage   Anything possessed by an organization that gives it an edge over its competitors.

Competitive Parity Budgeting Method   An advertising budgeting method where marketers estimate the level of funding that their competitors direct toward advertising and then fund their advertising budgets accordingly, essentially matching the advertising resources of their competitors.

Concept Testing   The practice of seeking consumer feedback regarding a hypothetical product offering or advertising message to gauge related interest and enthusiasm.

Continuity   An advertising scheduling strategy that involves the even, consistent delivery of advertising messages over an extended period of time.

Cooperative Advertising   An advertising arrangement where two entities, often the retailer of a product and its manufacturer, agree to share the costs of given advertisements, yielding reduced per-entity advertising expenditures and increased sales that will be enjoyed by both parties.

Cost   The amount of money that entities must spend to produce and/or provide goods and services.

Cost Per Thousand (CPM)   A term, abbreviated CPM, which reflects the advertising costs necessary for a given advertising vehicle to reach an audience of 1000 individuals. The "M" in CPM represents the Roman numeral for 1000.

Customer   Any party (e.g., an individual consumer, an institution) that purchases the goods and services of a given entity. The party may or may not be the end user of the purchased items.

Customer Relationship Management (CRM)   A marketing practice involving the delivery of personalized attention, service, and support to target audiences in an effort to establish lasting bonds with customers, ensuring their enduring patronage.

Customer Satisfaction   A primary goal of any business entity resulting from successful efforts to meet and, ideally, exceed the wants and needs of customers.

Demarketing   A practice where marketers, notably in situations of scarcity, seek to lessen the demand for given product offerings by reducing or eliminating advertisements, discounts, and other purchase incentives.

Diffusion   A term used to describe the gradual acceptance of a new product in the marketplace that occurs over time.

Direct Marketing   A promotional method involving the delivery of messages directly to consumers. Examples include direct-mail marketing, telemarketing, and catalog marketing.

Distribution   All elements involved with making products available to target markets. Examples include the transportation of goods to retail establishments, the warehousing of finished products, and the determination of hours of operation. Sometimes used as an alternative term for the place aspect of the marketing mix.

Electronic Advertising   Advertising that uses electronic media, notably including radio, television, and the Internet, to deliver promotional messages to target audiences.

Environmental Scanning   An externally focused activity where marketers seek to assess the environment in an effort to identify marketplace trends.

Exchange   A goal of marketing that involves the successful completion of a transaction between a buyer and a seller.

Flighting   An advertising scheduling strategy that involves the intermittent delivery of advertising messages to target audiences. It is characterized by intensive bursts of advertising, which are preceded and followed by periods of hiatus.

Four Ps of Marketing   The four interdependent components of product, price, place, and promotion that must be formulated for each product offering in an effort to attract target markets. Also known as the marketing mix.

Frequency   A measure of advertising effectiveness that specifically refers to the total number of times that individuals are exposed to a particular advertisement. Frequency (i.e., the number of exposures per individual) and reach (i.e., the number of individuals exposed) largely determine advertising impact (i.e., the degree to which given advertisements are effective).

Good   A tangible product offering.

Identity Management   A marketing practice involving the comprehensive management of all elements related to the establishment and maintenance of institutional and/or product identity, notably including branding and advertising.

Impact   A measure of the overall effectiveness of a given advertisement, which is largely determined by the reach (i.e., the number of individuals exposed) and frequency (i.e., the number of exposures per individual) achieved by the particular advertisement.

Integrated Marketing Communications   The coordination of all of the marketing communications efforts of an organization for the purpose of ensuring the consistent presentation of promotional messages to target audiences.

Intermediary   A participant in the process of routing goods and services from producers ultimately to the end users of associated product offerings. Also referred to as channel members, intermediaries include entities such as wholesalers and retailers.

Key Account   A customer who is responsible for a substantial portion of the total sales of a given entity and thus warrants special attention from the associated organization.

Line Extension   The addition of a new and typically related product offering to an existing array of products offered by an organization.

Macroenvironment   External forces within the marketplace that, although beyond the control of executives, have the potential to influence organizations. Such forces are often divided into four categories: political, economic, social, and technological.

Magazine Advertising   A form of print advertising that involves the use of magazines, typically circulated on a regular basis, to deliver promotional messages to target audiences.

Margin   The difference between the cost of producing and/or providing a product and the price received for the given offering.

Market   A broad collection of potential customers.

Market Leader   The entity or product, depending on the focus of the assessment, that possesses the greatest share of a given market.

Market Penetration   The degree to which a given product has acquired market share in a given market.

Market Potential   The overall capability of a given market to deliver customers for a given product, with such potential ranging from positive to negative from the perspective of marketers who are responsible for promoting the designated product.

Market Segment   A group of individuals within a market who share common characteristics (e.g., age, income, tastes, preferences).

Market Segmentation   The process of dividing a market into groups (i.e., segments) of individuals who share common characteristics. Market segmentation is the first step of target marketing.

Market Share   An entity's portion, expressed as a percentage, of the total sales generated by a given product in a given market.

Marketing   A management process that involves the assessment of customer wants and needs, and the performance of all activities associated with the development, pricing, provision, and promotion of product solutions that satisfy those wants and needs.

Marketing Concept   A marketing philosophy, which became prevalent in the 1960s and remains so today, that recognizes and appreciates the valuable role of customers in marketing, leading marketers to focus their attention on meeting and exceeding the wants and needs of their target audiences.

Marketing Mix   The four interdependent components of product, price, place, and promotion that must be formulated for each product offering in an effort to attract target markets. Also known as the four Ps of marketing.

Marketing Plan   A formal document that describes and assesses the current marketing performance of an organization and sets marketing goals and objectives for the upcoming period.

Mass Marketing   The practice of offering products to the market as a whole without regard for the individual tastes and preferences of consumers.

Mass Media   A term that refers to the range of media vehicles (e.g., newspapers, magazines, radio, television, and billboards) that can be used to deliver promotional messages to large target audiences.

Microenvironment   Internal forces within an organization that have the potential to influence the given establishment. Such forces include capital, personnel, institutional capabilities, and so on.

Need   Something that is required for well-being and possibly survival. A necessity as opposed to a desire.

New Product Development   The creation of a new good or service usually resulting from a systematic process ranging from idea conception to commercialization.

New-to-the-World Product A newly introduced product that defines an entirely new product category never before offered to the public.

Newspaper Advertising A form of print advertising that involves the use of newspapers, typically circulated on a daily or weekly basis, to deliver promotional messages to target audiences.

Niche Marketing A practice where marketers target and intensively focus on fulfilling the wants and needs of a very defined segment of the market in an effort to serve that particular segment better than any other entity in the marketplace.

Noise A term used to describe elements in the environment (e.g., competing advertising messages, distractions) that compete with the marketing communications of given establishments for the attention of target audiences. Also termed clutter.

Objective-and-Task Budgeting Method An advertising budgeting method that involves the independent, ground-up development of an advertising budget based on the promotional wants and needs of an institution. Advertising objectives are identified, along with the tasks required to accomplish those objectives, and a budget is formulated accordingly.

Outdoor Advertising Advertising that uses billboards, transit vehicles, street furniture, and other out-of-home media to deliver promotional messages to target audiences.

Outshopping A practice where consumers in a given marketplace forgo the goods and services offered by organizations in their particular community, choosing instead to purchase the products from other vendors in adjacent marketplaces.

Packaging The exterior boxes, cartons, wrappers, and similar elements that are used to aid in the transportation of products to given sales locations and in the presentation of offerings to potential buyers.

Percentage-of-Sales Budgeting Method An advertising budgeting method that calls for marketers to review sales for the previous period and determine an appropriate percentage that should be dedicated to advertising. The resulting amount then serves as the advertising budget for the forthcoming period.

Personal Selling   A promotional method involving the use of a sales force to convey messages to target audiences.

Place   One of the four Ps of marketing, which involves the formulation of all elements associated with making products available to target markets. Examples include the transportation of goods to retail establishments, the warehousing of finished products, and the determination of hours of operation. Sometimes referred to as distribution.

Portfolio Analysis   An activity involving the comprehensive review and assessment of an organization's product offerings.

Price   (1) The amount of money that must be paid by customers to acquire particular goods and services. (2) One of the four Ps of marketing, which involves all elements associated with pricing products in a manner that will be attractive to target markets.

Print Advertising   Advertising that uses print media, notably including newspapers and magazines, to deliver promotional messages to target audiences.

Product   (1) Any offering provided by an entity for purchase and consumption. A product can be a good (i.e., a tangible item), a service (i.e., an intangible item), or a hybrid (i.e., an item with tangible and intangible characteristics). (2) One of the four Ps of marketing, which involves the development of goods and services that will meet and, ideally, exceed the wants and needs of target markets.

Product Class   A collection of similar to diverse product offerings that serve related wants and needs (e.g., personal mobility—wheelchairs, walkers, and canes).

Product Deletion   The elimination of a particular good or service from a given product portfolio.

Product Differentiation   (1) The ability to distinguish goods and services from competitive offerings. (2) The development of distinguishable product features that allow offerings to easily be recognized by customers.

Product Form   A particular manifestation of a product and its closely related variants (e.g., aspirin—regular, extra-strength, and P.M.).

Product Life Cycle   A model that illustrates the four stages of a product's development: introduction, growth, maturity, and decline.

Product Portfolio   The overall collection of products held by an organization.

Product Positioning   The process of determining an appropriate and effective image for products to convey to customers in an effort to influence their perceptions of goods and services. Product positioning is the final step of target marketing.

Production Concept   A marketing philosophy, prevalent during the 1800s and early 1900s, that emphasized the production of goods and services, leading marketers to focus their attention on excellence in this area, typically at the expense of customers and their defined wants and needs.

Promotion   (1) All activities associated with communicating a product's attributes to target markets. (2) One of the four Ps of marketing, which involves the formulation of communications strategies and tactics that will effectively convey product attributes to target markets.

Promotions Mix   The five promotional methods used by marketers to reach target audiences: advertising, personal selling, sales promotion, public relations, and direct marketing. Also referred to as the communications mix.

Public Relations   A promotional method involving the use of publicity and other unpaid forms of promotion to deliver messages. Examples include press releases, open houses, facility tours, and educational seminars.

Pull Strategy   A marketing communications strategy that involves directing communicative efforts (e.g., advertising, sales promotion, direct marketing) toward consumers who, in turn, demand the associated products from establishments in the marketplace. Such activities essentially pull given products through channels of distribution, resulting in exchange.

Pulsing   An advertising scheduling strategy that involves the placement of a consistent but tempered number of advertising messages over a given campaign period, supplemented periodically by surges in the quantity of messages delivered to target audiences.

Push-Pull Strategy   A marketing communications strategy that involves directing communicative efforts (e.g., advertising, sales promotion, direct marketing) toward both intermediaries and consumers in the marketplace in an attempt to generate exchange.

Push Strategy   A marketing communications strategy that involves directing communicative efforts (e.g., advertising, personal selling, sales promotion, direct marketing) toward intermediaries who purchase the associated offerings and, in turn, promote them to their customers. Such activities essentially push given products through channels of distribution, resulting in exchange.

Radio Advertising   A form of electronic advertising that uses radio to deliver promotional messages to target audiences.

Rate Card   A document prepared by a media firm (e.g., a radio or television station, a newspaper or magazine publisher, an outdoor advertising plant operator) that lists various rates for given advertising purchases.

Reach   A measure of advertising effectiveness that specifically refers to the total number of individuals who are exposed to a particular advertisement. Reach (i.e., the number of individuals exposed) and frequency (i.e., the number of exposures per individual) largely determine advertising impact (i.e., the degree to which given advertisements are effective).

Relationship Marketing   A marketing practice involving the delivery of personalized attention, service, and support to target audiences in an effort to establish lasting bonds with customers, ensuring their enduring patronage.

Repositioning   The practice of altering the positioning characteristics of given product offerings in an effort to redefine the image associated with particular goods and services.

Retailer   An establishment that sells products directly to consumers.

Sales Concept   A marketing philosophy, prevalent during the mid-1900s, which emphasized salesmanship as a means of generating exchange, leading marketers to focus their attention on excellence in this area, typically at the expense of customers and their defined wants and needs.

Sales Promotion   A promotional method involving the use of incentives to stimulate customer interest. Examples include discount coupons, free gifts, samples, and contests.

Sales Representative   An individual employed by an organization to identify and contact customers in the marketplace who might have wants and needs for the goods and services offered by the employing establishment.

Segment   A group of individuals within a market who share common characteristics (e.g., age, income, tastes, preferences).

Segmentation   The process of dividing a market into groups (i.e., segments) of individuals who share common characteristics. Segmentation, also termed market segmentation, is the first step of target marketing.

Seller   Any party that offers products for sale to others.

Service   An intangible product offering.

Social Marketing   The use of marketing strategies and tactics to promote goods and services deemed to be beneficial to the health and well-being of individuals and society.

Substitute Product   A product that differs from a particular offering but largely, and sometimes completely, fills equivalent wants and needs. Laser vision correction, for example, could be viewed as a substitute for eyeglasses, with both products offering two different routes to better vision.

Supply Chain Management   A marketing practice involving the comprehensive management of distribution networks to ensure efficient and effective business operations that will ultimately yield goods and services of significant value.

Target Market   The name given to a market segment that has been selected (i.e., targeted) by an organization. Also referred to as a target audience or target population.

Target Marketing   A three-step process that involves the division of a market into segments (i.e., market segmentation), the selection of attractive segments to pursue (i.e., targeting), and the determination of an appropriate and effective image for products to convey to customers (i.e., product positioning).

Targeting The selection of attractive market segments to pursue. Targeting is the second step of target marketing.

Television Advertising A form of electronic advertising that uses television (e.g., broadcast network television, cable television) to deliver promotional messages to target audiences.

Test Marketing A practice where marketers directly or indirectly seek consumer feedback regarding their new products by allowing target audiences to experience the offerings prior to full-scale marketplace introductions. Such experiences are offered to customers via product samples, trials, small-scale market releases, and other means.

Top-of-Mind Awareness A marketing communications goal that refers to the first brands that come to mind when consumers think of products.

Transit Advertising A form of outdoor advertising involving the use of public transportation vehicles (e.g., buses, taxis, trains) to display advertising messages to vehicular and pedestrian traffic in the course of their passenger transportation activities.

Unique Selling Proposition (USP) A proposal forwarded to target audiences via an advertisement that touts the unique features and benefits possessed by a product offering for the purpose of attracting interest, attention, and exchange.

Value Added A term that refers to the enhancements and improvements offered by given products that eclipse the features and benefits of current offerings in the market.

Vendor Any party that carries a particular product offering and makes the item available to others for purchase and consumption.

Want Something that is desired but not required for well-being and survival. A desire as opposed to a necessity.

Warehouse (1) The act of storing goods for distribution or use at a later point in time. (2) A physical structure built for the purpose of storing goods for distribution or use at a later point in time.

Wearout The tendency for the impact of an advertising message to diminish over time, necessitating that marketers periodically alter their advertising messages to ensure sustained impact.

Wholesaler   An intermediary in a channel of distribution that is situated between the producer of a product and the retailers that carry the particular offering.

Word-of-Mouth Publicity   Publicity generated via communications between and among peers regarding the benefits, or lack thereof, of given product offerings.

Zapping   A practice, undesirable to advertisers, where television viewers use their remote controls to change channels during commercial breaks, thus avoiding exposure to advertisements.

References

Ansoff, H. Igor. 1965. *Corporate strategy: An analytic approach to business policy for growth and expansion.* New York: McGraw-Hill.

————. 1988. *The new corporate strategy.* Rev. ed. New York: Wiley.

Berry, Leonard L. 1999. *Discovering the soul of service: The nine drivers of sustainable business success.* New York: The Free Press.

Berthon, Pierre, James M. Hulbert, and Leyland F. Pitt. 1999. Brand management prognostications. *MIT Sloan Management Review* 40 (2): 53–65.

Blake, Robert R., and Jane Srygley Mouton. 1980. *The grid for sales excellence: New insights into a proven system of effective sales.* 2nd ed. New York: McGraw-Hill.

Booz, Allen & Hamilton. 1968. *Management of new products.* New York: Booz, Allen & Hamilton.

————. 1982. *New products management for the 1980s.* New York: Booz, Allen & Hamilton.

Calder, Bobby J., and Steven J. Reagan. 2001. Brand design. In *Kellogg on marketing*, ed. Dawn Iacobucci. New York: Wiley.

Day, George S. 1999. *The market driven organization: Understanding, attracting, and keeping valuable customers.* New York: The Free Press.

————. 2007. Is it real? Can we win? Is it worth doing? Managing risk and reward in an innovation portfolio. *Harvard Business Review* (December): 110–120.

Dutka, Solomon. 1995. *DAGMAR: Defining advertising goals for measured advertising results.* 2nd ed. (1st ed. by Russell Colley). Lincolnwood, IL: NTC Business Books.

Henderson, Bruce D. 1998. The product portfolio (1970). In *Perspectives on strategy from The Boston Consulting Group*, ed. Carl W. Stern and George Stalk Jr. New York: Wiley.

————. 2006. The product portfolio (1970). In *The Boston Consulting Group on strategy: Classic concepts and new perspectives*, 2nd ed., ed. Carl W. Stern and Michael S. Deimler. New York: Wiley.

Jain, Dipak. 2001. Managing new product development for strategic competitive advantage. In *Kellogg on marketing*, ed. Dawn Iacobucci. New York: Wiley.

Kaplan, Robert S., and David P. Norton. 1996a. *The balanced scorecard: Translating strategy into action.* Boston: Harvard Business School Press.

————. 1996b. Using the balanced scorecard as a strategic management system. *Harvard Business Review* (January–February): 75–85.

————. 2004. *Strategy maps: Converting intangible assets into tangible outcomes.* Boston: Harvard Business School Press.

Keller, Kevin Lane. 2000. The brand report card. *Harvard Business Review* (January–February): 147–157.

Kerin, Roger A., Eric N. Berkowitz, Steven W. Hartley, and William Rudelius. 2003. *Marketing.* 7th ed. New York: McGraw-Hill.

Kim, W. Chan, and Renee Mauborgne. 2005. *Blue ocean strategy: How to create uncontested market space and make the competition irrelevant.* Boston: Harvard Business School Press.

Kotler, Philip. 2003. *Marketing management.* 11th ed. Upper Saddle River, NJ: Prentice Hall.

Kotler, Philip, and Gary Armstrong. 2001. *Principles of marketing.* 9th ed. Upper Saddle River, NJ: Prentice Hall.

————. 2004. *Principles of marketing.* 10th ed. Upper Saddle River, NJ: Prentice Hall.

Kotler, Philip, and Fernando Trias de Bes. 2003. *Lateral marketing: New techniques for finding breakthrough ideas.* Hoboken, NJ: Wiley.

Lederer, Chris, and Sam Hill. 2001. See your brands through your customers' eyes. *Harvard Business Review* (June): 125–133.

Lehmann, Donald R., and Russell S. Winer. 2005. *Analysis for marketing planning.* 6th ed. New York: McGraw-Hill.

Levitt, Theodore. 1960. Marketing myopia. *Harvard Business Review* (July–August): 45–56.

————. 1965. Exploit the product life cycle. *Harvard Business Review* (November–December): 81–94.

————. 1980. Marketing success through differentiation—of anything. *Harvard Business Review* (January–February): 83–91.

————. 1986. *The marketing imagination.* Exp. ed. New York: The Free Press.

Lindstrom, Martin. 2005. *Brand sense: Build powerful brands through touch, taste, smell, sight, and sound.* New York: The Free Press.

Maslow, Abraham H. 2000. *The Maslow business reader*, ed. Deborah C. Stephens. New York: Wiley.

Mintzberg, Henry, and Ludo Van der Heyden. 1999. Organigraphs: Drawing how companies really work. *Harvard Business Review* (September–October): 87–94.

Osgood, Charles E., George J. Suci, and Percy H. Tannenbaum. 1957. *The measurement of meaning.* Urbana, IL: University of Illinois Press.

Porter, Michael E. 1998a. *Competitive advantage: Creating and sustaining superior performance.* New York: The Free Press.

————. 1998b. *Competitive strategy: Techniques for analyzing industries and competitors.* New York: The Free Press.

Raphel, Murray, and Neil Raphel. 1995. *Up the loyalty ladder: Turning sometime customers into full-time advocates of your business.* New York: HarperBusiness.

Ries, Al, and Jack Trout. 1986. *Marketing warfare*. New York: McGraw-Hill.

———. 2001. *Positioning: The battle for your mind*. 20th anniversary ed. New York: McGraw-Hill.

Rogers, Everett M. 2003. *Diffusion of innovations*. 5th ed. New York: The Free Press.

Schmitt, Bernd H. 2003. *Customer experience management: A revolutionary approach to connecting with your customers*. Hoboken, NJ: Wiley.

Schmitt, Bernd, and Alex Simonson. 1997. *Marketing aesthetics: The strategic management of brands, identity, and image*. New York: The Free Press.

Taylor, David. 2004. *Brand stretch: Why 1 in 2 extensions fail and how to beat the odds*. Chichester, West Sussex, UK: Wiley.

Index

301